Personality, Psychopathology, and Psychotherapy:
Theoretical and Clinical Perspectives
Henry Kellerman, *Series Editor*

Psychopathology and Differential Diagnosis: A Primer

VOLUME TWO
Diagnostic Primer

Henry Kellerman and *Anthony Burry*

COLUMBIA UNIVERSITY PRESS
NEW YORK

COLUMBIA UNIVERSITY PRESS
NEW YORK   OXFORD
Copyright © 1989 Columbia University Press

Library of Congress Cataloging-in-Publication Data
(Revised for volume 2)

Kellerman, Henry.
  Psychopathology and differential diagnosis.

  (Personality, psychopathology, and psychotherapy:
theoretical and clinical perspectives)
    Includes bibliographies and indexes.
    Contents: v. 1. History of psychopathology—
v. 2. Diagnostic primer.
    1. Psychology, Pathological—History. I. Burry,
Anthony. II. Title. III. Series: Personality, psychopathology, and
psychotherapy (New York, N.Y.) [DNLM: 1. Diagnosis,
Differential. 2. Mental disorders—diagnosis.
3. Psychopathology—history. WM 100 K286p]
RC438.K44   1988   616.89′09   88-6120
    ISBN 0-231-06702-X (set)
    ISBN 0-231-06096-3 (v. 1)
    ISBN 0-231-06704-6 (v. 2)

Printed in the United States of America

Casebound editions of Columbia University Press books are Smyth-sewn
and printed on permanent and durable acid-free paper

To my father, Samuel "Sol" Kellerman

To Madeleine, Theodore, and Alexander Burry

CONTENTS

PREFACE

This second volume, *Diagnostic Primer,* addresses the development of diagnosis, its purpose, and its relation to psychopathology and the understanding of personality. In addition, the important factors to consider in forming differential diagnoses are indicated in terms of principles and clinical examples. A persistent focus is maintained throughout on basic character structure and the essence of psychopathology as classified by the diagnostic nomenclature of *DSM-III* and *DSM-III-R.* Further, an integration is made of previously accepted diagnostic nosology covered by *DSM-I, DSM-II,* and diagnostic usage conventionally applied by clinicians that does not derive from official codification. This presentation and analysis of psychopathology and its corresponding diagnostic system includes specific psychopathological symptom clusters composed of traits, defense mechanisms, and emotion elements that when taken together comprise the major diagnostic syndromes.

What Is Meant by Diagnosis of Psychopathology?

There are two broad questions immediately relevant in the application of diagnostic principles to the domain of psychopathology. The first is, What is the diagnostic aim with respect to the codification of psychopathology? Is the diagnostic assessment designed to refer to a cluster of symptoms, a cluster of traits, a specific cause of behavior, prediction of outcome, a metapsychological interpretation of a personality aberration, or an aggregate of these? Such questions relate to whether diagnosis should include syndromal formulations, personality dynamics, etiology, prognosis, or some or all of these.

The second overlapping question relevant to diagnosis as a representation of psychopathology is, Should diagnostic statements specifically, and nosological categorization generally, be based upon purely descriptive behavioral phenomena or upon theoretical dynamic inference and interpretation—that is, metapsychology—along with supporting descriptive data?

The impetus for a descriptive nosology emanates from the work of Emil Kraepelin. By the turn of the twentieth century Kraepelin was utilizing descriptive classification, basing descriptive diagnostic statements on symptom clusters, age of onset, course of pathology over time, and outcome. Thus, Kraepelin's diagnoses were concerned with syndromal, etiological, and prognostic considerations as interpreted exclusively through observation of behavior. Sigmund Freud provided an alternate and profoundly different perspective to diagnostic classification based on his belief that descriptive taxonomy was an insufficient approach to the diagnostic representation of psychopathology. Freud revealed the usefulness of metapsychological inference in determinations of diagnosis. Such metapsychological inference requires highly abstract psychoanalytic conceptualizations in terms of a proposed psychic apparatus. This apparatus includes, for example, references to the intrapsychic agencies of id, ego, and superego as well as the dynamic factors involved in the system's functioning. Yet, the overriding effort in clinical psychiatry today is to compose a diagnostic nomenclature etched in a descriptive taxonomy. Such a descriptively based codification is thought to insure objectivity and reliability, but it seems to sacrifice understanding of the deeper structure that contributes to the formation and clinical significance of diagnostic entities.

The development of diagnostic formulations from *DSM-I*, to *DSM-II*, and from *DSM-III* and *DSM-III-R* leading to *DSM-IV* reveals that metapsychological dynamic inference continues to be minimized and even screened out as a factor contributing to the illumination of diagnosis. Denotative description has become the sine qua non of the overall differential diagnosis of psychopathology even though it is apparent that the ultimate and perhaps most useful method for formulating the diagnosis of psychopathology has not yet been approximated.

In order for psychopathology to be related to personality functioning, diagnostic representations of psychopathology need to reflect an organizational code for the entire domain of personality. However, this rather simple requirement based on parsimony and coherence dissolves in the face of a closer examination of the precise definition of the particular aspect of personality in question.

For example, is the diagnostic representation based upon denotative descriptive behavior? Is it based upon course of psychopathology over time, or on etiology? Or, is the diagnostic representation of psychopathology based upon different aspects of personality such as the operation of particular defenses, the presence of typical clusters of traits, the operation of emotions—the presence of which may or may not need to be inferred—or even the presumed influence of a preponderance of particular intrapsychic forces such as id or superego? When the diagnostic system relies solely on descriptive taxonomies, then, although the system can truly become a representation or code of aberrant behavior, it may reflect only a diminished or narrow view of personality.

With the advent of *DSM-III* and *DSM-III-R*, whether diagnosis is moving toward precise description or toward more precise understanding of the psychological meaning of each diagnosis aided by metapsychological inference is resoundingly clear—it is moving inexorably in the direction of pure description. To augment the narrow scope implicit in the descriptive approach, however, in this volume, *Diagnostic Primer*, a psychoanalytic and general psychodynamic understanding of psychopathology and personality, wherever possible, will be brought to bear on the overall issue of diagnosis.

Personality, Psychopathology, and Diagnosis

In creating diagnostic systems, the main issue is to understand what it is that is being codified. Is it overall personality style that is represented in diagnostic statements, or is the diagnostic system one that represents aberrant psychopathology measured against that which may be considered established personality and which is ubiquitous? In clinical usage, this distinction between personality style and psychopathology roughly corresponds to the respective difference between character structure on the one hand and symptoms or disordered behavior on the other.

The difference between a personality classification system and one formulated to classify psychopathology also suggests that the various terms used to refer to a general nomenclature need to be defined. Distinctions can be made between the terms nomenclature, classification, nosological, and diagnostic system. A nomenclature refers to a vocabulary of labels. A nosology is a specific kind of nomenclature, a particular classification showing relationships among designated diagnoses. Finally, the diagnostic system is basically a classification system of complex states.

These sorts of distinctions of systems and subsystems imply that the overall nosology would be unified and linked by theory, and therefore demonstrate a reasonable measure of internal construct validity and coherence. Yet, it should be noted (and is especially emphasized in volume 1, *History of Psychopathology*) that the history of psychiatric nosology including that of *DSM-III* and *III-R* is atheoretical; that is, the diagnostic nosology is not based upon theoretical metapsychological conceptions. Rather, it is a descriptive system that utilizes a vocabulary of labels, shows relationships among labelled objects and relates these to complex states exclusively in terms of empirical usage and clinical experience. As such, *DSM-III* and *DSM-III-R* are for the most part pragmatic and empirical approaches to the codification of psychopathology.

This present volume, *Diagnostic Primer*, therefore, is designed to address some complex issues of psychiatric nosology, and to contribute additional clinical and theoretical body to diagnostic nosology. Traditional diagnostic usage as expressed through *DSM-I* and *DSM-II*, as well as newer formulations arranged in *DSM-III* and *DSM-III-R* are considered along with useful diagnostic formulations not included in the current psychiatric nosologies. Further, it should be pointed out that in this volume the technique of multiaxial diagnosis is not reviewed or presented in detail. Rather, the idea of diagnostic levels becomes the linchpin of diagnostic organization with character structure accorded the central role in the expression of psychopathology and diagnosis.

This overall review also introduces metapsychological considerations in the analyses of diagnostic reflections of psychopathology. Thus, the diagnostic nosology reviewed in this work is infused with psychodynamic formulations that differentiate behavioral aberrations, refers to pathologic process, identifies levels of personality organization, and considers psychopathology in relation to the personality as standing in the foreground in bold relief.

Volumes 1 and 2 taken together demonstrate that all new attempts and alternate models for formulating and distilling diagnostic nosologies are efforts to approximate a single universe of psychopathology. This universe of psychopathology is perceived uniquely by theorists and clinicians both at different time periods and even during the same historical period. In fact, volumes 1 and

2 demonstrate that since diagnostic impressions and perceptions develop over time, changes in diagnostic statements generally represent a presumably more sophisticated reflection of attendant psychopathology. Thus, evolution of diagnostic nosology suggests new perceptions of psychopathology, new methods of establishing criteria of psychopathology, and even includes the elimination of diagnostic categories based upon newly developed sociocultural norms. Therefore, changes in diagnosis occur in concert with the continuing advances in the understanding of psychopathology and its differentiation. The organization of this volume, *Diagnostic Primer,* attempts also to show the shifting nature of diagnosis as such historical changes reflect new understandings of psychopathology and personality.

This diagnostic primer is suitable as a text as well as a reference work. It is usually the case that both clinicians and students need resources that are cogent and comprehensive, useful, and convenient, and that are cast in an applied practical way. It is intended that the nature of this two volume edition, *Psychopathology and Differential Diagnosis: A Primer,* is structured in a manner that encompasses these considerations.

Organization of Volume 2

Part 1, Character Structure, compiles and groups a basic complement of characterological types in terms of major underlying commonalities. An introductory chapter examines the deep structure of diagnosis. This deep structure of diagnosis enables the reader to appreciate a broad context that includes the matrix of personality out of which psychopathological manifestations are derived, and a diagnostic language emerges that is used to codify this wide variety of psychopathology into manageable and parsimonious proportions.

The remainder of part 1 sets forth twelve fundamental character types including those that have been conventionally agreed upon as basic by clinicians over the years, as well as those that have been recently considered by *DSM* codifiers to qualify as essential types. These twelve basic characterological types—also known as personality disorders—are grouped according to the ways in which each type manages emotion.

Chapter 2 presents the characterological types designated as emotion controlled, which include the compulsive, paranoid, and schizoid characters. In contrast, chapter 3 considers the emotion dyscontrolled character types. These are the character structures of hysterical, narcissistic and psychopathic. In examining the emotion controlled type in chapter 2, an analysis of developmental issues, defenses, anxiety, traits, and symptoms is made. This analysis enables the reader to understand that such character structures are similar in the vital effort each makes to control emotion. The analysis also permits the reader to see how each of these particular emotion controlled types retains its own distinctive configuration.

The same kind of analysis showing commonality of character structure as well as distinctiveness of type is presented for the emotion dyscontrolled types of hysterical, narcissistic and psychopathic characterology presented in chapter 3. Such analysis of commonalities and distinctiveness for the remaining six characterologies, grouped as emotion dependent and emotion avoidant character types is presented in chapters 4 and 5.

These five chapters comprise the first section of the volume on character structure and indicate contrasting groupings of the twelve character types. For example, in chapter 4, the emotion dependent types of dependent, passive aggressive and inadequate character are examined. These character types appear somewhat opposite to those presented in chapter 5 in which the emotion avoidant types of borderline, schizotypal and avoidant character are presented. Thus, in chapter 4 the analysis of dependency can be construed to unify the basic character structures of dependent, passive aggressive and inadequate personality, while an examination of developmental history, traits, behavior, defenses and symptoms shows that each of these character disorders also retains its distinctive configuration.

In chapter 5, emotionally avoidant aims can conceptually unify the character types of borderline, schizotypal and avoidant, and yet, the examination of developmental issues and features of personality enable each of these character types also to be viewed as distinctive.

Because of the fundamental importance of understanding personality and psychopathology through the formation of character structure, part 1 also includes clinical case material for each of the twelve basic character types. These clinical illustrations enable the reader to identify more closely the various clinical phenomena that are complexly integrated into each character type. For example, character structure includes considerations of the defense system. This defense system is composed of typical defenses designed to manage anxiety and emotion such as defenses of projection, denial, and reaction formation. Character structure formation also depends upon the more permanent etchings of the defense system's identifications and internalizations. The emphasis on character structure underscores the importance of character throughout all of the various other clinical diagnoses.

Part 2 of this volume—chapter 6—presents all the affect disturbances that are given in the *DSM* model as well as some mood or affect disorders considered by many clinicians to be important but excluded from *DSM* consideration. Among the mood disturbances are both those considered to have psychotic manifestations as well as nonpsychotic disorders, those that are bipolar and unipolar, as well as atypical depressions. In addition, an examination of depression viewed as characterological in nature is also presented, an example of a diagnostic entity not included in *DSM-III* or *DSM-III-R*.

Thus, in part 2 of this volume the entire grouping of all the affect, mood, and depressive disorders are considered in one place so that the reader may be able to sort out the basic *DSM* paradigm of mood, manic, depressive, bipolar, unipolar, neurotic, psychotic or characterological affect disorders. These depressions and mood associated disturbances follow the analysis of character structure presented in part 1 because it is frequently clinically observed that mood changes begin to occur during crises when pressure and stress unduly undermine character defenses and the fabric of character structure. In addition to mood changes during such crises, clinicians frequently note the appearance of anxiety conditions and a host of neurotic phenomena including special symptom disorders, such as phobias.

Part 3, accordingly, reviews neurotic phenomena. Chapter 7 focuses on anxiety disorders or general neuroses, considering both states of anxiety and individual phobias. Chapter 8 considers the disorders in which anxiety is managed through bodily phenomena and dissociation. Consequently, rather than characterological weakness resulting in affect disturbance or palpable anxiety syndromes, disorders appear that tend to bind or screen out such affect and anxiety. These disorders of conversion and dissociative reactions are presented in Chapter 8 under the *DSM* classification called somatoform and dissociative disturbances. Thus, part 3 comprising neurotic phenomena consists of two sections, one including anxiety disorders and the other covering conversion and dissociative disorders.

Schizophrenic disorders and other psychotic disorders are reviewed in part 4 under the geneal heading of psychosis. Particular symptoms and distinctive categories of schizophrenia and other psychoses are presented, along with several psychotic disorders that contain mixtures of thought and affective problems. Since the main affective psychoses are covered in part 2, this section on psychosis remains basically a compendium and examination of the schizophrenic and paranoid psychoses, as well as of psychotic mixtures of thought and mood disturbances.

The final part of the book, part 5, covers additional clinical conditions that either are newly considered in *DSM-III* and *DSM-III-R* or have been of such clinical interest to professionals and lay persons that they have been either selected from the *DSM* nomenclature or included here on the basis of their importance in clinical experience. In this final section are the syndromes of exhibitionism and voyeurism, sadism and masochism, narcolepsy and insomnia, anorexia and bulimia, and finally, the disorder of recent interest in adult psychopathology called attention deficit disorder.

The complement of psychopathological and diagnostic entities covered throughout this book are clinically relevant to adult patients and are the kinds of disorders that can generally be addressed psychologically and, for the most part can be treated psychotherapeutically. Even in the cases of psychoses and depressions, in which adjunctive medications are frequently helpful, the disorders included can nevertheless become further ameliorated with the application of an understanding of the vicissitudes of personality, psychopathology and diagnosis within a psychotherapeutic tradition. Because of the psychodynamic framework that informs the substance of this book, as well as the focus on the appearance of psychopathology during adulthood, many disorders in the *DSM* nomenclature have been excluded from consideration. Among these are, for example, the organic conditions, disorders of childhood, and the addictions.

In the planning and development of this volume, and in view of its contents, the sample of diagnostic entities selected for evaluation should help the reader cultivate a clinical sense that diagnostic language does indeed represent the broad and diverse domain of psychopathology and reflects in an organizational sense, a parsimonious code for the entire realm of personality.

ACKNOWLEDGMENTS

Several people were very helpful in the preparation of this manuscript. We especially thank Ann Horowitz and Betty Aroyou for their diligent and conscientious work in typing the manuscript.

Leona Mackler, Chief Librarian at the Postgraduate Center for Mental Health in New York City provided us, as always, with research materials as well as important citations. We extend our sincere appreciation to her.

Elizabeth Sutton and Louise Waller of Columbia University Press were exceedingly helpful throughout the production of this book, and their contribution is acknowledged with appreciation.

PART I
Character Structure

CHAPTER 1

The Deep Structure of Diagnosis

In volume 1, *History of Psychopathology*, several important themes were developed regarding the nature of diagnosis. The central theme concerned the principle that diagnosis was a reflection of psychopathology. Another basic theme revealed that certain behaviors and symptom clusters can constitute a type of personality. A third theme indicated that salient characteristics are identifiable in the personality, and that these qualities seem to appear universally in a few forms in response to stress. For example, it can be observed that throughout the history of the study of psychopathology, the phenomena of anxiety and depression were noted to be consistent manifestations of psychopathology. As such, the concern with behaviors involving anxiety and depression became important anchors in diagnostic formulations.

In a broader sense, surveying the history of psychopathology has lead to the inexorable conclusion that diagnosis contains a deep structure consisting of references to psychopathology, implications for prognosis and directions for treatment, and even what could be considered a morphological underpinning. This context or morphology can be both analyzed and synthesized in order to understand better the nature of diagnosis and its connection first to psychopathology and second to the wider concern of the study of personality.

On what basis is a diagnosis made? A diagnosis is certainly not solely the designation of a descriptive label. A diagnosis is, at least in part, a reflection of a person's functioning—a person's behavior. Thus, it has been a typical approach in the history of diagnostic nosological systems to base diagnostic statements on what a person does—that is, on how he behaves—and on what he says. What he says is another aspect that contributes to diagnostic formulation. For example, a person can be inert and yet reveal a great deal of diagnostic information by reporting fantasies, day dreams, or any other psychological or emotional data. In this respect, diagnosis includes, on the whole, observation of a person in order to identify patterns of behavior, verbal reports of internal states, as well as the important consideration of the reporting of historical material. In this sense, diagnosis relates to psychopathology and to the overall personality structure.

ELEMENTS OF DIAGNOSIS

Understanding the differential diagnostic formulation becomes substantially more meaningful when references are also made to specific psychopathology and sources of the personality structure. With this equation—the connection of diagnosis, psychopathology, and personality—clearly established, it becomes necessary to examine the deep structure of diagnostic concepts in the form of elements and features of diagnosis that contribute to diagnostic viability.

Just as it may be said that some psychopathology is more severe and some less severe, so too it is implied that some diagnoses are more severe and some less. Thus, a first element in the consideration of diagnosis concerns relative severity of psychopathology. Second, just as certain psychopathological manifestations seem to occur suddenly while others appear to have persisted, so too can diagnostic statements include the issue of whether the psychopathology is acute or chronic. In addition, some maladaptive behavior or psychopathology seems resistive to change while other maladaptive behavior appears amenable to change. The comparative extent of this plasticity in the person's experience is also reflected by diagnoses that imply the relative degree of the rigidity of the personality. Finally, diagnoses need not be immutable statements, because, in many respects, psychopathological manifestations themselves are subject to change, thereby also suggesting that the fundamental structure of personality can be an accommodating system.

This last point regarding change in diagnosis and implying possible change in psychopathology and personality can be referred to as *the diagnostic shift*. The diagnostic shift is a significant concept for two reasons. First, it ties diagnosis directly to prognostic and treatment implications. Second, the concept of the diagnostic shift reflects changes in personality and psychopathology on the one hand, and further, can imply a change in prognosis on the other.

So far, the equation involving the tripartite concept of personality, psychopathology and diagnosis and its extension involving prognosis as well as treatment generates a sense of an individual existing within an internal intrapersonal condition. Yet, all the terms of the diagnostic equation have been rather significantly influenced by events in the person's life, invariably involving other specific individuals. Thinking about diagnosis in terms of events in a person's life involving other people always raises the issue of the pivotal event that precipitated the presenting problem and the need for a diagnosis in the first place. This presenting complaint is another important feature in the deep structure of diagnosis.

Another way of characterizing the deep structure of diagnosis is to understand this diagnostic organization as an infrastructure. The infrastructure is a system organized on the basis of levels so that the wide array of diagnoses can be actually grouped in terms of levels of personality reference. Especially in the history of contemporary diagnosis of psychopathology—for example, in the *Diagnostic and Statistical Manual I, II, and III (DSM-I, II, and III* and its revision, *DSM-III-R*, leading to *DSM-IV*) and in other typical diagnostic understanding and usage not specifically codified in *DSM-I, II* and *III* but used conventionally nevertheless—there are a few basic levels of diagnosis. It is these levels that comprise the infrastructure of diagnostic nosology especially as diagnosis has been conceived in the last half of the twentieth century and particularly in the Western tradition. These levels are considerations of neurosis, character structure, psychosis, and, along a biological dimension, organicity.

CHARACTER STRUCTURE: THE CENTRAL DIMENSION

During the first half of the twentieth century, clinicians relied mostly on typical and conventional diagnostic terms when formulating their ideas of psychopathology. It was in 1952 that a vast array of common diagnostic concepts became organized into the standard form known as the *Diagnostic and Statistical Manual of Mental Disorders (DSM-I)*. The essence of this diagnostic form considered the behavior that was diagnosed in terms of particular psychopathology as reactions to stress. On this reactive basis, behavior became assessed more or less independently of consistent personality functioning that could be understood through theory. Thus, such standardized taxonomies were for the most part atheoretical. Yet, this nosological system could be considered as useful because it attempted to organize a vast psychopathological arena of behavior into manageable proportions.

Examples of the nature of diagnosed pathology as relatively atheoretical and as reactive conditions in *DSM-I* include the assessment of neuroses. Diagnoses in which anxiety was a central feature were considered anxiety *reactions*. With respect to specific fears, these were considered phobic *reactions*. Thus, in the end, although *DSM-I* attempted to gain diagnostic parsimony, the link between personality, psychopathology and diagnosis in the sense of the creation of an enduring and unified system was not achieved.

In *DSM-II*, which appeared in 1968, 16 years after the appearance of *DSM-I*, the diagnostic nosology involving anxiety revolved around the concept of neurosis with anxiety as its main feature. Anxiety reaction was now anxiety neurosis and phobic reaction was now phobic neurosis. In *DSM-II*, the focus on a unified system of personality exhibiting enduring patterns of traits became a clearer conceptualization. Consequently, personality disturbances could more readily be viewed as maladaptive patterns that were distinct from either neurosis or psychosis. In emphasizing maladaptive patterns, symptoms and syndromes became crucial to the *DSM-II* organization. Inexorably, therefore, the organization of *DSM* nosology has evolved so that what was *reaction* in *DSM-I* and *neurosis* in *DSM-II*, is now *disorder* in *DSM-III*. The concept of disorder in *DSM III* was designed to reflect a condition of typical trait patterns in an individual which are adhered to as a central aspect of personality functioning so that maladaptive or malfunctioning behavior is expected to result consistently.

Thus, in *DSM-III*, and perhaps more, even in the anticipation of *DSM-IV*, differential diagnosis is becoming more clearly organized as a derivative of personality and of personality maladaption expressed in terms of trait clusters. The purpose of *DSM-III* was to make diagnosis clinically useful by emphasizing descriptive clarity. Although in a specific sense *DSM-III* is not based upon theory, nevertheless, what can be imposed upon this descriptive taxonomy is the implied underpinning that reveals diagnosis as a reflection of psychopathology, or in a more fundamental sense, as a reflection of personality. (See table 1.1, p. 14.)

The Character Structure

In volume 1 on the *History of Psychopathology* of this present two volume edition *Psychopathology and Differential Diagnosis: A Primer,* it became clear that even during antiquity one's nature was assessed, perceived and described as a personality and even relegated to a personality type. Until the late nineteenth century, these personality categories were global admixtures of trait characteristics, inclinations, dispositions and behaviors, and more importantly, were based upon clinical description. When, in the twentieth century, considerations of personality became more specific, then the concept of character, character structure, and character defense surfaced as deeper etchings in the understanding of this inner organization called personality.

The character was seen as one's customary mode of behavior around which clustered traits and attitudes that were invariable, enduring, persistent, and defining. With the writings of the psychoanalysts Sigmund Freud, Karl Abraham, Wilhelm Reich, and Carl Fenichel, among others, it gradually became clearer to the clinical establishment that this syndromal formulation of character was based, at least in part, upon ongoing early developmental experiences in which the child was engaged in an inevitable struggle to reconcile internal demands and proclivities with the demands of the environment and external reality.

A rather simple example to illustrate the formation of a trait as it results from the reconciling of internal urges with the demands of reality concerns the formation of passive aggressive behavior. A passive aggressive character in terms of clinical behavior typically exhibits delayed reactions to demands of the environment. A passive aggressive person may indeed respond to external demands, but in a way that evokes the neurotic interpersonal condition, so that the probability vastly increases that the person who is the source of the demand will experience some frustration. A simplified version of this equation as it applies to the crystallization of the character traits is that the developing passive approach of the subject is designed to generate anger in the object.

This illustration of the development of a passive character trait as it appears early in one's experience reflects a response to a typical and relatively consistent interplay of reactions between parent and child. For example, a rather severe parent demanding immediate and efficient responses and requiring obedience and compliance can generate intense conflict in the child. Such a conflict produces considerable anxiety because the child cannot deny the demand, yet feels angry both at the implicit and explicit expectation for abject obedience. The child in fact does comply, but in the process of doing so, for example, accidentally spills the glass of milk on the table, and may also further complicate the issue by needing to go to the bathroom and then, finally, not be able to locate some article of clothing. By this time, the parent begins to seethe with anger but the child complies before the parent becomes overtly rageful. In this example, the child's method of compliance preserves its own interests and inclinations for independent development as part of the compromise effected despite the self-defeating passive trait that begins to become an important element of his character structure.

This parent-child interaction creates typical and repeating interactions and the particular compromise that the child makes becomes engraved as one of his personality contours, cast as the concept of character. When the amalgam of such parent-child interactions as well as the child's similar developing interactions with others further crystallizes, the total personality configuration then becomes entirely influenced by this core character. Thus, emotions, traits, defenses, anxiety, and even psychophysiological conditions become intrinsically aligned with the basic character configuration. It can be proposed that the particular character formation as the core of personality also becomes infused in whatever native or biological predispositional urges are present in the child.

Character Structure and Diagnosis

As described earlier, the deep structure of diagnosis reveals an infrastructure of particular levels that comprise significant and discrete arenas involving various global aspects of psychopathology. The first level is composed of one's psychological intactness with reality—a concern usually subsumed as psychosis; another level involves a concern with biological and brain intactness—a concern addressed on the level of organicity; the structure of symptoms and anxiety—assumed conventionally as neurotic functioning and labeled neurosis or anxiety disorder—comprises a third level; and last is the level of the mortar, cementing personality and revealing each person's uniqueness—the level of character. The character level is the foundation or the standard by which all other levels acquire significance by comparison. Considering character becomes important in a general sense to the understanding of diagnosis and specifically, in a clinical sense character becomes important because departures from the standard of characterological problems can be a measure of the extent of the clinical problem.

For example, when the passive aggressive behavior of the child no longer successfully expresses its underlying compromise—that of needing to maintain its growing independence by deferred compliance—but the child is still required to comply without any consideration of independence, then the release of anxiety can be predicted. In such an instance, the diagnostic consideration is that the child may then experience an anxiety reaction, anxiety disorder, or any other neurotic, anxiety-based symptom designation in the context of a passive aggressive personality. Even though this diagnosis will focus on the behavior and symptom that the child exhibits, it can be seen from this example that the symptom of anxiety that can be pathological, may also contain concomitant physiological responses, such as panic palpitations, sweaty hands, stomach sensations, hyperventilation, and so forth. This potential total anxiety syndrome is directly related to the vicissitudes of underlying character formation, and thus to personality. The entire syndrome is considered a neurotic one because of the flooding of anxiety and the resulting interference with adaptation. Yet, the underlying personality, to the extent that it is pathological, is diagnosed separately from the anxiety syndrome at the distinct level representing characterological functioning.

Once again, this brief clinical example illustrates that a diagnostic formulation reflects psychopathological material, which in turn reflects personality information, largely in the form of characterological structure. This example of the appearance of anxiety or neurotic symptoms embodies the idea of dystonic or alien experience. The dystonic or alien experience reflects the subjective sense of foreignness regarding the symptomatic occurrence as well as the discomfort and even anguish that emerge when the character formations are not sufficient to adapt to the stresses of reality. Another way of understanding this maladaption and subsequent dystonic experience of anxiety is to consider that the patterns of character structure involving trait clusters, emotions, and defenses originally designed to manage anxiety and coping have been rendered insufficient. Under such conditions, differential diagnosis reflects a concern with pathology revolving around the difference between character and neurosis.

Just as this example of the character structure and its relation to onset symptom behavior of anxiety illustrates a differential diagnosis between character and neurosis, so too a similar example can be offered by examining pathological manifestations of the psychotic level. In the case of a person who has tenuous ego boundaries—based at least in part on irrational parent-child interactions during the child's early development—pathological material erupts because the character structure cannot consistently sustain a typical behavioral response to stress. Consequently, inconsistent, labile, irrational, and highly idiosyncratic material can emerge. This idiosyncratic material goes beyond an anxiety flooding since the integrity of the character structure is significantly impaired. The idiosyncratic pathological material is called primary process and in some cases may be referred to as autistic. Such designations refer to the condition that exists in which the individual becomes largely governed by a set of internal referents that include fears, impulses, needs, and affects experienced in an exaggerated and unreal fashion. Thus, in place of an intact character pattern, a psychotic configuration is composed of fragments of that particular character pattern, decompensations of the character pattern, skewed responses derived from the character pattern, and large distortions in the very essence of the character pattern.

For example, the compulsive character is frequently described as someone with an inordinate need for closure and orderliness and with excessive concern with standards of conformity. These are persons who can have rigid and overconscientious capacity for work and are unable to relax. Such compulsive behavior frequently interferes with ongoing relationships in so far as concerns with the relationship are always secondary to concerns that involve striving and rigid orderliness. A compulsive character can be formed by a number of different circumstances and experiences of life that join to create this particular pattern of coping. In certain cases, the concern with striving is based upon great fears of incapacity. In cases where ego strength also is questionable with respect to its elasticity, durability, and synthetic and integrative properties, and environmental stresses prove overwhelming, then this particular compulsive character matrix cannot appropriately channel components of the inner world, such as fears, impulses, needs, and affects. A shattered inner regulatory governance then can produce a full-blown psychotic episode. A psychotic process can begin with the breakthrough of tensions that the character structure can no longer contain, leading ultimately to the pathological condition of psychosis.

In this case of psychosis, the character is fragmented and not merely affected by anxiety. The result is a projection of inner needs, impulses, fears, and affects that appear in the form of delusions, hallucinations, distorted, illogical thinking as well as affective disturbances. For instance, the particular compulsive character referred to above, who defends against strong inner self-doubt and defensively compensates with inordinate needs for closure and striving, exhibits a typical intact characterological organization. When such a person decompensates under the pressure of stress, a paranoid configuration in the psychotic sense can develop in which delusions of persecution or compensatory grandiosity may emerge. These delusions will reflect the paranoid projections of the patient's inner world. Understanding delusions of persecution, hallucinations, and confusion as they exist in the psychotic framework with reference to the context of character structure can permit a comprehensive clinical understanding of the entire psychopathological manifestation. Such a conceptualization of psychopathology further allows development of an understanding of this psychotic manifestation in terms of a characterological-developmental etiology. Fundamentally, pathological manifestations and symptoms are reflections projected from the inner world because of the loss of intactness of ego and impairment in the fabric of the character structure. This impairment of character structure is a loss of the interface between the demands of external reality with those of inner processes. What is left, therefore, are inner needs, fears, and impulses in the absence of the mediating material with reality—namely, the character structure which has decomposed.

Along with the example of the passive aggressive personality as a characterological framework that can allow neurotic manifestations, can be added the example of a psychotic manifestation that can occur when characterological structures are overwhelmed. Such examples suggest that the nature of the character structure is perhaps the salient component in the broad study of psychopathology and diagnosis.

Another example of character structure and the understanding

of diagnosis involves organic pathology. The appearance of organic pathology intrudes in behavior even when the character fabric is more or less intact. In this sense the patient is driven by the
pathology to function in uncharacteristic ways. For example, in a
deferential, dependent character, the very fabric of the characterological organization is composed of a cluster of traits that include
obedience, compliance, deference, needs for propriety, and a passive orientation. During occasions of pressure, the organic involvement shatters this coping style by an inexorable impulsivity revealing anger, impatience, low frustration tolerance, and poor
judgment—an imposed cluster of traits and behaviors completely
uncharacteristic of such a person's basic disposition. The discrepancy between the basic character disposition and the syndrome
developed by the organic involvement enables a clearer evaluation
of the difficulty such psychopathology engenders.

THE DIAGNOSTIC AXES OF DSM-III
AND DSM-III-R

This discussion of the salience of character in the infrastructure of
diagnosis reflects a basic clinical underpinning of *DSM-III* and *DSM-
III-R* nomenclature. In *DSM-III* and *DSM-III-R* each individual
case can be evaluated in five axes, the first two of which reflect
psychopathology. Axis I includes primarily clinical syndromes. The
second axis includes personality disorders and specific developmental disorders. Axis III includes physical disorders, Axis IV involves the severity of psychosocial stressors and Axis V assesses
the highest level of adaptive functioning achieved by the patient
during the past year.

In the work presented in this book, the main focus will be upon
Axes I and II, since these axes relate to basic character patterns as
well as clinical syndromes. Consistent with the approach to diagnosis in this chapter in which characterology is viewed as central
to the diagnostic process, *DSM-III* and *DSM-III-R* allow for a
diagnosis of the character structure on Axis II in every case, regardless of whatever other clinical syndromes, symptoms, or processes are involved that relate to Axis I. Although the importance
of character structure was only somewhat focused upon in *DSM-
I* and amplified even more in *DSM-II,* its importance as a ce-

menting component of diagnosis and personality in *DSM-III* and *DSM III-R* suggests that the appearance of *DSM-IV* some time in the future should underscore even further the unifying capacity of character structure in the understanding of differential diagnosis, psychopathology and personality.

In the following four chapters completing the first section, part 1, of this volume, the most typical character diagnoses—that is, diagnosis based upon actual character structure—are presented. The basic complement of character diagnoses are divided according to their commonalities. That is, there are certain basic character diagnoses that have greater similarity to one another than to other basic character diagnoses. Because of this inherent similarity structure between characterologies, those diagnoses with apparent kinship to one another are considered as a group, so that each can be appreciated with respect to its own defining properties as well as in terms of the differential diagnostic problem raised by the similarity of these types. The commonality of each of these clusters is considered in the chapter in which each is presented. These clusters of character diagnoses as presented here in some cases may not conform with the manner in which the *DSM-III* and *DSM-III-R* classification groups them. However, it should be noted that even in the *DSM-III/III-R* model, the organization of diagnoses represents an empirical approximation of the basic structure of diagnosis. In this respect, clinicians and theoreticians should be able to attempt refinements of basic diagnostic groupings with an eye toward better approximating these basic diagnostic groupings. Ultimately, the *DSM* classifiers can draw upon a body of theoretical literature in their quest to develop the most useful and representational diagnostic parsimony.

Four clusters of character patterns are considered:

1. compulsive personality, paranoid personality, and schizoid personality, which constitute emotion controlled types;

2. hysterical personality, narcissistic personality, and psychopathic personality, which constitute emotion dyscontrolled types;

3. dependent personality, passive aggressive personality and inadequate personality, which constitute emotion dependent or attached types; and

4. borderline personality, schizotypal personality and avoidant personality, which constitute the emotion avoidant types.

These various character patterns are so basic to the makeup of personality functioning that they are labeled personality disorders in *DSM-III/III-R*. In the analysis of basic character patterns in this volume, those listed in *DSM-III/III-R* as well as other traditionally accepted character patterns not listed in *DSM-III/III-R* will also be considered.

TABLE 1.1. Summary of the Deep Structure of Diagnosis

DERIVATIVE CODE
Diagnosis

Characterological disorders
Neurotic or anxiety disorders
Affect and mood disorders
Psychotic and schizophrenic disorders

VISSICITUDES OF BASIC LEVEL
Psychopathology

Severity issues
Acute or chronic course
Shifting levels
Dynamics and etiology
Fantasy/behavior correspondence
Control versus impulse

BASIC LEVEL
Personality (composed of character formations)

Typical traits and defenses
Customary modes of behavior
Enduring, persistent, defining personality style designed to manage
   anxiety and emotion

CHAPTER 2

Emotion Controlled Character Types: Compulsive, Paranoid, and Schizoid Character Structure

In this chapter, the character structures of compulsive, paranoid, and schizoid personalities will be considered together as a cluster based upon their significant underlying commonalities. These types are considered basic character patterns in which the need for strong control of emotion is the central determinant around which the multitude of traits reflecting the particular character pattern has cohered. A commonality shared by these three kinds of character patterns includes profusion of ideation in which an intellectual approach involving a dispassionate reliance on logic and analysis serves as a substitute for, and defense against, the experience of emotion. The purpose of this ideational and cognitive approach is to control the influence and pressure of emotion and through control, to avoid the unexpected which if present would be highly threatening and emotionally unsettling.

The need to control emotion generates a host of phenomena designed to fortify this control function. For example, the over-focus on ideation also serves to achieve interpersonal insularity which in addition sustains the accomplishment of a sense of control and safety from emotional arousal. This interpersonal insularity and highly constricted approach to interpersonal involvement reflects a second commonality uniting the emotion controlled types of compulsive, paranoid, and schizoid. Threatening aspects of emotional life are reduced when the function of the control patterns achieves its aims—mainly the containment of emotion. Such individuals may experience control of interpersonal interactions which in turn can reinforce a sense of security about overall emotional control and correspondingly reduce anxiety pertaining to the loss of emotional control.

Another phenomenon occurring in these emotion controlled characterological dispositions is the appearance of particular defense patterns. For example, in the emotion controlled types of compulsive, paranoid, and schizoid characterology, defenses involving intellectualization, projection, and insulation generally comprise the overall defense organization utilized to control the experience of emotion as fully as possible. In addition, particular clusters of defense mechanisms are utilized in each of the specific character patterns encompassing the emotion controlled types. These specific clusters of defenses contribute to the unique distinctiveness of each character type.

The point at which each characterological pattern crystallizes into its distinctive cast is theoretically determined by the respective needs for emotional control of each type. This personality distinction means that reasons for needing distance and control over emotion are quite individual in each type and for the most part, along with specific trait clusters and typical defense mechanisms, will constitute the differential diagnostic problems that can occur in distinguishing each character pattern. Each of the character patterns will be considered in the following sections.

Compulsive Personality or Obsessive Compulsive Personality

The compulsive or obsessive compulsive character structure as it is known in *DSM-III* and *DSM-III-R* respectively involves several distinctive tendencies that are rigidly maintained and when present can introduce distress in work or social functioning or at the personal level. A formal and serious attitude that closely conforms to convention and propriety is usually displayed by such a person in a manner that distinctly limits expressions of spontaneity, affection, or warmth. Thus, there can appear a withholding of feelings in favor of a formal and correct bearing that creates an ungiving approach both in a tangible as well as emotional sense. The compulsive's focus on organization draws upon a range of traits in which detail, rules, order, perfectionistic strivings, and expectations of others stand out. These traits can limit any ability to appreciate the nuances and shadings that enhance human interaction and understanding because of the inordinate focus on what it is that remains imperfect. In addition, such a social limitation can further interfere with a reasonable and appropriate approach to accomplishment that would fortify a sense of meaningfulness as a central feature of the person's value system.

The sense of entitlement that appears in the compulsive personality may actually reflect a need to dominate others. Very much in the spirit of a power struggle in which compromise is impossible, the compulsive person expects—and if contradicted, demands—conformity to his plan and direction. The negative feelings usually engendered in others by this rigid insistence that calls for yielding and adherence is not at all appreciated by the compulsive person. Thus, it appears that a prominent need exists in such a person to avoid the temptations and experience of feelings because such experience of emotion carries implications regarding loss of control and disruption of order. Since order and organization are essential and even reach ritualistic proportions in compulsive persons, pleasure and warmth of personal relating is usually eschewed in favor of dedication to work and the completion of tasks, no matter how bland or even unimportant. Yet, efficiency is most often limited in compulsive types because of an underlying focus regarding being found inadequate, disorderly, and wrong; consequently, compulsive rituals, procrastination, and rumination can interfere with productivity and the decisions necessary to proceed constructively can be frequently lost in hair-splitting displays of ambivalence.

Developmental Issues

Developmentally, the conventional psychoanalytic formulation regarding trait patterns and compulsive personality structure concerns the child's attraction to conditions of disorder which are presumably managed by the early exercise of the defense of reaction formation. The action of reaction formation is to turn into its opposite that which is attractive but prohibited, such as sexual attraction, anger, or dirtiness. In this defensive method of managing forbidden pleasures, an adherence to standards of conformity and orderliness presumably satisfies the person's need to eschew any potentially positive response to such attraction. From the psychoanalytic point of view, it is hypothesized that parental attitudes as well as conscientious toilet training fortify the compulsive character pattern. An attitude of coercion and pressure on the part of the parent—who overemphasizes the importance of compliance and submission of autonomous strivings in the child—has characterological consequences. This pressure toward conformity can create problematic angry resentment in the child, a resentment that is associated with the orderliness that is promoted and may even contain passive aggressive features. The pressure to comply ostensibly makes it essential for the child to control the resentment toward the parent generated from this interpersonal interaction with its characteristic struggle over power and submission. Any failure by the child to maintain control over such resentment would permit the release of anxiety. The anxiety is, in this case, a generalized emotional condition that threatens to betray the proposed underlying anger and resentment—specific emotions that need to be controlled in this compulsive personality.

In addition to reactions of anger and resentment, the emotions involved in sexual and competitive strivings that occur in later developmental phases can be regressively contained and ordered by the control emphasis of this compulsive characterology. Thus, a characterological network evolves that is utilized to control and manage an array of emotional propensities.

Compulsive Character in Contrast to Obsessive Compulsive Neurosis

The appearance of anxiety in personality functioning is a general signal of a salient sense that something dangerous and threatening is imminent. This signal function of anxiety is the basis of the principle that equates anxiety with a general state of tension in the personality. Yet, clinically the general state of anxiety presumably reflects an underlying, specific emotion that is sensed by the subject as the more basic threatening element underlying the anxiety. The design of the character structure is developed in large measure to prevent such anxiety and its associated emotion from surfacing or being experienced consciously.

The issue of anxiety in the compulsive character structure also helps to create a diagnostic distinction between the compulsive character—designated as the obsessive compulsive personality disorder in *DSM-III-R*—and that of obsessive compulsive behavior appearing in the obsessive compulsive disorder or neurosis. This distinction concerns the ego syntonic nature of the obsessional symptoms in the compulsive character. These symptoms are not experienced as alien and therefore they do not disturb the person. In the obsessive compulsive neurotic on the other hand, the obsessive symptoms are ego dystonic or ego alien—the symptoms do disturb the person and are sensed as unnatural intrusions. Such a distinction between the acceptable and disturbing quality of obsessionalism follows from the design of the compulsive character structure of preventing the emergence of anxiety. This control of anxiety is never so thoroughly achieved in neurotic functioning where anxiety is more likely to be palpably experienced.

The distinction between the ego dystonic or alien nature of the obsessional symptoms in neurotic functioning that cause tension, and the ego syntonic nature of the obsessional qualities in the compulsive character disorder in the absence of tension, also reflects the role of externalization in obsessional characterology; that is, the elaboration of compulsive traits in the character structure disorder enables the individual to localize the source of disturbance externally rather than internally. Therefore, the distinction made by the individual between the external versus the internal source of the problem and that individual's stance toward it, contributes to the differential diagnosis between personality and anxiety disorder. Focusing externally, the individual with a personality or character disorder seems to view problems and conflicts in living more in terms of the noncompliance and limitations of other people in contrast with the neurotic who seems to maintain a closer sense of suffering from problems arising out of the functioning of the self.

The Compulsive Trait Profile and Defenses

There are various traits and behaviors that comprise the compulsive character structure. A triad usually designated for the compulsive personality includes traits of orderliness, obstinacy, and parsimony. Thus, within the strivings toward orderliness, the compulsive character exhibits a perfectionistic orientation that includes efforts to operate by rules, exhaustive attempts at organization, and a rigid sense of clear priorities to the point that the importance of detail and organization begin to outweigh concepts and accomplishment. Efforts toward maintaining careful balance in all matters may accompany this orderly disposition with its emphasis on organization. Along with such needs for structure, compulsive individuals are generally devoted to work and productivity with focus on detail and minutia rather than showing a broader focus on particularly meaningful contributions. When this devotion to work is excessive, it can sometimes lead to indecision so that the extra internal demand to be precise actually undermines the completion of assignments. Clearly, this expansion of adherence to order and minutiae amplifies functioning in the intellectual range and places an endless network of strictures on emotional strivings that insure significant and excessive emotional control.

In addition, with such profusion of ideation and intellectual control, interpersonal relationships tend to suffer. These interpersonal problems occur first because of an interpersonal insularity in which relationship needs are less important than work needs, and, secondly, because the perfectionistic need usually overwhelms any empathic response to the partner in favor of a demand for compliance. The interpersonal demands and emphasis on conformity that such a compulsive person makes suggest the presence of covert and underlying resentment appearing as a demand or need for control. Thus, the interpersonal aim becomes one in which the subject seeks to control the object.

Not only is the demand for control and tendency to try to dominate others a covert expression of underlying hostility, but the additional tendency to become obstinate adds to the quality of hostility that is being indirectly expressed. The trait of obstinacy may appear as stubbornness, negativism, oppositionalism, or simply as a belligerent refusal to yield, supported by details and principles that are conceptually irrelevant to the interpersonal issue at hand. As an aggregate, these obstinate characteristics that are utilized to dominate people and circumstances strongly suggest aggressive efforts at control over external and interpersonal situations in which the submission of others is especially valued. In psychoanalytic terms, such a configuration of personality implies a tyrannical superego. In interpersonal terms, it means that such a person will simply need to have his own way.

Because of the traits of orderliness and obstinacy and their associated characteristics, the compulsive character in day-to-day functioning shows a relative reduction in the ability to express warmth and emotions of affection. Along with this limited expression of warmth a reduced capacity for spontaneity is seen and a cool, formal, and emotionally stingy approach is typically demonstrated. The characteristic withholding of tender and warm emotions in favor of cool detachment and focus on detail not only conveys hostility or emotional indifference but this withholding also reflects the compulsive's reliance on parsimony as a measure of controlled restriction in the expression of warmth or any pleasurable emotion. This character trait of parsimony also extends to the hoarding, saving, economic carefulness and nit-picking associated with compulsive characterology.

While many of the character traits in compulsive functioning convey covert hostility, the major aim is also clearly to secure control over emotions in any form of overt expression. Thus, the unexpected is avoided by a rational, unemotional disposition.

Finally, it should be noted that when the compulsive character structure fails and its main defenses of intellectualization, reaction formation, sublimation, isolation of affect, undoing, and displacement become overwhelmed by stresses, the differential diagnostic consideration at such a point in the absence of decompensation, will likely shift in the direction of depression. This diagnostic shift toward depression is likely to take place because of the extensive but partially failed attempt to submerge resentment and anger. Generally, the depression is also fueled by a failure in the compulsive's attempt to gain closure—a characterological aim—and a corresponding absence of pleasure. Pleasure is experienced by the compulsive person mostly as a kind of moral victory, often followed by doubts sensed in connection with the question of whether or not sufficient thoroughness or accuracy was achieved. The following clinical example illustrates the compulsive characterological syndrome.

Clinical Case Illustration

A 48-year-old male college professor was referred for treatment because of the sudden and persistent experience of tension and anxiety occurring to him on the way home each day after his teaching obligations were completed. This man had never before experienced such discomfort.

An assessment of his recent history revealed a classically successful compulsive pattern. However, after several years of marriage, his wife increasingly pressured him to decrease his work responsibilities and increase his family sharing time. He had relegated all responsibilities for raising their daughter to his wife while he devoted his energies and time to perfecting and completing assignments and work interests. He married at the age of 40, having been single up to that point. His time was always fully occupied. He stated that whatever relationships he had were short-lived and terminated when his partner pressured him toward greater commitment.

During treatment, it became clear that he married because he believed his wife would not intrude on his intense need to work and because he felt she was capable of managing the details of their life together without any extensive involvement from him. His anxiety broke through the compulsive defense structure after she finally issued an ultimatum that conveyed how fed up she was, demanded his participation in all family matters, and, in an overall sense, insisted on more intimacy, more time together, and, in a day-to-day practical sense, indicated that she wanted him to have leisure time without any work related behavior. For the first time, he felt he could not have his way with her. It was only a short time after this confrontation, where obviously his entire character defense structure was challenged, that he began experiencing anxiety and tension whenever he left the university campus to travel home.

In the course of therapy, it became apparent that his anxiety and tension were actually symptoms of underlying specific emotions consisting primarily of anger, dissatisfaction, and associated inclinations toward stubbornness and defiance. This cluster of anger attitudes and moods seemed related to the intrusion of and interference with his compulsive needs. In addition, his wife's ultimatum that he was required to change, or else, forced him to confront the challenge to his defense system. This defense system seemed to consist of the mechanisms he used to displace anger, exercising control through intellectualization and sublimation, and the use of reaction formation in distancing himself from the experience of family warmth and intimacy. Along with his anxiety, he also began to experience some depression.

The differential diagnostic problem in this illustration involved a focus on both the patient's anxiety and depression. In this sense, in the absence of his typical compulsive compensatory defenses, the surface or behavioral diagnostic problem included both the anxiety and depression. Yet, under closer scrutiny, and on the characterological level, it became clear that his basic diagnosis was that of compulsive character because of the dedication to work and thoroughness at the expense of interpersonal attachment. The traits involved in this characterological pattern were ego syntonic—that is, he viewed these compulsive work related traits as desirable, he felt comfortable with them and, indeed, even proud of them. At first he regarded the problem as his wife's pressure on him to be more interpersonally involved and less centered exclusively on his work. He felt this demand reflected her inadequacy in understanding the obvious importance of his performance and manner of conducting himself. He began to feel both helpless and furious, apparently because he could no longer have his own way. The tyranny of the superego was thus challenged: his wife was standing in the way of his inner drivenness to work.

In the course of treatment, his focus on his wife shifted to a focus on himself as he was gradually encouraged and enabled to recognize the disturbing aspects of his character traits. He began to experience some of his traits as the problematic elements of his life. It is proposed that when this compulsive person would be able to rely less rigidly on character traits designed to maintain emotional control, he would then be able to experience closeness and a better rounded participation in life. Under such circumstances his depression and tension would in all likelihood be reduced.

In this emotion controlled compulsive character type, the object of the ideational approach in the control of emotion operated effectively as long as this person retained an isolated position, even within his marriage. When the need for control and emotional regulation was sufficiently challenged, a stressful condition intensified and penetrated his character defenses. At the point of the breach in character defenses, anxiety was released because of the enormous sense of threat engendered by the challenge to his need for emotional control.

This illustration also portrays the role played by anxiety, defenses, and character structure in diagnosis and in the dynamic interplay of forces in the personality that can create psychopathological manifestations. Interference with the design of the compulsive character structure and its associated defenses toward control over emotion enabled anxiety to surface and the psychopathological aspects of characterology could be evaluated in the context of rigid personality functioning. The character traits revealed in this case illustration are experienced in everyday life as problems of living but obviously stand on a psychological foundation in which the ultimate diagnosis as a reflection of psychopathology reveals the substrate of personality.

In this clinical example, this man exhibited the essential characteristics defining the compulsive personality disorder and its characterological derivative behaviors. These characteristics include a serious formality restricting warmth and tenderness; preoccupation with order, detail, and organization at the expense of a broader conception of goals; a demandingness of obedience without awareness of the effects on those pressured; overinvestment in work at the expense of personal pleasure and interpersonal closeness; and, indecisiveness and extensive rumination over priorities emanating from fears of committing errors. He was also guided by a sense of righteousness and perfectionism and maintained a rigid, consistently unyielding approach.

This case illustration also reveals both the shortcomings in individual functioning imposed by the pathological aspects of character as well as the interpersonal disturbances that are an inevitable result of rigid adherence to the control imperative of such a character pattern.

Paranoid Personality

The control of hostility by ideation centering around criticality is proposed as the emotion controlled basis for paranoid characterology. This paranoid personality functioning is typified by mistrust and suspiciousness that persists in spite of the absence of realistic justification. Such a mistrustful person usually expects to be hurt, manipulated, or tricked by others and, in addition, expects others to be disloyal. Therefore, such paranoid types adopt a guarded and secretive posture revealing little if any emotional expression or personal information. This kind of paranoid person can become absorbed with an overfocus on external possibilities of threat or indications of potential danger and seems to detect motives and meanings in inconsequential circumstances or innocuous communications. Characteristic suspiciousness may become manifested in unsupported jealousy, and details can be scrutinized in an attempt to prove suspicions without considering the circumstances that must be realized to give proper meaning to such details.

Intense sensitivity is revealed by the feelings of being offended, insulted, and slighted that are characteristically experienced by paranoid types. Under conditions in which sensitivity is experienced, a tendency to counterattack may appear as a means of dissipating the distress of the sensitivity. In this and in other ways, minor problems are greatly exaggerated and grudges and resentments are maintained in persistent and unforgiving ways. Under the threat of danger or insult the capacity to relax may become exceedingly constricted. Further, a cool and unemotional disposition is often displayed with emphasis maintained instead on a kind of rational, impersonal approach with absence of humor or warmth.

As can be seen from the composite characteristics comprising paranoid behavior, themes of danger, harm, hurt, and their corresponding protective mechanisms—guardedness and suspiciousness—together suggest that such a person is usually occupied in the management of excessive anger and in avoiding the personal acknowledgment of such anger. The management of this anger and the avoidance of anxiety associated with it as well as possibilities of loss of control over this potentially frightening emotion make the issue of emotional control a major concern in paranoid functioning. Thus, a range of intellectual, analytic, and cognitive qualities are developed to provide a means for assuring the overall control and regulation of feelings. Thinking and ideation, however distorted, seem to be utilized to prevent emotion from appearing dominant in the individual's functioning. In addition, the distortions of ideation can become amplified, usually by reliance on projection, externalization, and displacement as a way of evacuating feeling. Such riddance of feelings then allows for an elevation of a cognitive approach with insulated personal relating.

Developmental Issues

Developmentally, in the genesis of the paranoid character structure, it is highly likely that a critical parent was focal in the family and that childhood development was harnessed to the identification with this pervasive critically scrutinizing characteristic of the parent. While the critical parent instills a sense of inadequacy in the developing child, the child's identification with this critical parent suppresses the child's feelings of inadequacy and insures the continuing importance of the critical mode in personality functioning. Thus, criticality becomes the key character trait of the paranoid personality around which all the other patterns of behavior form.

In a practical sense, the typical parental attitude of this paranoid type may consist of scanning the environment in order to detect and identify targets for displaced, projected, or externalized hostility. This displaced hostility can serve as a vehicle for projection of a cluster of emotions, including anger, jealousy, annoyance, irritability, hostility and aggression, all of which satisfy such a person's need to displace the hostility along with blame. In addition, in order to fulfill the paranoid need system, a sense of hypervigilance and suspiciousness is also usually developed.

Hypothetically, then, the child is confronted with an impossible dilemma. The only way to achieve harmony with the parent is by adopting this same orientation of blaming. Therefore, the parent and child presumably act in concert and agree on the identity of the enemy. Although, in other forms of character disorder the particular character type that the child adopts usually arises from compromises with parental demands, in the paranoid constellation, for all intents and purposes, there is no compromise with the need to blame. Blaming, as a trait in the paranoid character is presumably developed through identification with the parent. The blaming trait thus resembles and is considered an identification with the aggressor. The central dilemma raised is that the need of the child becomes one of either blaming as the parent does, or being blamed, by the parent. A special, albeit extreme, example is that of abusive parents who express violent outbursts toward their children. Such parents generally exhibit extremely poor frustration tolerance and an impulsive, labile pattern. A paranoid characterology is often found as the underlying structure of this explosive personality type with the need to blame as the central motive force. It is this need to blame that provides the indignation and deep unconscious rationale that ultimately permits the abusive parent to act out violently as the means of reducing or avoiding frustration. Through identification, the child then internalizes the blaming attitude, thereby setting the stage for an abusive stance in later life that resembles the abusive attitude of the parent—the aggressor. This identification with the parent serves to erase any possible experience of personal humiliation to which the child may be subject if separation from the parent rather than identification were to take place.

As in all character development, the issue of managing and binding anxiety is also, for the paranoid character, of paramount importance. In fact, the central anxiety of the paranoid character lies in the extreme and absolute need of such a person to project blame. The paranoid character apparently will always perceive the imperfections of others—whether real or fantasied. Such a person can then criticize these perceived imperfections as well as any other objectionable characteristics of others as a way to satisfy the basic craving to criticize and to blame.

The paranoid's scanning and scrutinizing of others also reveals an underlying guardedness that serves first and foremost to prevent any self-criticism. Thus, the paranoid blame syndrome contributes to an overall defensive maneuver of distinguishing the perfect self from the imperfect world. Both the guardedness and hypervigilance of the paranoid correspond to the person's sense of threat from others and the anticipation that others may bring harm or danger. The expectation of harm or danger from others is a result of the use of the projection defense in which the person's criticality is externalized. Projecting critical and aggressive emotions onto others enables the paranoid person to deny harboring these emotions. By projecting these critical and angry feelings onto others, the potential for harm and danger is always attributed to external sources. Thus, the paranoid must vigilantly guard against such externally perceived threats from others. In fact, paranoid characterological patterns of vigilant scrutiny become a central control orientation in the simultaneous seeking out, identifying, and guarding against aggressive potential from without. The projection of hostility also raises the question in the paranoid person of the loyalty of other people. Thus, suspiciousness about the closeness and motivation of others with respect to intimacy or friendship is a typical attitude of such a paranoid person.

The management of the critical impulse through its projection can often lead the paranoid personality to exaggerate difficulties, to take offense readily at minor criticisms, from others, or even to be likely to counterattack when such criticism is perceived. When this hypersensitivity surfaces the paranoid individual naturally is unable to relax. Among the protective measures that such a person

may invoke in the context of this hypersensitivity is to behave une-
motionally, to adopt a posture of objectivity, and to avoid more
tender expressions—along with an absence of humor. An investment in intellectualization with pronounced ideational activity is
typical in securing an aspect of aloof objectivity which insures necessary emotional distance and control, as well as interpersonal insulation.

The focus on seeing imperfection in the world also suggests that
the paranoid craving to criticize is nourished by the continued evidence of the presence of an imperfect world populated by imperfect people. The orientation toward external imperfection is of diagnostic importance because of the paranoid's unacknowledged
but central subjective experience of inadequacy—the underlying
core of the personality structure. The theoretical presumption is
that this core inadequacy is controlled by externalization which
then reflects that the really dangerous imperfection to be avoided
and eradicated is the imperfection that originates from within the
self. Control over the conscious realization of personal imperfection and its necessary denial seems to be largely supported and
fortified by reliance on intellectual and ideational investments as
well as by interpersonal distancing mechanisms that prevent exposure of the sense of personal imperfection and its correlated hostile self-blame.

The transformation of personal but unacknowledged inadequacy into an ensuing, overriding focus on imperfection external
to the self can have very specific consequences. For example, the
paranoid character usually finds it difficult to establish commitments; to commit is to accept the other person. In the sense of this
resistive stance toward acceptance of others, the paranoid character exhibits what might be called a buyer's regret whenever
something has been inadvertently accepted; that is to say, the paranoid person will attempt to reject the incorporated object. In
practical terms, this can mean simply always reneging on an already established promise or commitment.

In summary, the central anxiety concerning personal inadequacy in the paranoid character causes such a person to experience
imperfections as externalized in order never to acknowledge any
personal imperfections whatsoever. Regarding the paranoid's central anxiety position, inferentially, it may be said that the core of
the paranoid character—its central anxiety position—is a profound inferiority feeling that must be denied at all cost. The per-

son's core anxiety regarding this personal inferiority requires constant vigilance. This vigilance is directed externally, since denial of personal inferiority feelings are made possible by the projection of criticality towards the world, a projection that is consistently being fueled and reinforced. Thus, the interpersonal aim in paranoid characterology is to make continual distinctions between subject and object—that is, between self and other.

Defenses

In a theoretical sense, it is expected that when stresses overwhelm paranoid defenses—chiefly of projection and secondarily of rationalization, reaction formation, and displacement—the severe core feelings of inferiority and inadequacy flood the person and the experience of anxiety can surface. Such anxiety is frequently experienced as one bordering on fragmentation in which the person's tensions are felt as a personal disintegration. No longer is the pervasive imperfection seen in the external world; it is now floridly and uncomfortably personal. Of course, in such a crisis, there is an opportunity for the paranoid character to begin to correct basic distortions involved in the sense of personal and total imperfection. The prognosis here depends very much on the severity of the need to blame, that in turn corresponds to the severity of perceived personal inferiority. It may be assumed that the more rigid the identification with the paranoid parent the more guarded is the prognosis. In the guarded prognosis, the rigidity of the character is fortified by the amalgam of typical defenses previously indicated—projection, rationalization, reaction formation, and displacement.

The utilization of the defense of reaction formation contains deepest links to identification with the paranoid parent, usually of the same sex. The reaction formation presumably reflects a disguised attraction to this idealized parent who is also a confused figure, because the idealization can conflict with the sense of imperfection of the same parent. The rationalization defense provides logic for the need to blame along with the displacement mechanism which permits the accumulation of targets. Finally, the projection defense, which is the most instrumental of all the paranoid characterological defenses, provides the critical bridge on which shame toward the imperfect self is transformed into blame toward the imperfect world. The operation of such defenses, the issue of personal imperfection as the source of the anxiety dimension, and the various developmental considerations as well as trait developments of this character can all to some extent be seen in the following clinical example.

Clinical Case Illustration

A 36-year-old violinist who was an important instrumentalist in a major orchestra was referred to treatment because of a severe crisis in his marriage. His initial complaint was that his wife had become frigid, refused his advances, and was generally uninterested in any conjugal or affectionate contact. The patient entered treatment feeling agitated, depressed, and extremely angry. He complained of being humiliated in this relationship with his wife, minimized by her apparent decreased esteem for him, and he generally felt not in control of any aspect of their relationship. He was attached to their only child, and claimed that he could not sever his relationship with his wife because of the emotional difficulty it would cause the child.

The initial complaint concerning his wife gave way to a more historical review of his life although he sustained an emphasis on his marital relationship. It became clear that a large part of the problem in this marital relationship was the patient's highly developed critical sense. It was an exquisite criticality and became a serious problem in all spheres of his life. For example, he expressed criticism toward other orchestra members and was hypersensitive to any and all imperfections around him. This same quality of scrutinizing and monitoring his environment apparently was acutely experienced by his wife, who after three years of marriage became unable to feel any warmth towards the patient even though at the beginning of their marriage she, in fact, felt quite loving toward him.

He reported that his wife complained that all he knew how to do was criticize. In treatment it was suggested, and he agreed, that he seemed always satisfied whenever he expressed his criticism. This criticism was mainly composed of anger and hostility and would become invoked the moment he perceived what he considered to be stupidities in those around him. He would need to verbalize his dissatisfaction and only then could he feel satisfied. Yet, the satisfaction he experienced after expostulating his anger and criticism was not of a tranquil quality. Rather, it was the kind of stirred up satisfaction composed of vindication, justification, and the victory of righteous indignation.

Thus, this patient's pleasure circuitry, which was intricately tied into his critical character, was a persistent itch that needed to be scratched and this itch-scratch sequence appeared to contain sado-masochistic elements. It became clear that the characterology in which this critical trait was embedded was of a paranoid nature that included also jealousy, envy, and suspiciousness. The paranoid ideation was revealed, for instance, by the use of projective mechanisms, in which imperfections were always searched for and then detected as lurking in the world. His response was to displace anger toward the externalized object. In addition, he utilized an intrinsic rationalization which permitted him to avoid any insight. Through the use of his defense system he supported his sense of self-esteem—that is, self is good, world is bad— thus creating the possibility for sustaining the alien feeling toward the world. Accordingly, the patient necessarily lived with restricted affect and appeared, increasingly as time went on, as cool and objective in the absence of any display of tender feelings.

A developmental review demonstrated the various components of this man's paranoid characterology. He was the surviving child of a twin birth. His father was apparently quite inadequate, passive, somewhat remote, and very modest. Yet, he did express some affection and, as the patient saw it, was a good person. The mother, an intelligent woman, was however a highly critical person. She was so egocentric that she minimized others and would try to locate their weaknesses as a way of elevating her own family by comparison.

The patient indicated that his mother was so idiosyncratic that she would even wear articles of clothing that were in disrepair, never worrying about the opinions of others. Apparently, it was clear to the patient that his mother always justified her own behavior but always scrutinized the behavior of others. He quoted his mother as saying, "My virtuosity is in my senses—my eye and my ear." She could tell precisely when things were wrong around her. If she could not control something, she would be extremely irritable and would look for targets to blame. She was also a jealous, suspicious, and envious type.

During treatment, this patient also began to describe his mother as someone who desperately needed to protect a personal sense of vulnerability. He also parenthetically noticed that her protection of vulnerability was, perhaps, true of him also. He felt that he, as well as his mother, was completely unable to look inward and examine possible deficiencies in personality and behavior. He reported that his wife's major complaint over the years was that he could not ever see anything wrong in what he was doing but could only complain about what she was doing. Yet, in reporting such personal revelations, the patient was already beginning to look inward.

In the paranoid character, as, for example with this patient, criticality toward the world can diminish after a period of treatment. In this clinical illustration the patient's overall rationalization was the most difficult defense to manage. He would frequently say, "I still think I'm right," although he also was appreciating the fact that he was indeed becoming more empathic.

The major identification figure in this case was the mother and not the same sex parent. The mother was the dominant focal figure in the home and the patient's close ties with her became enmeshed in his identification and imitation of her major characteristic of criticality and denial of personal inadequacy. Although paranoid characterology is usually exceedingly difficult to treat, in this case, the father's contribution to the patient's development rested in the expression of affectional bonds between them and very possibly formed the underlying seed of empathy that was later to develop and emerge during treatment. It was this sense of empathy that seemed to provide the opportunity for greater introspection in this man as well as creating the condition that permitted a weakening of the paranoid defensive constellation. A new and vital acknowledgment of tension and anxiety, and a transformation into a less restrictive characterological pattern was then possible to approximate.

As can be seen from this example, this man exhibited many of the major characteristics associated with the paranoid character pattern. These characteristics include mistrust and criticality as manifested by guardedness, vigilance, avoidance of self-blame, jealousy, and the expectation of harm and disloyalty from others; hypersensitivity reflected by feeling easily slighted, exaggeration of difficulties, and a readiness to attack as indicated by his unprovoked criticality; and, highly restricted affect, resulting in a cool, objective, rational persona with an absence of more tender feelings. It became possible to view this character pattern in the context of understanding basic family relationships with primary figures—wife, child, mother, and father.

Another typical character pattern associated with the emotion controlled types is the schizoid personality to be considered in the following section.

Schizoid Personality

The characteristics comprising schizoid functioning focus on emotional and interpersonal distance and aloofness. Traits of affection and warmth that ordinarily facilitate the bonding of people are exceedingly restricted in this characterology and, in fact, are essentially absent. Not only is a bland, unemotional, unresponsive disposition and appearance generated, but closeness with people is avoided. Thus, meaningful relationships are virtually nonexistent; they are neither yearned for nor sought. Further, friendship is generally avoided and most activities are pursued alone. Yet, it should be noted that schizoid is not schizophrenic. Rather, the schizoid diagnosis refers to the clinical state of aloofness or remoteness.

In the schizoid character type, reactions to praise, criticism, and the feelings of others are markedly limited, reflecting the schizoid's general disinterest in emotion and people. Paradoxically, however, a rich fantasy life usually exists, through which ideation is utilized to contain and control emotion. This elevation of ideation over emotional acknowledgment, experience, and expression not only provides the schizoid person with control but also establishes a condition of emotional and personal self-sufficiency. The chief emotion fueling the fantasies of the schizoid character is generally that of hostility. The presence of fantasy reflects once again the importance of ideation as part of the intellectual and cognitive apparatus used to control the influence that emotion may otherwise have on behavior. The schizoid's use of fantasy also reveals the importance of employing ideational and intellectual resources to limit the presumed dangers in both the experience and expression of emotions and especially in the anticipated loss of control were these emotions indeed to be expressed. The self-sufficiency and striving by such a person to maintain personal isolation occurs within a cognitive context in which bizarre or unusual qualities do not enter overt behavior or speech and in which thought processes can remain logical, analytical, and coherent.

Developmental Issues

The family constellation that usually sets the stage for the development of schizoid character structure is perhaps the most clearly defined and easily understood of these three emotion controlled character patterns—compulsive, paranoid and schizoid. In the development of the schizoid character, the child finds itself in the confines of emotionally unresponsive parents. In this particular kind of family, the child experiences parents who generally perform vocational functions well and discharge their duties in the family efficiently. Yet, these achievements tend to occur in the absence of any demonstrable affection between the parents or between parents and child.

It seems quite clear that in a technical sense, in this emotionally antiseptic environment, the child develops the necessary qualities that permit normal functioning but remains apparently limited in the use of any important relational skills encompassing general interpersonal play, sexual relatedness, the deepening of relationships, and the general give-and-take of friendships.

Persons who develop this schizoid pattern are usually obedient and compliant, and in an overall sense also exhibit the traits of reliability and honesty and seek ways and means to conform. Thus, it may be proposed that the schizoid personality type presents a clear profile—that is, this type contains a highly specific trait picture. These character traits are clearly identifiable and the character structure is considered practically immutable.

Although one diagnostic criterion of the schizoid type concerns an alleged indifference to praise or criticism, nevertheless a more precise understanding of this schizoid type reveals that such a person can indeed experience criticism or pleasure covertly and yet either of these experiences affect the basic character mode only very slightly. In an object relations sense, early parental modeling was probably both perfectly efficient with respect to performance and profoundly inefficient with respect to the demonstration or exchange of emotion. It is on this emotionally muted basis that the experience of praise or criticism does not register terribly deeply or meaningfully with such persons. It is assumed that the child who develops this schizoid character is able to function quite well; performance expectations are met, and all jobs are done with proficiency. However, the experience of affection, and the overall sense of the deepening of relationships are, underdeveloped.

Defenses and Traits

Schizoid development results in the formation of a syndrome consisting of traits and behaviors that include coldness, aloofness, remoteness, shyness, avoidance of competition, obedience, intraversion, seclusiveness, and, of course, social isolation—a distinctly encapsulated personality. An additional aspect of the schizoid syndrome is an absorption in hostile daydreams and preoccupations, which is an example of a general gratification through fantasy that characterizes such a person's emotional life. This kind of fantasy gratification provides the person with release of emotion in a highly controlled manner.

One of the diagnostic criteria in the identification of the schizoid character is the phenomenon that a close relationship with no more than two persons, including family members, is likely to develop in the person's life. A similar diagnosis, to be elaborated later, is the avoidant character type. In the avoidant type, in contrast with the schizoid, close relationships are overtly yearned for and a desire for contact and involvement with people is certainly felt and expressed.

Another diagnostic observation of the schizoid character concerns the absence of severe eccentricities in overall behavior, speech, or thinking. Even if fantasy is hostile or bizarre, integrity of speech and behavior are nevertheless consistently logical and usually attuned to reality. Thus, the experience of fantasy is perceived by the subject as separate from the logical requirements of cognition. When this reality-fantasy discrimination becomes confused, yet another differential diagnostic clarification with regard to the schizotypal character—also to be described later—can be made.

The schizoid personality is emotionally attenuated, although there are several specific emotional conditions that together seem to comprise such a person's experience. These emotional conditions, rather than developing from object-relations concerns, grow out of the encapsulated schizoid position. For example, continual frustration foisted upon the schizoid person by another individual is one emotional condition that can be vividly experienced by this schizoid character type. This frustration will generate rage which will then become immediately translated into pervasive hostile fantasies. Further, if the schizoid position is threatened by any potential relationship that requires emotional interaction, then such a person can become highly anxious and fearful and will be likely to make attempts to escape from the relationship. The position of isolation that insures control, a sense of security, and the absence of threat is thereby reconstituted by the social withdrawal. In addition, in terms of the experience of sexuality, such individuals can experience erotic feelings along with compulsive masturbation which serves to gratify these sexual feelings in a self-contained way without any need for involvement with others.

In terms of the organization of defense in the schizoid character, especially with respect to effectively retaining the narrow schizoid emotional band—defenses of repression, suppression, isolation of affect, fantasy, displacement, and especially compensation permit a smooth schizoid functioning. The schizoid internalization and identification with parents who show limited emotional content provides the context for this rather bleak emotional organization.

Defenses of repression, suppression, and isolation of affect permit such a person to decathect and withdraw from any possible ongoing interpersonal interactions. In fact the operation of these defenses helps prevent the development of any cathexis. The defense of displacement also manages to transpose direct hostility into indirect fantasy. In fantasy the hostility is successfully played out in isolation in the same way that autoeroticism can generate gratification for such a person without reliance on other people. The key defense of compensation enables the schizoid person to neutralize depressive feelings because consistent, reliable, and well-defined work performance also reflects derivative compensatory aims. Thus, whereas adaptive work usually reflects healthy behavior, in the schizoid, able functioning is also a way of preventing a slide into depression. This sort of compensatory element is considered to be the linchpin of the ongoing pattern of the schizoid. Without such compensatory involvement, the impoverishment of the schizoid position could have a palpable emotional impact. The control and containment of emotion so vital to schizoid functioning would then be threatened so that the loss of ideational control over emotional containment would evoke anxiety and undermine security.

The following clinical example is an illustration of the schizoid character structure. In clinical experience varying degrees of the schizoid pattern are seen. When the pattern is a classic one, as described above, relatedness which is a fact of life for others is only an abstraction for the schizoid. When, however, the schizoid pattern is further removed from its classic position, even though usual trait patterns may apply, relationships may be possible. Yet, such relationships will produce complaints about the schizoid person involving his underresponsiveness, isolation, withdrawal, coolness, aloofness, and so forth.

Clinical Case Illustration

A 38-year-old male postal service employee entered treatment on the suggestion of a supervisor. The supervisor was recommending psychotherapy because of the patient's isolative behavior and overall lack of social responsiveness. As it turned out, the patient was a well-functioning employee in all aspects of his work. He was responsible, conscientious, and in a general sense, never abused the rules and regulations of his job.

Psychological testing revealed a classic schizoid pattern along with intellectual functioning in the superior range. This classical schizoid functioning included emotional isolation and adherence to authority structure in the extreme form that also involved traits of compliance and obedience. In the emotional and interpersonal sphere, relationships or interests in personal engagements were absent, and indications of a hostile fantasy life emerged along with attenuated emotional expressiveness and the absence of manifest anxiety. Defenses of compensation were evident which could account for the clinical finding that there was no real indication of depressive trends. The patient also acknowledged that he was a compulsive masturbator.

In the therapy sessions the patient reported that he was never part of any social relationship. Since his father's death at the age of 11, he was supervised by his mother and grandmother. The patient reported that for his entire life he had developed an emphasis on solitary activities. He relied on movies and adventure stories in magazines and books to provide the color and content needed to fill in his fantasy life. His relationship with his parents never involved physical affection, and as is typical in schizoid development, his parents, and especially his mother, cared for him in the technical sense of providing adequate shelter and nourishment. Yet, his parents rarely focused on involvements in his schoolwork, except in a highly cursory way, or on any other concerns he may have had that would convey the sense that he was understood.

The patient indicated that because of this consistent hands-off policy, he felt as though he could never approach his parents for consultation on emotional issues or even to initiate any normal interpersonal activity such as dinner conversation or just plain everyday discussion of family life.

In treatment, it became evident that simple interpersonal activity that usually helps generate feelings of trust and closeness was never reinforced, practiced, or valued in any important way in this patient's family. This patient could never initiate an approach to another person arising out of personal needs or feelings unless the approach would be an outgrowth of a work requirement or some operation necessary for daily life. Otherwise, the patient lived—more or less—in silence.

One of the central differential factors distinguishing the schizoid position from the paranoid in the development of basic characterology is the absence of malicious intent towards others in the schizoid pattern. In a thermostatic sense, the family context of the schizoid is a cool one, corresponding to traits of remoteness, isolation and aloofness, while the temperature context of paranoid development is a hot one, based not on warmth but on criticality, jealousy, and suspiciousness that in turn comprise the paranoid interpersonal

syndrome. Because of an absence of the characteristic mistrust of the paranoid, this schizoid person was indeed able
to incorporate and accept all available procedural rules and
regulations and any other structures that he could follow. He
then could depend on these structures in the most conform-
ing way in order to guide his life in the absence of processed
or internalized guiding figures. The paranoid person on the
other hand, would, of course, have great difficulty accepting
or taking in any guiding structure, because of basic needs to
criticize, blame, and externalize.

The fact that repression, suppression, and isolation of affect as important defenses of the schizoid act to continuously
block any possible ongoing attachments was also true in this
patient. He would, in fact, have some occasional sexual contact with women, but these contacts were always casual and
perfunctory, served an exclusively physical purpose, and were
terminated abruptly whenever his partner expressed any interest in continuing the relationship on a fuller basis. In addition, any anger he experienced on his job was knitted into
fantasy and hostile scenarios, but was never acted out. These
angry impulses seemed also to be displaced, as for example,
in his compulsive eating habits. The fact that compensation
played such an important role for this man as it does in the
schizoid condition generally was also expressed by his comment that he was never depressed and in 15 years on the job
never missed a day's work.

As is the case with the schizoid personality, this patient
emerged as someone whose sense of interpersonal boundaries
was the clearest and most definitive aspect of his social understanding. It was clear to him that he could never initiate
social conversation unless cued by the other person. His
nightmares would awaken him with feelings of terror and
startle reactions. Invariably, the content of these nightmares
consisted of crumbling walls where he became visible from
behind the wall as well as other such contents characterized
by boundary demarcations becoming vague, or broken, or in
some way permeable, accompanied by feelings of threat or
panic.

In this case illustration, this man exhibited typical characteristics of the schizoid pattern. These behaviors and attitudes include

aloofness, absence of warmth toward others, relative indifference
to the feelings of others or to praise and criticism, and no close
friendships to speak of—all with the absence of eccentricities in
thought, speech, and behavior.

In these three emotion controlled diagnoses of the compulsive,
paranoid, and schizoid characters, the strong control over emotion
is central to the development of each particular type. An intellectual, analytic disposition is emphasized, profusion of ideation or
reliance on ideation is highly valued, and an overall cognitive approach characterizes the patterns. In each case interpersonal insularity occurs and this insularity contributes to a sense of safety
and security. The particular differences of defense styles and early
development differentiate the particular types. However, the unifying thread that relates each type is the need to keep emotion from
becoming primary in behavior and to contain and control its
expression through reliance on intellective and cognitive capacities. Thus, the major purpose of each of the emotion controlled
character styles is to manage anxiety by controlling emotion. In
the next chapter emotion dyscontrolled types will be presented.
These constitute the counterpoint to the emotion controlled types
discussed in this chapter.

CAPSULE CLINICAL PROFILES OF
EMOTION CONTROLLED CHARACTER TYPES

In these character types, control over emotion insures safety and
security keeping anxiety in check. A central cognitive approach
and a profusion of ideation along with defenses of intellectualization, projection, and insulation enable the person to manage any
potential anxiety and emotion.

> **Compulsive:** A tyrannical need to control and dominate others
> is central. Perfectionistic attitudes along with traits of orderli-
> ness, obstinacy, parsimony, and an overinvestment in work con-
> tribute to a restriction of the expression of warmth in interper-
> sonal relationships. Spontaneity is avoided and an attitude of
> moral superiority is maintained.

> **Paranoid:** A central dynamic based on the need to criticize the
> world and external objects enables the person with this char-

acter to maintain an anxiety-free condition with respect to personal imperfections and a grave sense of inadequacy. Profound inferiority feelings are projected onto the "inferior" world, which is then related to in consistently critical terms. The self can be seen as good and the nonself as bad, permitting marked differentiation between the self and the world. Traits include the familiar paranoid cluster of mistrust, suspiciousness, and jealousy. Affect is restricted.

Schizoid: The central character operation involves distancing mechanisms as a way of managing anxiety. Needs for emotional distance are accompanied by traits such as remoteness, aloofness, and coolness. The person is not necessarily malicious toward others but an absence of warmth prevails. Insulated self-sufficiency is maintained. Typical defenses include repression, suppression, isolation of affect, fantasy, displacement, and compensation to insure the position of distancing and the avoidance of depression.

CHAPTER 3

Emotion Dyscontrolled Character Types: Hysterical, Narcissistic, and Psychopathic Character Structure

In chapter 2, the emotion controlled character types of compulsive, paranoid, and schizoid were considered in a cluster based upon a central, underlying commonality. This commonality was defined as an all-encompassing need to control emotion which was secured by the elevation of ideation and thought patterns in various ways. It was proposed that this preoccupation during development with the control of emotion through utilization of ideation was the fundamental condition by which the particular character patterns of compulsive, paranoid, and schizoid were germinated.

In contrast, the essential commonality of the emotion dyscontrolled types considered in this chapter is the singular importance of emotion and its elevation above critical, analytic thinking in forming the character structure of hysterical, narcissistic, and psychopathic personality disorders. There are several variations of the central tendency of loosening restraints over emotion or over reliance on emotion in the emotion dyscontrolled types. For example, a major commonality in the emotion dyscontrolled types considered in this chapter includes the person's persistent need to generate externally stimulating conditions. A profusion of stimulation insures the avoidance of a monotone internal condition or inertial experience. In these emotion dyscontrolled character types the experience of manifest anxiety is poorly tolerated. The creation of external stimulation is relied on to limit and avoid such anxiety. In contrast, the absence of externally stimulating conditions can create anger, depression, boredom, panic, and in some cases, the feeling of psychic paralysis. In the emotionally controlled characters presented in the last chapter, emotional insularity was assured by the overuse of ideation. In the emotionally dyscontrolled patterns of hysteric, narcissistic, and psychopathic character structures reviewed in this chapter, emotional insularity is avoided by the creation of external stimulation fueled by compensatory activity and the restriction of critical cognitive capacities.

In these emotionally dyscontrolled types, general anxiety is experienced with respect to the person's doubt about whether there is anything of value in the inner life. A persistent external focus is maintained by the person in order to avoid reflection related to inner concerns. As part of this external preoccupation, persons who are dyscontrolled along these character lines of development need to be involved in multitudes of relationships although not necessarily those that are intimate or deep. Such persons need to maintain a relatively high level of social activity and their superficiality of relating assists in the development of a multiplicity of external connections and focuses. In the emotion controlled types presented in chapter 2, an increase in the achievement of security and safety occurred through control of emotional life. In contrast, in the dyscontrolled types, the opposite is true; that is, when emotion is controlled the feeling of safety is threatened.

In terms of the central psychopthological signal variously referred to as tension, panic, or anxiety, the emotion controlled types of compulsive, paranoid, and schizoid become insular with respect to emotion by emphasizing ideation so that the emotional range is narrowed. Essentially, what is controlled are emotions of pleasure, criticality, and anger. The achievement of this control and its extension in efforts to control external circumstances tends to minimize surprise, excitation, and stimulation.

In contrast, in the emotion dyscontrolled types of hysterical, narcissistic, and psychopathic personalities, anxiety is managed by releasing emotion in order to avoid the experience of any significant insularity with respect to social interaction. In these dyscontrolled types, the emotional range is expanded so that at certain points, such persons sacrifice judgment, critical thinking, and analysis in favor of the satisfaction of releasing and exercising feelings.

Another commonality occurring in the dyscontrolled character patterns of hysterical, narcissistic, and psychopathic functioning concerns the cluster of defense mechanisms that typically predominates. This cluster of defenses operates to insure the condition of release of emotion and consistently increases the probability that externally stimulating conditions will prevail as a typical social condition. The specific defense mechanisms relied upon are repression, denial, regression, and compensation. These defenses are utilized extensively to prevent accumulations of critical feelings that tend to create social distance. Rather, such defenses assist in the creation of overly permeable boundaries enabling the person to experience as much stimulation as possible. In addition, these specific defenses permit a distinct and studied avoidance of depressive feelings as well as insuring a self-perpetuating action-oriented or motoric condition. The motoric condition enables persons of dyscontrolled character types to be ever involved in exercising and receiving stimuli, to be embedded in emotion and to minimize cognitive capacities.

Again, as in the previous chapter, it should be noted that the point at which each character pattern emerges with its own distinctive configuration relates to differing developmental issues involving the particular need for the dyscontrol of emotion. In the dyscontrolled types, the need for social accessibility and the continual spilling over of emotionality serves separate and specific purposes for each personality type. Along with the specific trait clusters and defense mechanisms that develop for each type—hysterical, narcissistic, and psychopathic—these separate purposes of the expanded disharge of emotion determine the differential diagnostic components that comprise and distinguish each type. In the following presentation each of the dyscontrolled character types—hysterical, narcissistic and psychopathic—will be considered in detail.

Histrionic Personality or Hysterical Personality

Histrionic or hysterical characterology displays innumerable signs of the person's immaturity. This characterology relates to an essentially dependent core in which thinking, planning, analysis, and other secondary process attributes have not gained equality with the need for emotional satisfaction. The experience of emotion and reference to feelings as the basic guide for decision making, which is almost casual and automatic in its operation, are attributes consistent with this immature quality that marks the histrionic character style. This character type also values praise, approval, attention, and rapid gratification of desires. Thus, limited ability has developed to allow for sustained tolerance of frustration or the ability to withstand removal from the center of attention.

The hysteric's naive reliance on appearance relates to preoccupations with emotional exaggeration, dramatic expression, craving for recognition, and especially recognition based on attractiveness and utilization of a sexually seductive type of self-presentation. Emotions and relationships that are engaged are usually characteristically shallow with manipulativeness more likely relied upon than articulate persuasion. Verbal expression itself tends to be global and inarticulate in its nonspecificity, and the desire for stimulation is considerable.

Developmental History

In the development of the hysterical characterological pattern, a family history usually reveals a major dynamic that can be described as a labile family mood. This lability in the family is frequently identified with the mother who allegedly lives her life on the basis of what is clinically considered to be a magical thinking style. The formulation of the concept of magical thinking refers to the presence of a positive, euphoric mood based upon wishful thinking. This wishfulness is frequently met or even accompanied by its opposite inclination—that is, numerous disappointments that result in a dysphoric or disappointed mood. This sort of lability—a swing from euphoria to disappointment—differs from manic-depressive psychosis in its depth and scope and in that the disappointments are quickly forgotten and replaced by additional hopeful and magical wishes.

A child in such a family can experience one parent as histrionic or hysterical and the other as quite naive, unchallenging, and apparently accepting of the overly major histrionic or dramatic tone that is established for family life. The child who is drawn to the more dramatic parent demonstrating the overtly emotional role, may, in terms of object identification, begin to seek gratification through a group of histrionic characteristics. These include tendencies to adopt attention-getting devices, to develop a gregarious social orientation, and to learn the overall hysterical pattern that includes becoming helpless and dependent on others as well as becoming demanding and arbitrary in decision making. This arbitrariness can arise gradually out of an experience in which instant gratification becomes a prominent need at the expense of a more considered and time-consuming decision-making process that would require delay of gratification.

Since gratification through the intense experience of emotion—with only limited inhibition by cognitive or ideational processes—is a central striving for the hysterical person, defenses are utilized that can encourage perceptions that reinforce romantic and magical wish fulfillments. The defense mechanism of repression eliminates awareness of the original figures toward which romantic inclinations were focused in early development, and with the utilization of displacement allows a striving for childlike romantic and magical impulses to be discharged on contemporary figures. The basis for such discharge of romantic impulses onto contemporary figures presumably has its genesis in the child's attachment to the opposite sex parent, a constellation frequently referred to in the psychoanalytic literature as the oedipal drama between daughter and father. This underlying drama contributes to the prominance of traits involving dependent and romantic strivings in the hysterical character structure. Such romantic and magical wish fulfilling efforts can be clinically characterized as naive and childlike and represent the hysteric's exaggerated investment in romantic strivings. Romantic strivings and a rather elevated or aristocratic view of one's destiny and entitlement exemplify the use of the defense of compensation in the hysterical character structure. The defense mechanism of compensation is likely to limit anxiety that would otherwise surface if awareness of the limited substance in achievements, maturity, and relationships were overtly faced by the hysteric personality.

Parallel with repression and displacement which operate on the internal impulses and wishes of the hysteric person, the defense mechanism of denial also becomes central to the entire hysterical characterological pattern. The evolving hysterical personality employs denial so that unpleasant realities and those external factors that would impede expansion of emotional strivings are vigorously screened out. Intellectual, cognitive, analytic, and thought-based capacities are successfully minimized by emphatic use of this denial defense mechanism.

It is out of such a dynamic of displaced magical wishes and the use of denial of reality factors that the central diagnostic component of the hysteric emerges. This central component is a high index of suggestibility in the hysterical structure in which emotional responses are taken more seriously than thoughtful analysis. With such a high suggestibility quotient, romantic fantasies are usually fortified while critical and evaluative faculties are sacrificed. In contrast, in the paranoid personality, the critical-evaluative faculties are the ones depended upon most strongly in keeping with the paranoid need to rely on ideational control factors. Whereas in the paranoid personality the critical-evaluative function is overdeveloped as a way of rejecting any ego dystonic material, in the hysteric personality, the proclivity to suggestion, persuasion, and influence is overdeveloped for the same reason—to reject ego alien material. Persons with a hysterical character structure must be able to accept almost anything in order to retain and enhance the powerful need for a dependent orientation, to diminish serious investment in thoughtful decision-making, to permit quick gratification, and to ensure an endless incoming stream of stimulation from the outside.

Character Trait Development

In terms of character trait development, the hysteric characterological type can be impetuous, petulant, easily bored, dramatic in gesture and behavior, arbitrary with respect to decisions, and generally impatient. The need for speedy gratification and the need to foster an environment free of decision making also then creates the possibility in such a person of more frequent irrational outbursts, a focus on a host of complaints, and even the experience of somatic symptoms such as aches or overall feelings of weakness. Utilization of these sorts of conversion mechanisms enhances the dramatic quality of the hysterical profile.

The child growing up with a parent who demonstrates histrionic character patterns is confronted with the imperative to learn either to be a victim or an indulged person. This sort of dichotomy between victim or aristocrat promotes an alternation that corresponds to the lability in the personality of the hysteric. There is a release of positive emotion associated with the indulged role and a release of dysphoric emotion associated with the role of victim. The hysteric utilizes denial in order to reinforce the indulged role and to minimize the role of victim. The constellation of reduced negative perceptions then allows good feelings to be continually reinforced as they are fueled by the romantic, magical, and wishful impulses that dominate over thinking. The hysteric's use of denial mechanisms and high suggestibility quotient fortify such a focus on the positive and magical preoccupations. The repeating problem that such a person encounters is that sooner or later inevitable factors of reality impinge on this characteristically uncritical, shallow style so that disappointment, consequently, is inevitable. Thus, the lability of mood can also be seen as composed of acutely felt wishes sensed as always on the verge of being gratified. This focus on yearnings for gratification, especially in the romantic sphere, as well as the ready display of feelings associated with a focus on wishes, support a quality of exhibitionism. Yet, in spite of the drama of this framework of intense emotional responding, the suppression of thoughtful faculties allows a naive, uncritical perpetuation, if not acceptance, of the emotional strivings and expression that seem to dominate histrionic functioning. These features of an emotionally oriented, gratification-seeking, cognitively underdeveloped character structure reveal the central dependency needs that form the core of the hysterical posture.

In the early history of such a person it is often evident that the parent seeks to avoid the manifest experience of anxiety at all cost. This excessive concern with the denial and avoidance of anxiety is consistent with an essential focus on dependency needs and with impairment in the development of effective regulatory mechanisms enabling tolerance of frustration. In addition, it may be hypothesized that a child in such a family is exposed to models exemplified by the parent who expects magical solutions without showing any effort involved in the numerous steps required to achieve actual mastery. In the pursuit of gratification, the defenses of denial, repression, and compensation serve to ward off depression, neutralize anxiety, and screen out any perceptions that would contradict the stance of dependent-like magical thinking. Thus, the external stimulation sought by such a person is selectively screened to achieve gratification, dependency, and reassurance.

With such a wishful need system and the inevitability of disappointments, hysterical personalities can often become angry, experience irrational outbursts, and exhibit impatience. They can be, at the least, demanding and inconsiderate in the emotionally driven pursuit of their view of happiness and, at the other extreme, can create suicidal dramas as a result of their disappointments. The suicidal dramas are generally not designed to end life; instead they function to attract attention and reflect such a person's need for manipulation and the achievement of secondary gain. The somatic complaints of pains and weaknesses of various sorts are similarly designed to engender attention, care, and special stature in a dependent context. In the following presentation, a case illustration is offered that contains many of the classic hysteric components that together comprise the hysteric character structure.

Clinical Case Illustration

A 37-year-old single woman sought treatment because of her latest disappointment over a broken engagement. This was the third time she was engaged in a ten-year period. She reported that her first fiancé, to whom she was engaged when she was 27, was extremely immature. He would invent tales about alleged achievements that were transparently false. Even though this patient was warned by friends and family to be wary of him, she did not agree with such negative perceptions; nor did she believe any admonishments or concerns.

Soon she was disappointed in the relationship and discovered that indeed, her fiance, in fact, was quite untrustworthy. She became irritable, impatient, and morose, and announced to her family and friends that life was not worth living. Her despondency was short-lived, even though it caused concern among friends and family with respect to suicidal implications. Her histrionics abated immediately upon another involvement, approximately one month after the breakup of her engagement.

The patient described a series of love affairs lasting until the age of 32, when she became engaged for the second time. She enjoyed calling herself a romantic. In most of these encounters, she would assume a dependent posture, expecting others to take on special responsibilities for her, and then would feel disappointed and angry when each one of her relationships ended in failure.

Her mood swings ranged between exaggerated and grandiose gestures of self-love to dispirited pessimism. During euphoric periods of grandiose self-love, she would describe her hopes and ambitions for success. In the course of treatment, she began to notice that she required a great deal of adoration from others and that although this need seemed odd to her, nevertheless she would quickly put it out of her mind. When she was disappointed, she became angry and would experience humiliation and depression—feelings that were very difficult for her to bear. She readily agreed that her feelings of superiority were sometimes quickly converted to profound feelings of inferiority whenever she felt disappointed. This transformation actually exhausted her.

Historically, she described her father as a person not to be considered seriously, as someone who was weak and submissive to her mother. She said "my mother, myself" and explained that she felt very similar to her mother, especially in terms of ignoring rules and regulations whenever it suited her achievement wishes. She described her mother as someone who could only focus on personal distress and who was singularly involved in an idealistic and romantic view of life.

The patient reported that her mother spent many years with "tons of boyfriends." The patient laughingly referred to this picture as a self-portrait, meaning that she too had tons of boyfriends. In the analysis of her character and behavior, it became evident that this woman could be tilted toward love and romance by the slightest positive feedback and frequently suspended any critical judgment when she would be complimented or otherwise praised. The strong suggestibility component in her personality is visible also by her comment, "I just can't see their faults and I never could." This suspension of critical judgment on the part of the patient along with her high suggestibility quotient tends to reveal her character dilemma. While swept away and flooded with stimuli generated by romantic fantasies, she is unable to govern such fantasies by carefully scrutinizing information. For example, she does not notice any contradictory evidence or think conceptually and analytically about the people and circumstances she engages. Thus, the defenses of denial, repression, and compensation continue to be exercised in the service of neutralizing any anxiety that would otherwise be generated in such a situation that calls for independent judgment, critical reasoning, and evaluation. Emotions are utilized to define situations, while thinking is restricted. The patient tends to employ magical thinking and because of underemphasized cognition establishes a position of dependency. The limited development of conceptual and analytic skills and non-manipulative interpersonal connections seems to prevent the assumption of more personal and independent adult responsibility. These dependent and wishful characteristics also seem to reflect poor regulation of early gratifications. In addition, such characteristics often result in vague somatic complaints along with feelings of tiredness, weakness, and fatigue, all of which appeared in the complaints of this patient. These physical complaints can foster secondary gains of attention, reduced expectations for accomplishment, the need for extra help in a wide range of personal functioning, and the consolidation of a dependent orientation in the absence of any serious pressures to plan and think more realistically.

In summary, this patient exhibited most of the typical hysterical dynamic. This dynamic resulted in the development of traits that included petulance, impatience, anger, and a high suggestibility index, along with an absence of critical judgment. She was at once experiencing both grandiosity and inferiority depending on the extent of the success she had in gratifying her wishes. When approaching success, she would feel euphoric and when unsuccessful she would feel inferior and disappointed. In addition, she was exhibitionistic, required adoration, and, in an overall sense, was self-centered. The defense cluster of denial, repression, and compensation seemed apparent in her attempts to sustain a positive wishful stance.

As in the case with most hysterics, it was troublesome for her to solidify any relationship because of intense dependency needs and the bane of her existence was the consistent, periodic experience of disappointment.

In the following section, the emotion dyscontrolled character structure of narcissistic personality functioning will be presented as the second character pattern in the triad of the emotion dyscontrolled types that include hysteric, narcissistic, and psychopathic. In this narcissistic personality, self-centered strivings for admiration are even more crucial than those present in the histrionic characterology.

Narcissistic Personality

For the first time, the narcissistic personality has been officially codified in *DSM-III/III-R* as a bona fide characterological pattern. In the past, narcissistic characteristics have been for the most part amalgamated within the diagnostic concept of hysterical personality, in addition to which they have also been assigned a general developmental role in other characterological patterns. Since the 1960s, however, as interest and research in object relations theory has increased, greater clarity has accrued to the entire narcissistic constellation, culminating in the 1980s with the diagnosis of narcissistic personality occupying the focus of many professionals.

At the descriptive level codified by *DSM-III* and *DSM-III-R*, the narcissistic personality disorder embodies traits of self-aggrandizement, expecting special or unique treatment by others, and preoccupations in fantasy with extraordinary achievement, and an extravagant self-estimate of intelligence and attractiveness. On the basis of such grandiosity, the narcissist expects recognition and admiration. When such entitlements are not met, and when slighted even in minor ways, anger, shame, deflation, humiliation, and emptiness are experienced. Relationships with people are manipulatively designed especially to furnish positive acknowledgment and feedback based on the narcissistic person's ostensible special status and superior attributes; therefore, exploitation, limited feeling for the position of others, and grandiose expectations reflect the narcissistic character's deficiencies in empathy and extremely restricted understanding of interpersonal conventions. Extraordinary needs for attention, admiration, and compliments involve the person of this character type in easy exaggerations of the talents that are possessed, perception of the envy of others, and the tendency to consider ordinary problems as uniquely special in importance.

Hysteria and Narcissism: A Comparison

Symptomatically, in behavior as well as etiology, the narcissistic and hysteric personalities share certain commonalities, and yet the differences in the two states are certainly great enough to warrant their separation. The essential commonalities of the two characterologies will be considered followed by a discussion of major differences.

As indicated in the previous section on the hysteric, and in terms of the present discussion of the narcissistic pattern, both the hysteric and narcissistic characters share focal points of concern with respect to the expectation of special entitlements from others. In addition, both types then experience a euphoric tinge in the anticipation of gratification of these entitlements and also can experience sudden despair when confronted with disappointment. Both the hysterical and narcissistic persons can be quite sensitive to minor slights, and can become easily angry when ignored. This anger usually covers a deep sense of hurt arising from the experience of deflation and loss of self-esteem when expectations are not met. For the hysteric, such deflation of self-esteem concerns a threat to dependency needs in the face of disappointment, while for the narcissist a more central fragility of the integrity of the self may be involved.

In both types, achievements are frequently overvalued largely because of profound self-doubt. Such doubt is managed by compensatory needs, and both the narcissist and hysteric share fantasies of conquests that can include themes of power, success, and adoration from others—a compenstory feast.

Behaviorally, both types also express exhibitionistic needs that require constant reinforcement, attention, and gratification. This exhibitionism also contains elements of grandiosity and an intense wish for love and recognition. In addition, ironically, both types also show an underdeveloped sense of empathy and a corresponding disregard for others. Thus, ample similarities between the narcissist and the hysteric can be cited with regard to behavior and symptoms.

The importance in distinguishing between the narcissistic and hysteric character structure can be appreciated when the differences between behavior, symptoms, and etiology are examined. Whereas the hysteric is highly suggestible and screens out negative information concerning, for example, romantic wishes toward the love object, the narcissistic personality shows rather limited tendencies toward suggestibility. The narcissistic person is not as malleable, is more strident, and is capable of utilizing rational and intellectual techniques calculated for purposes of gaining sought-after admiration. This difference with respect to the more thoughtful or analytic qualities of the narcissistic character creates an important distinction between the two character types. The narcissistic personality is one that can generate cool indifference in interpersonal relations and can develop a complex of symptoms with respect to the experience of disappointment. The hysteric, of course, also can become dispirited in reaction to conditions of disappointment. Such disappointment experiences are short-lived however, and the hysteric then rebounds with new wish fufillment fantasies. Thus, critical thinking and access to cognitive analysis and planning usually achieve greater development in the narcissistic person as compared to the hysteric, although in areas affecting self-esteem and self-doubt, the emergence of intense feelings that override the utilization of intellect is characteristic and typical of both.

In contrast to the hysteric, the narcissistic personality treats disappointment in a way that reveals the most important aspects of its particular character. For example, disappointment is usually responded to with feelings of emptiness, anger, depression, and even humiliation, which together constitute a trait aggregate or special syndrome rather than a simple, short-lived, emotional state of despair that is more characteristic of the hysteric. What becomes evident about the narcissistic personality is the appearance of a syndrome that includes feelings of inferiority, shame, and an idiosyncratic existential emptiness occurring in response to conditions of disappointment.

Implicit in the qualities of personal feelings in narcissistic types is that the release of such a complex underpinning to disappointment suggests that the narcissistic personality, as is frequently acknowledged, is essentially a disorder of the self; that is, narcissistic characterology is a personality disorder that reflects identity concerns, personhood issues, and finally, profound self-doubt. The difference between the hysteric and the narcissistic personality types with respect to etiological and developmental factors concerns the fragility about self that is especially relevant to the narcissistic character type, but is less central as an etiological consideration and developmental manifestation of the hysterical character type.

In the hysteric character type, the absence of a critical psychic agency permits a high suggestibility quotient; that is, the hysteric views the interpersonal experience through rose-colored lenses according to wish fulfillment needs. In the narcissistic personality this need for ideal love is also present and exists as a high priority need issue. Yet, the operation of a range of defenses such as intellectualization, projection, rationalization, and even sublimation along with repression, denial, and compensation create in the narcissistic character a greater need to criticize and an increased obsessional concern that can generate a more rigid boundary structure. Through the use of defenses of repression and denial, recognition of many aspects of the inner sense of inadequacy and the limitations of accomplishments can be avoided. Projection allows the narcissistic character to externalize onto others the devalued sense of self as well as the criticality that is harbored toward this core personal inadequacy. Concurrently with repression, denial, and projection, compensation acts to promote the idealized self in grandiose fashion. Similarly, compensation promotes strivings to participate in special situations and to be involved with special or idealized figures as a way of enhancing self-evaluation. Intellectualization, sublimation, and rationalization are utilized to gain a sense of accomplishment, to view personal achievements as special, and to explain away deficiencies or the criticisms of others through a process of justification. This entire narcissistic defense structure is employed to manage the inherent deflated sense of self and also to establish a clear sense of interpersonal boundary structure.

Theoretically, beneath the complex defensive structure, the narcissistic personality contains a fragile identity underpinning along with this more rigid interpersonal boundary structure, whereas the hysterical personality is thought to contain a more resilient personality underpinning with a permeable interpersonal boundary structure. In the most derivative sense, as an overall personality configuration, the hysteric seeks to achieve goals through dramatic gestures and emotional manipulativeness, while the narcissistic character may also seek to achieve goals through rational and intellectual styles—albeit within an emotionally dyscontrolled mode—and with an emphasis on achievement strivings.

While the characteristics utilized in striving toward goals differ between the hysteric and the narcissist, the goals in psychological terms also reflect important diagnostic divergencies. For the hysteric, goals tend to relate to the achievement of acceptance and recognition along with romantic connotations in order to feel safe, cared for, and worthy. For the narcissist, striving is aimed toward special accomplishments, recognition and admiration to compensate for fundamental self-doubt and an inner sense of emptiness. In addition, striving for the narcissist seems to serve as an integrating force insuring a sense of coherence to fortify the essentially weak and fragmented sense of self.

On a prognostic level, it is apparent that with a more fragile personality underpinning and less permeable interpersonal boundaries, the narcissistic character type will be more resistant to change. Further, because of profound identity concerns with respect to this fragility, the narcissistic character type can experience what is typically described as narcissistic rage reflecting a more basic experience usually referred to as narcissistic injury. Thus, the narcissistic character resistance to treatment is presumbly greater, interpersonal success is predictably less, and overall prognosis apparently more guarded, as compared to the hysteric, even though levels of overt achievement in the narcissistic person may be substantial. A major factor accounting for this more guarded prognosis is that the narcissistic character type typically shows considerably less emotional investment in others, in contrast to the hysteric whose curtailed rationality paradoxically encourages greater emotional investment in and dependency upon ameliorative attempts such as psychotherapeutic intervention.

Developmental Considerations

Developmentally, the fragile personality underpinning reflected by profound self-doubt and identity concerns suggests more primitive fixations and an even earlier onset of the narcissistic maladaptive pattern. For example, a narcissistic character type presumbly develops motives based upon experiences with parents who are likely to act indifferently or negatively to actual accomplishments. Yet, it is thought that such parents seem always to extend hope that special achievements will be recognized and acknowledged as valuable in the future. Thus, the child experiences the first glimmer of a particular repetition compulsion; that is, on a behavioral level to continue to strive for the attainment of some important goal that will ostensibly and finally establish self-worth, while at the same time trying to master the tension and anxiety caused by the fact that moment to moment solid, realistic achievements are somehow complicated and involve strangely ambivalent responses from others.

Since theoretically the feedback from parents does not permit simple enjoyment of accomplishments, interpersonal expectations become both more limited and at the same time more intense; that is, this seeming paradox of acceptance–non-acceptance by the parent is resolved by the operation of the repetition compulsion—expectation of devaluation leads to greater compensatory attempts for special recognition. Thus, it is presumed that the need for recognition can become elaborated into a host of special derivative entitlement wishes in which the narcissistic personality type expects compliance from others and can become surprised, enraged, or humiliated when people are not consistently receptive. It is proposed that such an ambiguous response from others awakens an important developmental theme: the sensitivity associated with narcissistic injury.

A final effect of the narcissistic wish sequence of seeking recognition but receiving an ambiguous or negative response is that interpersonal relationships can become shallow and governed by the desire for such admiration and recognition rather than determined by interpersonal warmth, care, and affection. It is when such wishful entitlements of the narcissist are unfulfilled or frustrated that the complex narcissistic reactions of rage, deflation, hurt, shame, and humiliation may ensue. The following clinical case is presented that reflects many of the dynamics of the narcissistic character.

Clinical Case Illustration

A 45-year-old male university professor who was the chairperson of a humanities program experienced depression and anxiety due to a series of disappointments in his role as administrator. A tracing of his history soon revealed that for most of his life this patient experienced a fragile sense of self. He would become periodically depressed, always in response to disappointment at not achieving personal goals. He described his relationships with others in grandiose terms and seemed to be using florid defenses of denial and compensation to justify his grandiosity. He was fond of describing his achievements, and especially described the high esteem his program evoked and he himself engendered. He made it quite clear that he was most concerned with the special status of his program and conveyed the implication that this special status aggrandized him in a direct way. A quality of exaggeration was evident in the one-dimensional presentation of his achievements.

The onset of his presenting problem of depression and anxiety concerned the university administration's decision to reject his application for the position of dean. Apparently, one of the committee members confided that his image was of a person who was nonempathic, opportunistic, and that he was seen as someone who had not made sufficiently solid achievements. Rather, he was considered to be untrustworthy. Rumor had it that he persuaded others to ghostwrite material for him.

He was extremely wounded and depressed by this exposure. Like other narissistic persons in their fantasy quest for power, he felt completely entitled to success. In addition to his depression over this actual disappointment and the gaping fragility this disappointment revealed with regard to his sense of self, he became very angry and experienced his disappointment as a humiliating defeat. He also parenthetically reported that his wife was not understanding. She suggested that his colleagues and friends all probably felt what she had been feeling: that his cool indifference toward others, along with an exhibitionistic aggrandizing need for constant attention and admiration, was just plainly wearing everyone out.

This patient was unable to utilize his denial defense, and his compensatory fantasies of aggrandizement—composed of needs for power, admiration, success, and the achievement of a special, recognizable niche—were now nullified. What was left for him was the actual rejection by the university committee and the rather devastating revelation by his wife that confirmed his insubstantiality. The combination of these factors meant that his worst fear would be confirmed: that is, the experience of a profound self-doubt combined with self-devaluation that resulted in an unshakeable feeling of emptiness and worthlessness.

This patient exhibited some major characteristics attributed to the narcissistic personality including the primary polarity between overidealizing the self on the one hand and devaluing it on the other. He showed entitlement problems, an absence of empathy necessary for adequacy in interpersonal relating and a tendency toward experiencing sudden and brittle anger with respect to disappointments. The essential impact of his childhood can be condensed into a single formulation: no matter what he did in the present it was never quite enough. His parents would typically refer to what he could do in the future. This family posture—displaying lack of realistic encouragement and empathy, and instead emphasizing the value of a future, hypothetical special achievement—can characterize the developmental history of the narcissistic personality.

In the following section, the third character pattern in the triad of emotion dyscontrolled types—namely, the psychopathic character—will be presented. This diagnostic character pattern has been also called sociopathic or antisocial. The designation psychopathic is used here to focus on the theoretically defensive regressive nature of the disorder. This regressive nature creates difficulties for such a person in terms of understanding boundary structures. Thus, this psychopathic dyscontrolled character pattern can be examined in a psychological sense and not necessarily seen solely from the point of view that considers certain behaviors to be delinquent or criminal. In this psychological sense, the psychopathic type will be understood and examined in the context of emotion dycontrolled character formation.

Psychopathic Personality

The emotion dyscontrolled character disorder referred to here as psychopathic type has been variously called antisocial reaction, as well as dysocial reaction in *DSM-I,* and antisocial personality in *DSM-II.* In *DSM-III* and *DSM-III-R* it is referred to as antisocial personality disorder. In all of the psychiatric nosological systems, this psychopathic type has been characterized by antisocial behavior, that is, by the kind of behavior that ultimately leads to legal and social difficulties.

In the codification of *DSM-III* and *DSM-III-R,* the antisocial qualities of this disorder involve a pre-adult history that includes some representations of the following dysocial behaviors: school truancy, suspension, delinquency, various criminal activities and inability to adhere to rules in general, as well as a disposition for fighting, substance abuse, and casualness in relationships. Inabilities to function in socially adequate terms are reflected by diagnostic criteria drawn from among excessive job loss, unemployment, absenteeism, irresponsible parenting, overtly illegal activities, inability for sustained personal heterosexual attachments, and predelections for overt aggression, financial irresponsibility, impulsivity with incapacity for adequate planning, lying, manipulativeness, and recklessness without a sense of guilt.

This compilation of the behaviors contributing to the current *DSM* diagnostic criteria of the psychopath overwhelmingly relates to social implications typified by antisocial behavior associated with impulsive, acting out patterns. In spite of the antisocial qualities traditionally associated with the psychopathic diagnosis, the character structure of the psychopath nevertheless is psychologically complex, containing implications not solely reflecting social disturbances. For example, the psychopathic character type also contains a specific profile composed of an intertwined network of personality traits, impaired cognitive skills, mood imperatives, dispositional characteristics, inadequate and incomplete identifications, as well as specific etiological referents. In this overall personality sense, the psychopathic type described here in characterological terms is primarily viewed, along with all other character types, as essentially a psychological type and only secondarily in terms of the social implications of behavior.

Treated conceptually in this psychological manner, the psychopathic personality, like other character orientations, engages in a specific complement of behaviors, utilizes a particular mode of defense, and is to some extent presumably guided by unconscious forces that contribute to an attempt to accomplish a central adaptive task. This task, as in all the character disorders, is basically to manage anxiety. Thus, the consequences of psychopathic behavior which can be defined as antisocial are—from the psychological point of view—a secondary consideration and frequently are not terribly explanatory. Further, such social concerns can deflect important focus away from the underlying psychological conflicts that are actually responsible for the antisocial, sociopathic, or dysocial acting out.

It can be proposed, therefore, that the psychopath should not be considered solely as an antisocial or delinquent type. Rather, in terms of character, a psychological dimension needs to be emphasized in any diagnostic consideration of the acting out of dysocial or antisocial behavior. Thus, explanatory, etiological, diagnostic, and prognostic concerns would involve an analysis of underlying conflicts as well as traits, defenses, and character structure designed to manage anxiety. In psychological terms, such an analysis would reveal the individual stamp and inevitable qualities of the psychopathic diagnosis.

Trait Behavior

To distinguish the psychopathic character pattern, it is necessary to consider the particular trait constellation that is typical of this personality disorder. In the psychopathic type, a central characteristic is a motoric style in which the person seems to need to physically move and thus functions by seeking to resolve conflicts always in terms of motoric activity. Because of this need for movement and consequent motoric behavior, traits such as impulsivity, aggressivity, promiscuity, addictive tendencies and correlated cognitive deficits such as poor attention span and poor frustration tolerance are some obvious qualities expressed on the trait and attitudinal levels of the personality. Along with these traits are many corresponding behaviors such as lying, fighting, frequent disruption of relationships, frequent job changes, overall irritability, abrogation of financial obligations, underachievement, selfishness, and callousness. Additional traits that are typical include manipulative behavior, a tendency to blame others, an apparent hedonistic style, impaired judgment, a tendency not to learn from experience, an overall irresponsibility, and limited if any guilt regarding the behaviors utilized that cause distress to others.

It can be seen from this constellation of trait behaviors and needs that the probability of antisocial behavior in such a personality profile can be high, and that it can be easy to overlook the psychological aspects of the disorder and to focus instead solely on social implications. In contrast, a psychological conception of acting out as an aspect of a central defensive and characterological style accounts for the greater probability of antisocial activity and also provides an understanding of personality functioning as it is distorted by the psychopathic character structure. To focus on delinquency—an outcome of the personality disorder rather than its essential character structure—seems to create a bias toward typical social remedies such as punishment and segregation. In contrast, focusing on the concept of acting out can lead to a series of further questions regarding the psychological nature of the acting out, its causes, and components.

Before discussing the nature, the cause, and the components of the acting out, it is useful to review the organization of the defensive constellation utilized by the psychopathic character type.

Defenses

In the psychopathic character type, the defenses of repression and compensation work in tandem: to keep important knowledge suppressed and out of awareness—the job of repression—and, to help the person pretend that he is involved in important activities—the work of compensation. A further important third defense in the psychopathic constellation is the defense of regression. An active regressive defense enables this type to exercise, fortify, and reinforce the motoric need. It is the defense of regression and its derivative conditions of poor attention span and poor frustration tolerance that give the psychopathic type its stamp of emotional dyscontrol and impulsivity. Finally, the defense of comparmentalization permits the psychopathic person to act out even when some awareness of consequences do in fact exist. That is, the knowledge of consequences can exist, as it were, in one compartment, while the urges and impulses toward action operate out of another entirely independent compartment.

The central acting out phenomenon of this type can be defined as an attempt by the person to *do* something rather than to *know* something. The *something* is perceived as important and is kept elevated in importance by the use of compensation. The *doing* is the motoric substitution for the *knowing,* and is assured by regressive operations. This particular configuration of acting out, that is, doing something rather than knowing something, addresses the psychopath's central motivation. This central motivation involves anesthetizing specific current anxiety as well as deflecting potential anxiety about fears of the deadened inner life. Thus, through the use of repression regarding this core anxiety of a deadened inner life, the character structure is well defended and smoothly integrated. It is this successful defensive operation against anxiety in the psychopath that establishes the characterological features, including a trait configuration of an impulsive, action oriented style with components of aggressivity and promiscuity, and a defense constellation including repression, compensation, and regression.

Acting Out

Within the framework of understanding the psychopath as a character disorder with traits, defenses, and specific etiology, an analysis of the nature, cause, and components of acting out can be considered.

THE NATURE OF ACTING OUT

The nature of a predisposition toward acting out is understood with respect to the presence of a motoric orientation in the personality. From a characterological perspective, action or motoric behavior keeps the person on the move so that doing things is a substitute for thinking. Because of a significant reduction in time utilized to reflect, carefully plan and assess alternatives in the context of tranquil thought, the individual is governed by intuition and impulses that prevent him from considering important personal issues. Therefore, it can be assumed that the probability of experiencing tension and anxiety would increase were this individual to stop and reflect. In addition, the elevation of emotion over reflection in the operating style of this psychopathic emotion dyscontrolled type reveals impairments regarding planning, learning, abstraction, and conceptualization, as well as inadequate use of thought to determine the most constructive choice of action.

From a psychoanalytic point of view, the motoric behavior that displaces more considered thinking is not a random kind of motor behavior. Rather, this behavior presumably contains symbolic meaning that corresponds to a specific psychological conflict. Thus, the acting out is a psychological phenomenon that can be understood and can illuminate the person's defended state. Because of this deterministic approach in viewing acting out, the nature of the acting out can be specific as to cause, and, in addition, the acting out can have specific components in its expression.

THE CAUSE OF ACTING OUT

In discussing the nature of acting out with respect to its deterministic underpinnings and symbolic behavior, the question arises as to the specific cause of acting out as the central behavior of psychopathic character. It is assumed, of course, that the cause of such acting out and action orientation is designed to manage tension and anxiety. The question becomes, What is it about the psychopath's particular intensity of anxiety that makes him uncomfortable to the point of needing to continue moving and behaving, but at all costs not to remain still? The answer to this question regarding the cause of acting out lies in both theoretical considerations and empirical observations. Empirically, clinicians observe that psychopathic types report the experience of a deadened internal sense—that is, an estimation of the inner self consisting of emptiness or silence. The etiology of this profound self-concept of inner silence will be further elaborated in the later section of the clinical illustration. However, on a theoretical level, the cause of the acting out leads to a discussion of the elevation of emotion and action over thought and planning in psychopathic personality functioning and points to a constriction in the development of internalized structures such as ego strengths.

Coupled with the poor models available for internalization in terms of object relations, the impaired and diminished ego strengths of the acting out characterology are assumed to contribute to an impoverished inner sense. This tenuous inner sense would necessarily involve a highly diminished sense of self that together with poor ego strengths offer little of the comfort and tranquility that would be needed to stop moving, to consider, and to reflect. The need to protect this vulnerable inner life can create the all-important interpersonal aim characterizing the psychopathic person—to prevent any external source or object from controlling the subject. To be controlled by others means to be stopped. Thus, a grave experience of dread may be associated by the subject with any involvement in the internal world. From this theoretical viewpoint it is clear that the imperatives of acting out characterology prevent typical introspection and reflection.

Theoretically, the psychopath's motor orientation and corresponding acting out behavior can be better understood in light of the intense anxiety generated by alleged inner sensations of deadened feelings and abject silence that must be avoided at all costs. This, then, can be proposed as the central cause and the source of the motoric fuel the psychopath utilizes to keep moving, and reveals the absolute necessity to employ regression as a defense in order to maintain this motoric childlike condition, the display of poor frustration tolerance, and corresponding needs for immediate gratification.

The motoric orientation, therefore, is pleasurable because it insures relief from the potentially intense anxiety of being still or motionless. Because of this avoidance of the expected experience of inner emptiness under conditions of stillness, the self-reinforcing condition of pleasure through consistent and immediate gratification in so-called play is constantly fortified.

These issues of the nature and cause of acting out in the psychopathic character type can now lead to an examination of the components of acting out within the context of the acting out process.

COMPONENTS OF ACTING OUT

When considering the components of acting out, it is important to examine the issue of impulse since it is impulses that are acted out, and the clinical question concerns the nature of these particular impulses. From a psychoanalytic perspective the conventional understanding of the nature of impulses considers two classes of impulses. These are impulses related to anger and impulses related to sexuality. In terms of anger impulses, in a practical sense, such impulses most frequently appear in the form of an ever-present, mild dissatisfaction, so that in the psychopathic character type, a person who experiences this persistent mild dissatisfaction is motivated to push ahead, so to speak, in order to stay ahead of the dissatisfaction—in order not to experience it. The sensation of such a person is that something from within is pushing, and this sensation is a major factor contributing to an overall action orientation.

The nature of this ever-present, mild dissatisfaction, is directly related to the proposed core anxiety of the psychopathic character, that remaining still or motionless is terrifying because of a perceived deadened inner life. Thus, the management of this core anxiety consists of a sense of continual discomfort or mild dissatisfaction that is only relieved by moving and by staying out in front of the tensions. This sort of action orientation also increases the probability that such a person's judgment can be negatively affected. In this sense of the possibility of an ever impending presence of impaired judgment, the person's inappropriate behavior also reveals a limited appreciation of boundary conditions. This issue of impaired judgment, of course, becomes more of a problem when the impulsive condition of the psychopathic character reaches the intensity level of anger or rage, rather than one of merely mild dissatisfaction.

Under such anger conditions, consequent behavior increases the likelihood that the person will need the assistance of external controls. At such an intensity point, the need for external controls, of course, substitutes for the absence of sufficient inner controls. Among the inner controls weakened in the characterology of the psychopathic personality are those derived from impaired ego strengths and defective internalized structures reflecting the incorporation of incomplete identification figures.

A further internal regulator of some importance that is typically defective in psychopathic functioning is that of conscience. Thus, an additional controlling mechanism that is severely compromised is the capacity of meaningful reference to concepts of right and wrong and standards of conventional morality as guides for choice and behavior. The defective mechanism of conscience and corresponding limited guilt is accordingly unavailable to permit anticipation of negative or punitive consequences with respect to behavior. The pressure of emotion then, as opposed to reflective planning, is further solidified as the main mechanism in determining behavior and insuring impulsive choices.

The psychopath's restricted development of standards as guides for behavior and the limited development of inner structures to allow thought and reflection interfere with the importance usually given to consequences in learning from experience. The capacities that are lacking are usually masked beneath a charming facade that has been derived from the persuasiveness and manipulativeness developed in place of more substantive strengths. The experience of inner emptiness which combines with the limited structures for delaying anxiety can promote a repetitious, motorically based acting out of impulses at the slightest signal of anxiety or emotional pressure. The fateful consequence of the acting out disposition is the impairment in strengthening internal resources, a defect that reinforces reliance on regressive functioning.

In contrast to the action orientation of the psychopathic character, when sufficient controls do exist in a person, then the anger impulse can be expressed directly or the anger may be translated into hostility, which is processed in a way that enables a measure of inner control. This more normal inner control over hostility and anger which is usually expressed directly toward an object is typically managed, more or less, by the defense of displacement. Thus, hostility is carried through fantasy and rumination and managed by means of this entire fantasy displacement process.

In the psychopathic type however, such a sequence is unfortunately most frequently short-circuited and the dissatisfaction, anger, or hostility leaps directly into intrusive behavior, usually in the form of aggression. Of course, the difference in the psychopath versus more adaptive types, is that in the psychopath, the feelings and impulses, whether anger or sexual impulses, translate into immediate behavior upon the action orientation need. In contrast, in more adaptive types, impulses are displaced into fantasy, or remain on a cognitive level, generally in thoughts, and can become expressed in verbal rather than action terms. Thus, the components of acting out include the psychopath's sense of inner numbness, severe impairments in cognitive and ego structures, internalizations and moral referents that create an inadequate, foreboding inner world, an action orientation that addresses the anxiety resulting from this sense of inner deadness, and an acting out pattern in which the use of thoughts and fantasies is eliminated, so that impulse leads directly to behavior that is frequently experienced by others as intrusive or invasive.

With respect to sexual impulses, the same imperfections of reflection, ethical considerations, inner controls and the need to act as a means of avoiding anxiety lead to impulsive involvements rather than those regulated through fantasy, displacement, or sustained feelings. Interpersonal relationships, including sexual and parenting patterns tend to be remarkably casual and superficial, reflecting the gratification of action rather than investment in forthought, planning, and consequences. The sequence of usually short-lived interpersonal involvements is typically sustained by the charm and manipulativeness that the psychopathic type relies upon in the absence of richer, more thoughtful, cognitive and analytic capacities.

In the following section, a psychopathic character sydrome will be presented that shows some of the features of the psychopathic behavior pattern presented above.

Clinical Case Illustration

A 49-year-old business man was referred for psychotherapy because of his philandering, gambling, and incessant activity seeking. He was an extremely loquacious person, who in one session reported his entire history, facts related to his marital relationship, children, business, and extra-curricular activities. What was most revealed, however, was the psychopathic characterological structure that identified his personality. The most evident and visible characteristic to emerge was his incessant action oriented need, which in the first session was revealed through a compulsive talking style. He was intelligent and charming, and his poor judgment in social interaction, as illustrated by his inability to listen, could only somewhat be overlooked because of his charm. His ten-year marriage was eroding and his charm was apparently wearing thin.

Early in treatment, the psychopathic character formations became increasingly apparent as he described two nightmares. In the first, he was chased by a knife-wielding attacker, but felt paralyzed and could not run. The second was a nightmare in which he was underwater and drowning. In these nightmares of ultimate paralysis in the face of mortal threat, such a person's central defense becomes inoperative and in the case of the psychopathic character this central defense is identified as regression. The defense of regression usually insures an action orientation. In the absence of the regression, the action orientation propensity is unavailable to the subject. This vulnerable condition—the absence of action orientation—means that the psychopathic person experiences a stopping and an abiding stillness which in the dream develops into the extreme—that of paralysis. Hence, these nightmares reveal the true nature of the psychopathic character with respect to such a person's core anxiety—that of feeling inwardly inert or inorganic, that is, not alive.

Generally such persons, and this man in particular, have had historical experiences with parents who were either unable to offer guidance, were themselves delinquent and acting out, or were concerned and anxious but hopelessly unknowing with respect to implementing guidelines. When the child internalizes this sort of an absence of structure, the probability increases that such a child will begin to engage in behaviors that generate short cuts, that reflect a paucity of any rich and varied internalizations, and will show a need for immediate gratification. Excuse making, glibness, and other correlated personality qualities begin to appear. These are essentially substitute traits for planning, thinking, postponement, and the general development of an enriched inner life.

This man reported just such a developmental history. He described his mother as someone who was overly concerned with rules and regulations but who he reported was stupid and toward whom he developed contemptuous feelings. The patient felt similarly toward his father, calling him weak and uninteresting. He also reported that, although he was usually the smartest of his classmates, his grades were poor because he could not sit still for an appreciable amount of time to do his homework. He indicated that he loved the business world because he could constantly use the phone, move around, and be involved in a great deal of action. He said, if he had a middle name, it would be *action*.

This person demonstrated the way in which underlying psychopathic ingredients appear in derived form in the person's everyday life. In this case, the entire acting out process in the form of action orientation and the reliance on compensatory behaviors were the ingredients that stirred his motivations and, in a sense, kept him as far away from his inner life as possible.

In the *DSM-III/III-R* equivalent of the psychopathic character, the antisocial personality is described as one who engages in delinquent activity, illegal activity, persistent lying, promiscuity, drunkenness, or substance abuse, and so forth. Included also are school delinquency, underachievement, and fighting. In the group above 18 years of age, characteristics such as inconsistent work behavior, absenteeism, irresponsibility, inability to develop a meaningful relationship, irritability and aggressiveness, poor planning, impulsivity, recklessness, and disregard for the truth are some characteristics and trait patterns attributed to this type. The difference between the *DSM-III/III-R* model for this type and the present discussion of psychopathic character lies in the behaviorally oriented and sociological conceptualization in *DSM-III/III-R* in contrast to the psychological perspective of the psychopathological character structure of the psychopath offered here.

Commonalities in Dyscontrolled Diagnoses

In the three dyscontrolled diagnoses of the hysteric, narcissistic, and psychopathic characters, a determined and typical dyscontrol of emotion is important in the identification of each type. Rather than needing to monitor and exercise consistent control over emotion as in the controlled character types, these dyscontrolled types seem to create, generate, or at least become involved in, endless stimulating conditions that are externally derived. Without the experience of stimulation, persons who express the characteristics of dyscontrolled character types can experience feelings of panic and paralysis as well as self-devaluation that can lead to extreme dissatisfaction and a sense of emptiness. Consequently, references to feelings play a much greater role in determining behavior than do applications of thought, analysis, planning, and other cognitive qualities. In addition, the activity resulting from externally stimulating conditions serves compensatory needs, which in turn permit such persons to achieve interpersonal contact. In this interpersonal respect, such persons can develop many relationships, although not always those that are intimate or deep. The management of anxiety in such dyscontrolled types concerns the prevention of social insularity, self-doubt, and the feeling of inner emptiness.

The dyscontrol aspect of emotion thus serves its central purpose of fueling a sustained compensatory syndrome of each of the respective dyscontrolled characters. When these compensations, regressive defenses, and denials operate well, a feeling of safety is insured. Finally, these character types are variably successful in avoiding protracted depressive feelings because of the constant search for impulse gratification. Thus, the strong dyscontrol of emotion as a central characteristic of such character types provides the major commonality in character development around which clusters of traits congeal in a manner that unifies the dyscontrol types of hysteric, narcissistic, and psychopathic characters, along with providing each type its distinct cast.

In the following chapter emotion dependent types will be presented. These include characterological syndromes of dependent personality, passive aggressive personality, and inadequate personality, and are grouped together under the heading of emotion dependent types.

CAPSULE CLINICAL PROFILES OF EMOTION DYSCONTROLLED CHARACTER TYPES

Elevation of emotion over critical, analytic thinking characterizes emotion dyscontrolled character types. Each of them needs to create externally stimulating conditions to insure endless opportunity for emotional experiences. In this way emotional insularity is avoided. Self-doubt is a major problem, and typical defenses utilized to shore up impaired ego strength and create personal reassurance include compensation, repression, denial, and regression.

Hysterical: Intense needs for rapid gratification of desires are evident along with a corresponding low level of frustration tolerance. Along with cravings for recognition, an immature dependent core of the personality as well as inadequacy feelings are often managed by grandiosity. The histrionic trait cluster includes petulance, impatience, anger, and dramatic style. An overinvestment in magical and romantic strivings limits feelings of disappointment and victimization. Denial mechanisms also fuel a high suggestibility quotient.

Narcissistic: Self-centered strivings for admiration are intense. Self-aggrandizement covers great self-doubt and a fragile identity underpinning. Conflict between an overidealizing self and a devaluing self is central. Entitlement demands are frequent and, when thwarted, a reaction of rage, depression, and especially feelings of shame and humiliation appear. Relationships are often shallow. The narcissistic person shows a limited tendency toward suggestibility and can employ an intellectual style.

Psychopathic: An intrusive and hedonistic style along with poor judgment and planning ability reveals the impulsive character of this person. Acting out or action orientation increases the probability of antisocial behavior. Regression is mainly utilized to maintain the typical motoric style and to obtain a reduction of anxiety regarding a deadened inner self through a continuous search for stimulus filled experiences. The psychopathic person uses blame and is manipulative. Learning from experience and moral referents are usually impaired. Defenses of repression, compensation, and compartmentalization are also employed.

CHAPTER 4

Emotion Dependent Character Types: Dependent, Passive Aggressive, and Inadequate Character Structure

In the organization of the development of character structure, and for heuristic purposes, the basic groupings of character patterns can be considered as opposite types. For example, chapter 2 presented the *controlled* character types of compulsive, paranoid, and schizoid. In chapter 3, a discussion of *dyscontrolled* types was presented consisting of hysteric, narcissistic, and psychopathic. Similarly, in this and the next chapter, two additional groupings can be conceived as polar, opposite, or at least discrepant types along the dimension of emotional dependency or interpersonal reliance. In this chapter, the character pattern of dependent character, passive aggressive character, and inadequate character share a cluster of characteristics concerning needs for nurturance, dependency, reliance on authority figures, protection, and the striving to express emotion without any overt appearance of negativity, such as anger; these character patterns are designed to avoid conditions of emotional chaos or threat to the primary and existing nurturing bond. In contrast, the next chapter will present character types that can be grouped under the commonality of emotion avoidant types in which reliance on nurturant figures tends to be avoided largely due to specific fears of involvement. These emotion avoidant types are the borderline character, schizotypal character, and avoidant character.

In the emotion dependent character types presented in this chapter, perhaps the classic representative of this group is the dependent personality which will be considered first.

Dependent Personality

In the dependent character, consistent efforts are made by the person to achieve safety and security. These efforts to insure safety and security constitute the major operations of this kind of personality. The dependent character is newly derived in *DSM-III/ III-R*. In previous diagnostic nomenclatures such as *DSM-I* and *II,* any dependency features of the character, whenever exaggerated, were subsumed either under the passive aggressive personality, the hysterical personality, or the inadequate personality. Yet, empirically, there is a growing consensus that the dependent personality structure has a clear enough configuration to warrant its own analysis and classification.

The dependent character structure is arranged so that the person avoids meeting challenges on any independent footing and, therefore, the responsibility for decision making is shifted to others. Limited self-esteem is usually associated with this need to rely on others for guidance and life's basic decisions. The need to depend, which becomes central for this character type, requires such dependent individuals to devalue personal capacities and to avoid displeasing those upon whom they depend. Consequently, the expression of hostility or the involvement in controversy is consistently avoided.

Thus, in the context of dependent functioning, passivity is emphasized, the advice of others is sought and followed, and agreement with authority figures is easily expressed. Initiative and spontaneity are minimized in favor of following, and abuse is sometimes accepted by such persons in order to insure building a store of love and approval—a method of achieving the important gain of security. Because of the striving to avoid self-direction, such dependent persons find it exceedingly difficult to tolerate solitude. Individuals of this type, therefore, are sensitive to any signs that a dependent relationship might end. In this respect, the possibility of abandonment will usually generate extreme anxiety for such persons.

The dependency profile becomes more visible when viewed within the interpersonal matrix. In projective psychodiagnostic testing terms and in personality trait theory, such a person would be labeled a need dependent type who exhibits a host of attitudes associated with dependency, including needs for nurturance, protection, reliance on authority figures, and the inclination to avoid any emotional turbulence. It is in the effort of the dependent character type to create and sustain conditions in which the central dependency requirements can be gratified that dispositional tendencies toward passivity and deference develop. These need dependent tendencies of passivity and deference are designed to evoke protective responses in parental or authority figures. Such protective parental responses include making decisions, providing structuring, offering direction, ordering the world in clear, predictable terms, and the retention of childhood conditions in which the relationship with the responsible parent is essential, and in a transferential sense, continually recapitulated. When the dependency condition is in fact successfully reproduced, the dependent type does not have to rely on himself and has managed to avoid or limit any anxiety experienced in connection with self-direction and the possible loss of the protective figure. The reluctance toward self-reliance on the part of the dependent person is important to note because it is a direct link to the etiological and developmental conditions of the dependent character structure.

Developmental Issues

Developmentally, the dependent character structure begins to assume its particular cast when the self is perceived and experienced as helpless, and when parental figures are inordinately needed for balance and stability. In the absence of a parent or authority figure on whom to depend, ambivalence increases and foreboding anxiety with a sense of emotional chaos can be experienced. This experience of emotional chaos comprises palpable anxiety, confusion, and the feeling that one is helpless, lost, and abandoned. The dependent person therefore needs to prevent any confusion and ambivalence from gaining in ascendency. Further, such a person must keep emotion under at least some control, and must, therefore, remain attached to a parental figure. The figure that becomes the focus of attachment may be either a natural parent or some representational figure who is relied upon for direction, decision making, and nurturance. When such need dependent conditions are met, the context of safety and security that is provided enables the person to experience a better sense of self. This elevated sense of self can occur as long as the integrity of the interpersonal dependent conditions are insured, since the achievement of safety and security neutralizes any anxiety concerning the issue of abandonment.

The trait of passivity is naturally utilized so that in the dependent person decision making essentially replicates original parent-child interactions; that is, the parent or parent substitute figure assumes responsibilities for choices to be made. The dependent personality also portrays the essence of the dependent condition in fantasy. These fantasies can reflect magical solutions to problems in which the self is not credited with mature implementation of behavior that leads to attainment of goals. Rather, activities that lead to the achievement of goals are either ascribed to an authority figure or are entirely absent. Thus, when fantasies result in accomplishment of goals in the absence of necessary implementation behavior, then there are only magical solutions to problems: the person is gratified in fantasy simply by a magical leap from dependent need directly, more or less, to goal satisfaction.

In the etiology of the dependent character structure, anxiety about abandonment, loss of love, and the possibility of independent functioning becomes essentially regulated by the overprotective parent. Such a parent is not usually aware of the importance to the child of gradually learning to tolerate frustration, building strength out of enacting individual choice, and tolerating and rectifying mistakes by relying on inner resourcefulness. In this interpersonal pattern, as the child develops, the parent continually gratifies the child's needs by directing behavior and offering reassurance, often in subtle ways. The child becomes convinced through this pervasive gratification that the presence of the parent and respect for the parent's knowledge is the only way to satisfy reliably the need for love, security, safety, and overall nurturance.

In a practical sense, this type of parent runs interference for the child even in only moderately untoward circumstances, attributes importance and uncertainty even to relatively innocuous requirements of life, and checks all of the child's products, from feces as an infant to homework assignments in the child's developing life. In such cases it is typical for the mother to be the one who is overly involved and for the father to be relatively passive. The dependent position also can be induced through abundant advice-giving and supervision or excessive monitoring and other less obvious influences that are based on subtle but continuing guidance from the parent.

Emotions and Defenses

Negative feelings in the dependent type can become quite visible during the psychological experience of separation. It is the experience of separation that generates pronounced anxiety in this type and it also, parenthetically, offers a model of the psychological effects of separation anxiety. Separation events that may occur for the dependent character as life proceeds can include attending a new school, leaving home for college, moving to a new neighborhood, and the death of a parent. During such separation events the negative emotions displayed are likely to include sorrow, as well as anger and rage. Some psychophysiological reactions that can appear may include symptoms of insomnia, digestive disturbances, as well as sexual problems such as impotence. The presence of feelings of helplessness, as well as the appearance of physiological reactions, also contribute to the experiences of anger, panic, and depression.

The defense of denial, as well as that of compensation and the central internalizations involving control by the parent, can also become disrupted during separation experiences thereby intensifying the dependent person's fears and fortifying the sense of frustration and anger. An analysis of the dependent personality with respect to the emotions of anger and depression and the defenses of denial and compensation yields a consistent psychological principle: dependency generates anger. This principle enables appreciation of the covert anger that frequently is masked by the compliant, cooperative, apparent goodness in the self-effacement of the dependent person. Covert anger develops from the fact that a dependent attitude must be adhered to because of the constraints of the character structure. Resentment also accrues from the numerous occasions that inevitably occur when dependency needs are not sufficiently met. Under such conditions, anxiety as well as anger may become mobilized.

The principle that dependency generates anger also provides an explanation for typical rebelliousness during adolescence. Even reasonably well-adjusted adolescents who are separating from the childhood dependency relationship become oppositional, generally dissatisfied, and angry. In contrast, the dependent personality type who forgoes this typical agitation of adolescence and instead retains the childhood dependency position, in all probability will indeed experience less of a turbulent adolescence. The central position of the dependency type, therefore, is based upon the presence of conditions that insure safety and security and avoid the evocation of emotions of anger and depression. Such anger and depression then, can be generated from the release of anxiety usually caused by experiences of separation and the threat of abandonment.

While the various traits established to maintain the dependent posture, such as passivity, submission, obedience, lack of initiative, self-effacement, and reliance on others for guidance and decision making, seem fairly obvious, these and other traits of dependency are linked to reliance on specific defense mechanisms. For example, the defenses of displacement and repression are usually mobilized whenever anxiety threatens to arise in connection with the experience of anger concerning possible separations. In addition, suppression and denial can be utilized to regulate the anxiety that would emerge in the dependent person if the essential limitations of functioning and necessary yielding to others were to be seen realistically. Instead, the defense mechanism of denial insures the successful avoidance of unflattering or self-defeating character patterns that the dependent personality must maintain. Rather, by virtue of the use of denial, these dependent qualities are viewed as necessary or normal interpersonal features. Further, a sense of strength, safety, and security is gained by the dependent person through the operation of the defense of compensation. Compensation completes the defensive management of anxiety regarding feelings of helplessness to potential separation experiences by providing a sense of well-being and security. This defensive network helps to neutralize any anxiety such persons may experience regarding the limitations of behavior, devalued confidence, angry submissiveness, and immature stature.

In the following clinical illustration, most of the conditions considered in the description of the etiology of trait development, interpersonal needs, and system of emotions and defenses that comprise the personality pattern of the dependent type can be seen. On an empirical level, this kind of clinical example is easily identifiable, and contributes to a further rationale for viewing the dependent character as a rather unique personality—not merely a character type whose traits can be encompassed solely within either passive aggressive or inadequate personality structures.

Clinical Case Illustration

An 18-year-old young man left his first semester of college after only six weeks. His reason for leaving was the sense of unfriendliness and coldness he experienced in the college environment generally, as well as in his dormitory specifically. The patient entered therapy feeling anxious and somewhat depressed. He was accompanied to his first therapy session by both of his parents. His overtly dependent behavior in the first few sessions as well as his considerable stress regarding his brief college experience made it clear that he was suffering with classic separation anxiety. In the reporting of his history, it also became clear that his entire life was organized as a safety and security net composed of parental guidance and their close checking, monitoring, and overall supervision of most of his activities.

A classic illustration of this young man's dependency orientation is exemplified by his first day of kindergarten. He remembered this experience vividly and described a dramatic scene in which he began to whimper at the intimation that his mother was going to leave him there. He reported that as his mother actually moved toward the door, the whimpering turned into sobbing. As she stepped out of the door the sobbing then became heaving. His mother reentered the classroom and remained with him in the classroom for the first weeks of kindergarten.

This memory of separation anxiety corresponded also to feelings of dread, alienation, tension, and loneliness which he also felt during the first six weeks of college. Only after he was reassured that he could both attend a college close to home and also live at home did the separation symptoms subside.

During therapy he recognized that indeed he always seemed to need parental protection. The observation that his mother would always help him with his homework along with subsequent discussions of his mother's pervasive influence enabled him to conclude that his experience throughout his life was never quite age appropriate. Despite his new insight concerning the absence of self-reliance, he nevertheless admitted that it was a deeply gratifying thought to feel protected in the bosom of the family.

Therapeutic exploration gave this young man an opportunity to review the role dependency played in his friendships during the span of his childhood, during latency, and in early adolescence. He was self-effacing and assumed an inferior position in social relationships. When unsure of homework assignments, he characteristically checked with others for ideas and then presented the challenge to his mother who was expected to help furnish the direction needed to insure completion of assignments. Apparently, these experiences contributed to a sense of personal immaturity compared to peers, and levels of confidence were noticeably limited. In grammar school he never volunteered for parts in class plays but accepted whatever parts were left. During later adolescence, relating to girls was ignored because of his fears of rejection, hurt, and disapproval. This kind of social avoidance apparently served to protect him from obvious risks that might have engendered loss of esteem.

In college for the first time, he experienced an emotional disequilibrium. It as a time for independent decision making in the absence of a well-known, reliable figure to offer guidance. His anxiety level and self-doubt accordingly intensified. The analysis of these college experiences revealed also that a significant increase in ambivalent feelings surfaced and constituted an obsessional symptom fueled by his self-doubt. In a practical sense, this obsessional ambivalence appeared in the form of an inability to make decisions as to how to study, which readings to do first, and how to spend his money. His obsessional ambivalence seemed to reflect the degree of helplessness, confusion, and anxiety that was mobilized by the sudden loss of a specific figure to depend on and the expectation of independent decision making implied by the circumstances.

Thus, the central point in this profound experience of separation anxiety and self-doubt concerned the fact that there was no one he could depend upon, be passive with, and toward whom he could be deferent. In an existential sense, his helplessness in this newly found, independent condition of college life could not offer him his usual gratification of helplessness within a dependent-nurturant context. He then experienced a kind of emotional chaos in which he felt he had lost his bearings. There were no magical solutions to problems that could mask the challenges facing him, and his new role required implementation behavior with which he had very little experience. He became anxious and angry. His feelings of anger also corresponded to memories of angry outbursts he had whenever he felt his parents were not offering the level of support he required. On the defense level, his customary compensatory and denial defenses were disrupted, and therefore, tensions could not be managed by his typical dependency character configuration and its attendant system of traits and overall defense operations. The chief purpose of the dependent character, to insure safety and security and to avoid anger and depression, had thus failed him.

As can be seen in this clinical illustration, dependent character structure is frequently straight forward and easily identified. It is not usually subtle either in its symptom picture or in the translation into behavior of the person's need system. In contrast, the passive aggressive character to be presented next can indeed be quite subtle and even intriguing in terms of the overall complexity in the development of trait behaviors that act to manage the person's central anxiety.

Passive Aggressive Personality

Unlike the dependent character, which was only recently considered in *DSM-III* as a separate personality configuration, the passive aggressive personality is a character disorder that has been viewed as a separate structure in virtually all the diagnostic nosologies. This passive aggressive personality contains a cluster of traits designed to help the person express hostility indirectly or passively and thereby generate irritation, frustration, and anger in the interpersonal interaction. These passive aggressive traits can create great difficulty for the subject in day-to-day living. Traits such as procrastination, oppositionalism, tardiness, incompleteness, and stubbornness are examples. In *DSM-I* the entire complex of traits, behaviors, and emotions of the passive aggressive character was divided into three parts, or three distinct syndromes.

These were the passive aggressive personality, dependent type; the passive aggressive personality, passive type; and, the passive aggressive personality, aggressive type.

Briefly defined, the passive aggressive personality, dependent type, was one who consistently deferred to the authority figure, thereby creating a clear dependency situation. Yet, this deferential attitude was intended also to be an expression of hostility. Thus, the direction offered by the authority figure was actually resented, and predictably, this deferential attitude within the passive aggressive interaction would invariably cause the object to feel angry. In contrast, the trait of deference in a dependent character—described in the previous section on the dependent character structure—usually generates feelings of affection, concern, and satisfaction in the object and an absence of the feeling of anger.

The second subdivision cited in *DSM-I* was the passive aggressive personality, passive type. This passive aggressive person engaged in typical procrastination and delay tactics designed, at the very least, to frustrate the object; these delaying tactics could also generate rage reactions in the object. In the expression of the passive aggressive syndrome, it was the passive type who represents the classic understanding of passive aggressive characterology.

The third component of the passive aggressive personality considered in *DSM-I* was the passive aggressive personality, aggressive type. Within this aggressive configuration of the passive character, rather than expressing withholding as the typical communication of hostility, the subject expressed defiance, and, most of all, displayed destructive behavior. Examples of such traits include quarrelsomeness and overtalkativeness that borders on compulsive talking, but is not derived from compulsive character conflicts. Thus, overtalkativeness corresponds to low-level but persistent argumentativeness and interruptiveness, containing the motive of hostility toward the object. Another typical trait in this aggressive type was a tendency for the subject to be involved in actual physical fighting, to be quick tempered, and to engage in so-called preemptive strikes in which the object is taken by such surprise that an experience of defeat surfaces in the recipient of the attack before any other rationale for the attack is able to crystalize. As a differential diagnostic issue, this destructive aggressive behavior is not to be confused with psychopathic acting out. In psychopathic acting out, the destructive acting out behavior is motivated by compelling motoric needs, intense needs for experiencing external stimulation, and the inability to exercise frustration tolerance. In the passive aggressive, aggressive type, the aggressive destructive behavior is governed entirely by the need to convey and decisively concretize hostility toward the object. A motoric impulse imperative is absent in this passive aggressive, aggressive type, and frustration tolerance is generally carefully calculated and calibrated so that aggression is expressed sufficiently but not excessively. This calibrated character of the aggressive display is one aspect of the essence of passive aggressive functioning.

In *DSM-II* these various subdivisions of the passive aggressive pattern were amalgamated into the overall passive aggressive type in which the entire syndrome is considered together and in *DSM-III* this consolidation persisted. The *DSM-III* and *DSM-III-R* diagnostic composite of the passive aggressive personality is based on the characteristic demonstration of passive resistance that is mobilized when reasonable standards for performance are expected. The compromise with expectations or demands is characteristically effected by procrastination, delay, forgetting assignments, and accomplishing less than promised, or less than is obviously appropriate. This passive aggressive type may also engage in quarrels if asked to do something he wishes to avoid and may claim that too much is expected of him. Another cluster of behavioral strategies includes efforts to sabotage the work of others, the presence of a resentful attitude toward helpful suggestions, and a reflexive critical stance toward authorities as a matter of principle.

The Passive Aggressive Character Compromise

In the genesis and development of the passive aggressive personality, the essential ingredient without which the organization of passive aggressive traits, emotions, and defenses could not have coalesced, concerns the issue of gratifying authority in a technically correct but actually insufficient way while avoiding punishment. The essence of the subject's strategy concerns a hostile separation from authority that avoids retaliation. The classic example of the development of the passive aggressive personality concerns the parent, either the demanding father or pressuring mother, who insists that the child comply with the parental wish entirely and immediately, and is willing to threaten the child in a way that indicates there is no choice but for the child to comply. The child must gratify the parent's wish. Yet, in order for the child to salvage any autonomy, some measure of defiance and empowerment needs to be expressed by the child.

The compelling striving of the child to adhere to the wishes of the authority while simultaneously needing to assert some measure of autonomy and self-empowerment leads to a continued reinforcement of this neurotic interaction—that of combined adherence and defiance. Thus, diagnostically, the passive aggressive personality type is associated with the emotionally dependent one. In the passive aggressive pattern, as far as the child is concerned, the basis for interpersonal relations becomes thoroughly characterized by the perspective of relying upon the typical passive aggressive maneuver. Thus, in expressing the passive aggressive pattern, emotionally dependent responses are also gratified and the passive, covert quality of the aggression does not threaten the dependency status.

For example, the father wishes that the child finish his meal immediately, because the family is late for an appointment. The father's demand is intense and the child knows from experience that he must comply. The child begins to eat quickly so that the father can see that compliance is forthcoming. The child finishes the meal but inadvertently tips over his glass of milk with his elbow. The father becomes furious, but what can he do? The child was eating fast; he simply had "an accident." Understood psychologically, of course, it is proposed that the accident is equivalent to the child saying to his father, "watch this," then picking up the glass of milk and deliberately and slowly pouring it all over the table.

The dynamic thread that motivates the compromise—complying by eating faster while defying by hostilely spilling milk—reflects the child's management of anger in the face of the father's aggression. Since the child is dependent on the authority, he dare not oppose it or express anger directly. Instead, a passive means of directing anger is utilized, while the safety of the child's dependency is preserved. The effect of the anger as delivered is reflected by the feeling of frustration invariably experienced by the authority in the interchange. At the same time that compliance by the child is observed, corresponding aggression is covertly discharged. A sense of individuality and autonomy, therefore, is secured by the child through the design of this character structure.

Other behaviors by the child that can generate hostility in the parent will involve a multitude of procrastinations, a range of accidents, and numerous forgotten agreements. The idea is to frustrate the authority, to withhold in order to express defiance, to be obedient as well as tardy and stubborn—all while retaining the formality of compliance. In addition, further behavioral paradoxes include to promise and yet procrastinate, to agree and yet to be incomplete, and to remember along with forgetting—as in the incomplete accomplishment of tasks. These ingenious polarities also reflect an obsessional ambivalence in the passive aggressive character that encourages the perception of authority in a wide range of interpersonal contexts. This character type, as all character configurations, is designed basically to manage anxiety and to preserve one's identity. The level of pathology is reached when a self-defeating outcome can occur because of the endless compromises that must be effected to achieve the management of anxiety and assertion of individuality.

The Identification Process

In the passive aggressive character, one of the more deleterious effects of the identification process concerns the phenomenon in which the developing child begins to identify with the demanding authority figure and internalizes autocratic and tyrannical impulses. Second, in the development of the passive aggressive character, traits of defiance, oppositionalism and procrastination will ultimately generate inefficiency in occupation and work so that the passive aggressive trait profile also frequently correlates with underachievement. Thus, the passive aggressive character structure assumes a masochistic or self-defeating cast and the particular passive aggressive behavior persists even when more self-assertive and effective action is possible. In the case of the passive aggressive character, the chief defense of displacement in the expression of anger toward the authority, as well as repression which manages the fear of the authority, are constantly operating so that hostility can be conveyed in an unconscious but persistent manner. Thus, the fear of the authority figure is repressed while in a transferential sense the anger toward the authority figure is constantly being displaced onto the object.

Family constellations in such character development can consist of one parent who is fairly demanding, pressuring, or aggressive, while the other may assume a relatively passive stance. The demanding parent acts out the aggressive component and the other the passive one. The entire passive aggressive model is thereby conveyed through the processes of internalization and identification.

In the following section, a clinical illustration of the passive aggressive character will be presented. In this case, the vicissitudes and dynamics described above can be discerned and traced in a way that establishes the entire character configuration concisely.

Clinical Case Illustration

A 30-year-old psychiatrist applying to a psychoanalytic training institute was required, as part of the application process, to undergo psychological testing in order to rule out significant pathology. The test results revealed classic passive aggressive characterological patterns both in the projective tests as well as in the applicant's clinical behavior. Especially interesting to note was the examiner's reaction to the applicant's overall approach; that is, to the applicant's test-taking, typical response patterns, and demeanor. On the one hand, the examiner reported that the applicant was quite compliant and would answer all questions more or less with brevity and courtesy. Yet, there was a gratuitous quality also reported, along with a lengthy discussion of classic passive aggressive features and behavior.

For example, to simple questions requiring yes or no answers, the applicant was forthcoming and efficient in his responses. Yet, when questions required discussion and explanation, the applicant became overthoughtful, more deliberate in his speech patterns and required the examiner to wait an undue amount of time for responses. In addition, on the Rorschach Ink Blot Test, where the applicant was required to report whatever perceptions came to mind, a typical passive aggressive response pattern as well as passive aggressive clinical behavior emerged. For example, the applicant became obsessively interested in each and every detail of the blot but did not demonstrate obsessive ambivalence. Rather, the concentration on exploring each detail of the blot as well as overall perceptions were clearly in the service of a passive aggressive motive—to comply with instructions while simultaneously defeating the authority and to effect an individual stance while simultaneously complying with the technical demands of the situation.

Thus, the examiner was engaged in writing many extra pages, needed to wait an unusually lengthy amount of time before a response was offered, and had to wait inordinately for the response to be defined, explained, and completed. The examiner was a trained psychologist who was able to conceptualize the passive aggressive diagnosis during the actual testing and gathering of data, and even though he understood that such a passive aggressive response pattern along with its corresponding clinical behavior is designed to generate anger in the interpersonal interaction, nevertheless, the examiner's response was typical. The examiner could not prevent himself from becoming increasingly frustrated and angry as the subject, who was highly successful in the performance of the passive aggressive drama, inexorably increased the passive aggressive network of trait patterns.

The traits that emerged during testing involved procrastination reflected in time lag measures, oppositionalism, and stubbornness as well as many figure-ground reversals, in which the background of the blot is treated perversely as though it is the foreground. In addition, although the subject behaved deferentially, his aggressive and hostile intent was constantly betraying itself. The examiner felt entirely frustrated, overworked, and angry. Yet, this successful passive aggressive character performed within socially desirable conditions so that his hostility could not be easily identified as a violation of civility. The abundance of responses offered by the applicant to the test qualifies as overtalkativeness and even as disguised quarrelsomeness. Yet, none of his behavior was obsessional or psychopathic. Throughout, defiance was expressed in the guise of obedience—a typically ingenious passive aggressive device.

In this example, the urges to preserve autonomy and to avoid an overt aggressive confrontation with an authority figure revealed a range of passive aggressive symptoms and character traits. These characteristics were designed to manage anxiety stemming from several key issues: the perception of a demand for compliance which, in turn, is resented; apprehension regarding the expression of anger by the subject so that anger is discharged covertly; striving to maintain a status of protective dependency as the source of security; and fear of loss of autonomy—a cause for great concern by the subject and, in turn, resented. The passive aggressive solutions to such dilemas contain endless compromises, calculations, and calibrations that drain undue energy from potentially productive behavior.

At the end of the examination, the applicant, who was a trained psychiatrist was required to pay for the examination. Rather than paying with a personal check, the applicant payed in cash which inadvertently slipped from his fingers and landed on the examiner's desk with a rather loud thud, so much so that his hostile intent became clear both to him as well as to the examiner. The applicant quickly apologized, and said, "That's the problem, isn't it?—passive aggressive to the bone." The applicant then briefly described his professional history and how he had, over the years, through his internship and residency as well as his first professional job as a psychiatrist, continually engendered hostility in others. He also revealed that colleagues had actually told him that he demonstrated classic passive aggressive behavior. He now wished to engage in psychoanalytic training, believing he could resolve this passive aggressive behavior in his own psychoanalysis. The prognosis in this case seemed quite good. When the unconscious passive aggressive behaviors spilled over and became glaringly evident to the subject, he was then able to acknowledge the problem and discuss it.

In the following section on the inadequate personality, which concludes the presentation and analysis of the triad of emotion dependent types, a conception will be presented of the inadequate personality that will contrast the passive aggressive character structure and the character structure of the inadequate personality. The passive aggressive person manages to preserve some sense of autonomy, while the inadequate personality, in contrast, can be viewed as a person who has been defeated in the struggle to preserve autonomy. Even though some autonomy is salvaged in early development, interpersonal satisfaction for the person with an inadequate personality is attenuated and an enriched personal experience becomes limited along with a restricted potential in the achievement of goals.

Inadequate Personality

Although the diagnosis of inadequate personality does not appear in *DSM-III* or *DSM-III-R* as a distinct character diagnosis, it is included here because it has been historically important and was included in both *DSM-I* and *DSM-II*. It has been used clinically as a separate diagnosis by tradition and is consistent with those character styles reflecting emotion dependent types. In addition, it is a clearly defined characterology and can be discerned from a clinical point of view with reliability and utility. It can perhaps be expected that there is a good probability of this diagnosis reappearing as the *DSM* nosology evolves. Most importantly, professional mental health workers, including diagnosticians and psychotherapists, frequently confront individuals in clinical settings who in their symptoms, etiology, behavior, expression of affect, and in practical daily life demonstrate the manifestations of this well-delineated inadequate personality character diagnosis.

In general terms, inadequate characterology rests on traits of dependency, passivity, and withdrawal so that effective reactions to the various challenges facing the individual are rarely produced. Actual deficiencies of physical or intellectual sorts are not present in this inadequate personality so that the psychological sense of inadequacy and ineptness characterizing this type is no more than a means to justify disengagement from working, relating, or responding effectively and productively.

It is evident in the early *DSM* models that the inadequate personality is an emotion dependent type allied closely to the dependent character, sharing some traits of the passive aggressive personality, and even appearing similar to borderline functioning. Of course, on a differential diagnostic basis, the inadequate personality is not a borderline character in so far as, developmentally, early familial ties were in fact presumably available, were somewhat supportive, and reflected a reasonable abundance of affectional activity. As a result, in the inadequate personality the ego is not brittle, and, therefore, the problem of control of anger can be better managed because of the smoother use of overall defenses. In contrast, the borderline condition is not an emotion dependent constellation, defenses are not quite as efficient or integrative, anger is not managed consistently, and the ego lacks plasticity.

The inadequate personality diagnosis resembles the borderline condition in the underresponse to demands of the environment. This underresponse can also be mistaken for the tentativeness of the borderline character, the remoteness of the schizoid character and even in some cases, the dramatics that can be seen in the hysterical character. Such an amalgam of traits in the inadequate personality generates a profile of disorganization, which, in the absence of psychosis also can be mistaken for a generalized borderline character pathology.

The condition of underresponse characterizing the inadequate personality is actually an underresponse to all aspects of functioning. In early *DSM* nosology aspects of underresponse included those in the intellectual, emotional, social, and physical spheres. As a result of such underresponsiveness, concepts such as underachievement become prominent in the analysis of inadequate character. Additional concepts psychologically descriptive of inadequate character include inadaptability, ineptness, poor judgment, lack of physical and emotional stamina, and social incompatibility. In the sense of practical everyday living, such incapacities are translated into highly constricted reactions in relationships, underachievement in school and at work, and even poor responses in sexual functioning. Additional traits typically displayed in inadequate characterology include excessive and weepy sentimentalism, and, most importantly, an inappropriate sobriety in authority relationships. This latter point is extremely significant and constitutes the major problem for the inadequate character type. Inadequate character types may be quite bright. Yet, on intelligence tests that require assertiveness and consistent high-level functioning they may score significantly lower than their potential justifies. For example, abstraction capacities in such persons are usually ample and this ability to think abstractly corresponds to a high level of intelligence. However, the inadequate character type will behave quite concretely in interpersonal relationships and frequently needs to be guided through tasks on a step-by-step basis. Deference to authority also accounts for the reduced initiative taken by the inadequate character on such tests and in life generally. Initiative as a trait is therefore not very visible and such an inadequate dependent person consistently seeks direction and guidance from figures in authority who in turn need to be quite literal and specific in their instructions. This dependent need raises the question of the historical antecedents, the genesis of the inadequate character structure, and differences from the dependent personality.

Developmental Issues

There are several variations in the natural history of an inadequate personality character formation. Typically, a relatively ineffective father figure, who is either silent or in other ways unavailable, coexists with a mother figure who is primarily absorbed in satisfying her own needs. Presumably, the effect of the child's interaction with such a mother figure is that the child is usually left to its own immature and inadequate coping devices. As some point, the mother usually usurps the child's activity, ostensibly because the child was not performing well enough, not completing tasks, working too slowly on them, doing them incorrectly, or in some other way not organizing the work. When finally, this interference pattern becomes established as a typical mother-child interaction, then the child is left feeling that it cannot really do anything right. This interaction contrasts with the mother who generates dependency character structure where tasks are in fact accomplished and completed, albeit only in the presence of and with encouragement from the overwhelmingly protective and nurturing parent figure.

In this course of the natural history of the inadequate personality character formation, the child develops unelaborated and unsophisticated defensive patterns. Despite the development of all necessary defenses, the child's internalizations and the operation of autonomous functions remain underdeveloped. Such a person generally remains somewhat childish or immature, regressively clinging to a posture of constriction and limitation. Such persons also tend to proclaim their feelings with a compensatory air of importance. They fail to recognize the shallowness, immaturity, and basic inappropriateness of these responses, and this sort of behavior reflects a regressive rather than an age appropriate point of view.

The compensatory operation of the inadequate personality permits such a person falsely to experience ego gratifications based upon an exaggerated sense of importance; however, on a practical basis, such persons are, of course, effectively incapacitated. This incapacitation is defined as the underresponse in virtually all areas of life and constitutes the chief characteristic of inadequate personality types. Compulsive and obsessional methods are also instituted that contribute to childlike levels of functioning.

Secondary defenses that are utilized are those of denial and rationalization. The inadequate character employs defenses of denial and rationalization to justify characteristically immature behavior. In the following case presentation, a classic illustration of the inadequate personality type displays many of the salient characteristics inherent and typical in this character configuration. The character picture will include aspects of the personality relating to behavior, trait, emotion, defense, and etiological considerations.

Clinical Case Illustration

A 28-year-old man was referred for psychotherapy three weeks after he moved into a sublet apartment. This was his first experience away from home and he was apparently unable to live on his own with any measure of success. When he lived at home his mother would awaken him in the morning so that he could get to work on time. Now, on his own, he consistently arrived late to work. He was not diligent about keeping appointments and rather than prepare meals for himself would eat in restaurants, thus depleting his finances.

Family and friends realized that he was unable to meet the most simple demands of life. His response to this dilemma was to make jokes, and he did not seem unduly affected by his failures. He denied and rationalized his predicament, and retained an inappropriately compensatory stance by maintaining an exaggerated sense of importance about the new living arrangement he was undertaking.

It soon became clear that the character structure of this patient reflected a typical inadequate personality type in whom compensatory defenses enabled the warding off of any depressive feelings, while permitting him to deny the potential effects of his poor performance. This defense cluster of compensation, denial, and rationalization, along with his deferent response to authority, his ambiguous relationship to his parents, as well as his overall regressively inadequate behavior secured the diagnosis.

He was obviously an emotionally dependent person whose immaturity became mostly visible when he made some pronouncement or when he expressed a knowing smile regarding an event of ostensible importance when, in fact, the event

was not important at all. He was not psychotic or schizophrenic so that the inappropriateness of his behavior was
clearly a function of his social immaturity and developmental
inadequacy. His interpersonal behavior, therefore, with respect to maturity level, was shallow and reflected a profound
lack of social experience.

With respect to etiology, he described his mother as a person who dominated the family, who was quite vocal and intrusive, and criticized, albeit offhandedly, most of the decisions and activity in which he or his father became engaged.
He reported that rather than guiding him, his mother left him
to his own devices, especially in schoolwork. Yet, she would
be there at the end either telling him that his work was too
abbreviated or that his handwriting was poor, and she would
then go ahead and fix it. He said she was affectionate, but
even there, only on her terms. She would embrace him but
not wait to be embraced. She would occasionally kiss him
but not wait for a return kiss, and she was evidently a compulsive talker.

Apparently, this man grew up with only a few friends, never
exercising the active role in maintaining contact with any of
them. He reported feeling on the periphery of peer groups,
and also indicated that academically he barely scraped through
high school and then college. He was unable to complete reports on time, was routinely unable to sustain homework activity, and consistently became tired after minimal effort. He
felt his father did not provide any counterbalance to his
mother's overall dominance of the household and he was disappointed by his father's silence. Finally, in this classic picture of the inadequate personality type, the patient's typical
response to authority was as child to parent. For example,
he would become quite literal with his employer, feeling that
he had to answer any question to the letter, and would never
show any initiative, always preferring to be told exactly what
to do.

Generally speaking, this man showed consistent underresponsiveness with respect to all levels of functioning: intellectual, behavioral, social, and interpersonal. Yet, he did not
exhibit a fragile or brittle ego, was neither emotionally particularly expressive nor remote, and did not express either
schizoid, borderline, or narcissistic symptoms. His work was

minimally fulfilled, well below his potential, but he simply was not able to meet obvious standards of work, even though he was actually quite bright. Yet, he was able to work on his own, and in that sense was not classically dependent. Rather the nature of his dependency was special in the sense that the inadequate personality type requires consistent and perennial boosting. The fact that his behavior was annoying was not consistent with passive aggressive characterology primarily because he did not act with any significant reservoir of anger. His aim was not to frustrate authority; rather, it was to please authority.

In the three emotion dependent diagnoses of dependent, passive aggressive, and inadequate character structure, traits such as nurturance, relation to authority figures, and dependency issues generate a condition in which the person attempts to express emotion in less than direct or age appropriate terms. In the emotion dependent character structures, emotion is neither dyscontrolled nor avoided. Dependency is either rebelled against, as in the passive aggressive character, ignored but needed, as in the inadequate character, or sought after in direct ways, as in the dependent character. These three basic character types—the dependent, the passive aggressive and inadequate—constitute a cluster of characterological formations in which the salient variable around which character forms concerns emotions regarding dependency and the vicissitudes of behavior addressing such dependency needs. Anxieties that are managed by any one of these three character formations are only successfully addressed when such dependent needs are dealt with in ways that are characteristic of each type.

In the following chapter, the character types labeled emotion avoidant types will be considered. In these character formations a reliance on nurturant figures is prohibited because of early failures in development as well as early chaotic experiences. In the adult years, a clear derivative conflict in such persons generates fears of interpersonal involvement. These emotion avoidant types are the borderline character, the schizotypal character, and the avoidant character.

CAPSULE CLINICAL PROFILES OF EMOTION DEPENDENT CHARACTER TYPES

These character types share typical needs for dependency and nurturance and usually do not express emotion or conduct interpersonal contact in age appropriate terms.

Dependent: Magical solutions to problems are sought and corresponding poor implementation ability and poor intitiative are shown. Dependent persons seek an authority context in order to gain structure and direction. Passivity and limited self-esteem appear. Inability to be alone and strong deferent needs also reveal potential for intense separation anxiety reactions. Nevertheless, compliance masks underlying anger. Reliance on others fuels the hope of avoiding emotional turbulence. Denial and compensation facilitate maintenance of the dependency structure, helping to minimize and manage anxiety.

Passive Aggressive: The predominant need to express hostility indirectly creates typical irritability in others but also serves to preserve a measure of autonomy in this person who is basically fearful of authority figures. The typical passive aggressive trait cluster includes procrastination, oppositionalism, stubbornness, withholding, overtalkativeness, quarrelsomeness, and interruptiveness. Anger is controlled through repression, displacement, and compromise.

Inadequate: Ineptness and underresponse are seen in all aspects of functioning. The ego is intact although an emotionally dependent position is central. A passive and withdrawn stance is necessitated by an underresponse to the demands of life. Poor judgment and overall social awkwardness is seen. Deference to authority is typical. The inadequate person is generally unable to initiate instrumental activity in order to accomplish even minor goals.

CHAPTER 5
Emotion Avoidant Character Types: Borderline, Schizotypal, and Avoidant Character Structure

In this chapter, a final character grouping, of borderline, schizotypal, and avoidant personalities will be presented, along with an analysis of the way in which each type manages anxiety through the avoidance of emotional and interpersonal stimulation.

In the case of the borderline personality organization, ego fragmentation and ego deficiencies, identity confusion, and emotional lability all contribute to circumstances of boundary insecurity in which interpersonal involvements need to be limited in order to avoid overstimulation of feelings and dysphoric reactions. Classification of the borderline personality as an emotion avoidant type is largely based on the overwhelming nature of emotional arousal that the borderline personality struggles to avoid because of inadequate integrative ego resources. In comparison, the schizotypal character structure embodies a largely idiosyncratic eccentricity in which the expression of emotion is inappropriate or constricted, cool, and aloof. Social signals can be seen as demands and further encourage social isolation. Therefore, from the position of idiosyncratic, unusual, and cool functioning, an emotionally avoidant posture as well as a socially avoidant one is maintained in the schizotypal personality. Consequently, anxiety evoked by the threat inherent in emotional closeness is diminished if not denied by schizotypal functioning.

The last of the emotion avoidant types presented in this chapter is the avoidant character structure. In this type of personality functioning, expression of social interest or emotionality itself is inhibited by fears of interpersonal rejection, humiliation, and embarrassment. This level of sensitivity to rejection can only be neutralized when interpersonal signals of clear acceptance are offered. Thus, the existence of consistent and pervasive fears in connection with emotional expressiveness classify this avoidant characterology as an emotion avoidant type.

The first character structure to be discussed is that of the borderline personality which has recently been officially codified as a defined characterology.

Borderline Personality

Prior to codification of the borderline personality disorder in the current nomenclature represented by *DSM-III/III-R*, a history of clinical entities had been proposed by various investigators that reflected important aspects of what eventually emerged as the borderline personality organization. Among the clinical syndromes that were precursors of the current diagnosis of borderline personality were psuedoneurotic schizophrenia, latent or incipient schizophrenia, and the "as-if" personality introduced by the psychoanalyst Helene Deutsch. The borderline quality between psychotic and neurotic spheres is suggested by these preliminary formulations but, more precisely, a condition identified with the triad of pananxiety, pansexuality, and pandefensiveness was indicated by such diagnostic formulations. This triad comprised extensive and intense anxiety with a shifting defensive facade so that aspects of obsessional, hysteric, dependent, or depressive dispositions could periodically and alternately predominate. This sort of an unstable facade both reflected and encouraged emotional lability and also related to the incomplete and confused self-identity that was part of the syndrome. An important aspect of the confusion in identity of this syndrome was the individual's sexual confusion. This sexual confusion contributed to the pansexuality included in these early formulations. In psychoanalytic terms, such pansexuality referred to the polymorphous perversity or immature sexual variety displayed by those unable to achieve stable, consistent sexual orientations. Many of these early observations have persisted in more recent conceptualizations of borderline psychopathology.

In the current *DSM* nomenclature, the borderline personality configuration actually is not a diagnosis intended to denote the border between neurosis and psychosis. Despite the general consensus that the borderline personality is considered to be marginal, this marginality is understood to be a function of unstable interpersonal, vocational, academic, and other life experiences, along with instability of mood and identity. A comprehensive description of borderline pathology consistent with *DSM-III-R* terminology includes criteria drawn from a range of possible features. These criteria include: marked instability of mood in which departures from the customary levels of depression, irritability, or anxiety occur; intensity of anger reflecting lability with deficient regulation and insufficient controls; self-defeating impulsivity that can encompass addictive propensities or sexual acting out as well as impulsivity and inappropriateness in any number of daily activities; overt self-damaging involvements such as suicidal threats, gestures, behavior, or self-mutilation; intense but unstable relationships incorporating emphatic idealization and devaluation; confused sense of identity in terms of either self-image, sexual identity, career goals or values; preoccupations with empty feelings or boredom; and persistent fears and concerns regarding abandonment.

Ego Functioning in the Borderline Personality

Borderline character structure reflects an underdeveloped or deficient condition of the ego in which a quality of fragmentation persistently precludes a sense of integration. Such an ego condition does not necessarily imply the presence of primary process breakthroughs or profound psychotic manifestations as in the presence of hallucinations or systematic delusions. There is usually no substantial associative disturbance in the borderline condition. Instead, a quality of logical integrity is retained at the surface of thought; indecisive ambivalence is not usually a major problem, and autism is absent.

The deficient ego, however, does produce impairments for the borderline person with respect to the expression of affect. For example, a chief characteristic of the borderline personality is the eruption of anger to stimuli that would usually be considered innocuous or mild. In this sense, a clear trait of the borderline character is the frequent display of temper. Thus, as would be expected in such a person, interpersonal relations can become quite intense and problematic. The poor confidence and identity confusion in the context of ego deficiency of the borderline character type contributes to the phenomenon of projecting idealization and devaluation—alternating aspects of self—onto others; minor disappointments can therefore precipitate outbursts of anger. This frequent loss of patience and expostulation of anger in the borderline person reflects lability of affect and mood shifts. These shifts are quite noticeable, and, in part, provide the rationale for avoiding interactions that may evoke such impulse. Hence, on the level of behavior, the borderline type is an emotion avoidant type.

In seeking isolation and in trying to avoid stimulating conditions, the borderline personality is in a dilemma. The dilemma raises a contradiction of personality needs that creates a difficult conflict for such a person. The paradox is that despite the need to avoid emotionally stimulating conditions, this kind of person finds it difficult to tolerate isolation and emphatically fears abandonment. Such fears of abandonment sometimes can lead to serious distortions in the perception of other people's motives and consequent frantic and manipulative behavior in the borderline person. The conflict between the fear of becoming absorbed in the emotional stimulation of interpersonal involvement and the fear of abandonment is reflected by alternations between avoidance and overinvestment in others. This avoidance and overinvestment in others parallels the experience of alternations between devaluation and overidealization of people.

Such intense conflict of fear of both involvement and abandonment can also create a regressive and dyscontrolled posture in persons with borderline characterology. The dyscontrolled position offers the borderline person immediate relief from the intensity of this conflict between fears. As a result of such regressive or dyscontrolled acting out, not only do identity impairments become prominent, but severe impulsivity problems as well. These impulsivity problems can include a variety of difficulties in everyday living that encompass drug abuse, gambling, excessive spending, stealing, and truancy. Such impulse behavior also creates a need for the clinician to differentiate between psychopathic character structure and borderline personality in assessing the diagnostic problem. In the borderline personality, a disorganized quality characterizes the acting out since it is ego insufficiency and fragmentation that contribute to patterns of self-defeating acting out.

For example, among the acting out proclivities of the borderline personality, self-mutilation and suicidal threats or gestures can occur, whereas the psychopathic character does not usually engage in such directly self-damaging behavior. Further, in the borderline personality, controls are tenuous or shifting, allowing for idiosyncratic or even bizzare acting out, while substantial anxiety persists because of the core fragmentation of aspects of ego and self. In contrast, in the psychopath, the acting out nullifies anxiety.

Deficient and fragmented ego functioning characterizing the structure of the borderline personality is reflected in the impaired controls and affective lability already described. In addition, defective ego functioning is represented by a pervasive experience of anxiety as well as by disorganized acting out, and fears of abandonment. Another consequence of fragmentation of the ego is the impairment of self-image and self-esteem that also appears as confused self-identity. A highly devalued sense of self emanating from ego fragmentation is periodically mastered by a compensatory narcissistic process of idealization, entitlement and specialness, with the idealizing effort toward self-integration most often seen as a projection invested in other people.

The Borderline Trait Profile

Typical of the disorganization generated by a deficient ego are shifting moods and irregular controls, so that a broad spectrum of traits can be seen in the personality profile of the borderline. Sometimes these traits appear as aspects of obsessive behavior (stubborness, overinvestment in order, addictive qualities), histrionic behavior (manipulativeness, suicidal threats, suggestibility, overinvolvement in others), paranoid qualities (mistrust, blaming), narcissistic phenomena (idealizing and devaluing of others, expectation of special entitlements), and even schizoid behavior (striving for isolation). The borderline personality may also become severely pessimistic and may experience depression which can also lead to suicidal attempts. It should be expected that the borderline experience of unpredictability and the sense of being flooded and overwhelmed by shifts of emotion consumes enormous psychic energy. In this depleted psychological condition, along with the borderline's ego deficiencies, there is then only limited energy available to encourage introspection, to delay gratification, to

evaluate the nature of expectations from others, or, in the interpersonal sphere, to reflect sympathy and empathy toward others.
Therefore, the relationships maintained by persons with borderline
characterology invariably contain the cast of a distinct lack of depth,
concern or generosity toward others. Thus, the relationships developed by borderline types can generally be characterized as superficial because of the lack of feeling shown toward others and
the consequent absence of genuine interest in other people.

A collateral problem experienced by the borderline person concerns the identity question of "Who am I?" Consistent with this
underdeveloped sense of identity, the borderline character is afflicted with the experience that the self frequently can be defined
by a variety of role assignments in an "as if" posture. This sense
of an indefinite and changing identity is the basis for a feeling of
irreality so that, for example, the borderline person may split the
identity of self into self-loathing that is inwardly directed while
identifying valued behavior with others. This kind of split in identity implies an actual loss of identity. To minimize the dispiriting
effect of such role shifts, borderline persons seek to remain free of
roles generally and thus free of role confusion. The least complicated way to remain role free is, of course, to remain alone and
isolated. However, the social isolation that such a person may create because of diminished and inconsistent self-identity can bring
to the surface pronounced feelings of emptiness, boredom, and
abandonment. The pain engendered by these feelings causes such
persons to engage in efforts to escape social isolation. Since identity concerns do in fact exist, tenuous personal boundaries raise a
grave sense of threat in response to seeking interpersonal involvement. Consequently, movement toward interpersonal closeness can
be experienced as a serious danger while the condition of solitude
can be an equally intolerable condition.

Defensive and Developmental Features

On a defense level the borderline personality utilizes a rather primitive defensive organization of regression, projection, and splitting.
Reliance on regression by a defectively integrated ego assures repeating impulse dominated behavior such as outbursts of anger
and contributes to lability and acting out. Use of projection diminishes anxiety regarding self-doubt and identity confusion as in-

sufficiencies and confusion are attributed to external circumstances. The use of projection also facilitates the externalization of the powerful devaluing and idealizing trends. These attempts to devalue and idealize are associated with efforts to secure a sense of integration and personal substance and to attempt mastery of feelings of emptiness and abandonment. In addition, it is assumed that the absence of significant positive introjective experience contributes to the primitive defensive structure of the borderline person and the relative insufficiency of this structure with respect to ego development.

The use of splitting as a defense also reflects the incomplete sense of self in borderline characterology which is apparent in the frequent surfacing of disconnected idealized and devalued aspects of self. These unintegrated parts of the self reflect the fundamental fragmentation underlying borderline personality organization. The defense of splitting allows an impression of wholeness to be artificially attributed to the self as well as to others through projective identification. This reliance on splitting enables a consequent reduction in anxiety concerning the lack of integration that would otherwise intensively appear. Conflict and, most importantly, confusion about the positive and negative aspects of oneself and others, crystallized in the devalued and idealized images, can be neutralized by the defense of splitting, since this defense eliminates recognition or acknowledgment of opposites and contradictions.

In terms of the etiology of borderline character structure, the early life of the borderline person is likely to be characterized by identification with parents who were themselves socially underdeveloped, interpersonally insensitive, egocentric, nonintrospective, impulsive, and largely inconsistent with respect to limit setting. External structure, such as rules for living, particularly regarding such typical activities as bedtime behavior, meal time, bathing, homework, and so forth, would most likely be inconsistently implemented. Under such inconsistent or unstable conditions the child is thought to develop deficiencies in ego structure and functions with ensuing significant disorganization of the personality. Yet, these disorganizations develop within the confines of nonpsychotic ego development, since some early care and bonding is apparently sufficiently present.

Affectional ties in early life, however, would be inconsistent just as were the structure and reliability provided by the parents. For example, early abandonment experiences may alternate with the occurrence of efforts toward overcontrol of the child. Thus, the child's striving toward autonomy and individuality are consistently thwarted. In this type of overcontrol, the developing child is treated as an extension of the insecure or underdeveloped parents. Overcontrol by the parents compromises the child's growth and development of stable individuality while gaining for the parents a greater sense of completeness, control, and worthiness. The phenomenon of merging is also thereby theoretically experienced by the child. Such merging experiences in the context of accompanying insecure personal boundaries and weakened self-identity are likely to contribute to the highly intense interpersonal reactions as well as the exaggerated fears of abandonment that characterize the borderline. Expressions of harshly derisive attitudes by parents may also be displayed as part of an inadequate parenting style contributing to the development of fragmented feelings of self and tendencies toward devaluation. Impairments in the affectional bond generated by the various interpersonal strains between parents and child within the borderline developmental context also reduce the capacity for cohesive ego development for the child and force reliance on shifting clusters of personality traits. Components of this shifting personality profile include lability in emotional expression, confusion of self-identity, and inconsistent regulation of control.

In summary, a fragmented perspective toward the world and confused self-identity are typical for this character pattern; to manage the anxiety derived from such fragmentation and loss of self and to aid organization, people and experiences are defensively split into good and bad and can also be interchanged between such categories of good and bad without awareness of contradiction. Interpersonal relationships are intense and unstable reflecting domination of processes of idealization and devaluation. Because of early inconsistencies and limitations in affectional experiences, such persons may experience merger phenomena with controlling and thwarting parents, and may find it difficult to maintain whole object contact. An aggregate of part-objects accumulates, which can create a cast of almost grotesque internal images which consist of distorted, threatening, and frightening characterizations. These internal images can also generate anger. It is such an array of fears that qualifies the borderline character as an emotion avoidant type. Anxiety is allayed therefore when avoidant reactions predominate. In this object distorted perspective, the borderline personality is haunted by a sense of incompleteness, unfulfillment, part-object contact and fears of abandonment, and yet is always in search of the elusive good and whole object. In the following clinical vignette, a borderline personality can be discerned that includes many of the characterological and behavioral characteristics discussed above.

Clinical Case Illustration

A 39-year-old man in an agitated condition was assessed at the outpatient department of an urban hospital. The differential diagnosis to be determined included the need for a distinction between catatonic excitement, organicity as it primarily generates impulsive conditions, or a borderline personality disorder with respect to frequent angry outbursts. In addition, an assessment of ego strength and ego integrity was required in order to understand whether any psychotic process was involved. This man was accompanied by his elderly father who reported that typically throughout the patient's life there occurred outbursts of anger and that, in general, the patient was somewhat of a loner. The father also reported that from time to time his son became terribly unhappy about being isolated and lonely.

Psychiatric and psychological evaluations ruled out the presence of a psychotic process, although an assessment of ego functioning showed brittleness, rigidity, and exceedingly low frustration tolerance. Catatonic excitement and organicity were similarly ruled out. The patient was judged to be a severe borderline character. He had never established any enduring relationship, either with boys when he was growing up or in his adult life with a woman. He was a chain smoker, and used codeine enhanced cough medicine as a sleeping aide. His father felt that the son was addicted to the codeine and psychiatric evaluation also established that his dependency on his cough medicine along with other behaviors suggested an addictive problem that can be typical of borderline personalities. His cynicism seemed to reflect paranoid-like ideation; his isolation seemed schizoid-like and it became clear that he exhibited a multiplicity of traits of a mixed clinical picture, such as that characteristic of borderline conditions.

The patient's father indicated that as a child the patient had frequent accidents and was extremely moody. His school record was poor throughout his educational experience which ended in the third year of high school at which point the patient refused to attend classes. At first, he would overvalue his teachers and try to comply with their requests. When this became difficult to accomplish he would become quickly disillusioned with these teachers and turn against them. This repetitious sort of behavior seemed reflective of the primitive splitting defense so typical of the borderline condition.

Analysis of interview and test data indicated that he really did not see himself as a distinct personality and was unclear with respect to his particular role in life—an indication of identity confusion. The one issue that he was certain about was his antipathy toward his parents, whom he said were never clear, never consistent, and, he implied, never instructive about anything he needed while he was growing up.

This clinical and diagnostic picture of the borderline character contains many of the major features associated with this person's apparent character disorder. For example, the patient was generally unkempt, agitated, unclear about his goals, and terribly unfulfilled in life. Essentially, he was unable to be comfortable or to find a place for himself. This incompleteness in his life also applied to the area of interpersonal relationships. Socially, the patient functioned in a superficial manner, sometimes trying to be intensively involved with someone for short periods of time and then invariably withdrawing into emotion avoidant reactions and isolation. Thus, bonds with people could never really be permanently or deeply secured.

The *DSM* nomenclature in the *DSM-III/III-R* version has for the first time included the borderline personality as part of the basic complement of personality disorders. In the following presentation the second emotion avoidant type, schizotypal character, also included in *DSM-III/III-R* for the first time as part of the basic complement of personality disorders, will be examined.

Schizotypal Personality

Apprently, a sufficient clinical consensus has qualified this diagnosis of schizotypal character to reflect a particular configuration of traits and behavior justifying its consolidation as a bona fide character diagnosis to be included among the basic character types already codified in conventionally accepted nosological systems. Essentially, clinicians have felt that there are patients who function stably in a preschizophrenic state, even though they exhibit thought processes, emotions, and characteristic interpersonal behavior that if exacerbated could crystallize into a schizophrenic configuration. Yet, the apparently stable, enduring nature of this schizotypal character configuration does not, in fact, deteriorate to meet the criteria for schizophrenia; neither does it derive from schizophrenia through a process of remission. Thus, the delusions, hallucinations, autism, and confused thinking associated with incoherence as well as loosening of associations—that is, a number of the generally accepted definite signs of schizophrenia—are absent from the schizotypal characterology. Nevertheless, various eccentricities and unusual qualities do appear persistently in the schizotypal character, although not with full schizophrenic expression. The likelihood of social isolation and unusual affect expression as well as peculiarities in behavior limit interpersonal contact for such schizotypal persons. Such a constellation places the schizotypal personality in the emotion avoidant type of character structure.

Elements of the Schizotypal Personality

In the *DSM-III* and *DSM-III-R* nomenclature, characteristics of schizotypal personality functioning include various idiosyncratic representations. The presence of paranoid ideation or traits, such as suspiciousness or ideas of reference—the conviction that innocent events pertain to the individual—can be expressed along with unusual, magical beliefs including the possession of special means of influencing others and powers of paranormal communication. Unusual perceptions and sensations—illusions, not delusions, because of lack of full, fixed persuasive belief—as well as eccentricities of speech, such as oddly abstract or vague patterns also may appear. Eccentricities in behavior and appearance may be displayed, including, for example, manneristic rituals or lack of self-care. Emotions may be constricted or expressed inappropriately, fostering either profound social discomfort or isolation—hence, the categorization of the schizotypal personality as an emotion avoidant type.

The absence of illogical thought processes, delusions of persecutions, hallucinations, and other such symptoms, help differentiate schizotypal characterology from schizophrenia. In the schizotypal, nonschizophrenic configuration, ideas of reference can exist, but they do not reach the proportion of full-fledged delusions. Rather, they may include pronounced magical thinking frequently seen in persons with regressively immature eccentricity or with exaggerated dependency needs. This sort of magical thinking can in turn include placing special value on superstitions, beliefs in clairvoyance or telepathy, and fantasy preoccupations that are quite important to the individual but are, nevertheless, highly idiosyncratic or even bizarre. Yet, in spite of peculiar or even paranoid thinking, expressions of the thought process reflect a relative intactness with essential integrity and logical presentation. Along with this nonschizophrenic thinking process, the schizotypal person is involved in a great deal of wishful thinking and in this respect can even experience some derealization episodes. For example, such a person, imagining a relative or friend three thousand miles away, is likely to assume that the other person, at that precise moment, is correspondingly thinking of him. Such correlational thinking contains a syncretistic element—that is, the belief that the fact of correlation is equivalent to the condition of causation. This sort of correlational and magical thinking is also a function of the feeling of social isolation and reflects a collateral and intense investment in wishes and fantasy.

In terms of verbal communication, then, schizotypal behavior can in fact include some circumstantial thinking and digressive and vague speech. Yet, in the absence of the breakdown and loosening of associations and/or incoherence that would be typical of schizophrenic cognition and speech, the schizotypal type congeals with an intact characterological configuration.

In terms of emotion, this schizotypal avoidant type can express affect that is silly or inappropriate, aloof or cold, and can react without the necessary and accompanying facial gestures that typically invite social intercourse. However, in terms of differential effects, the constricted affect of schizotypal functioning nevertheless remains modulated and is not the same as flat or grossly inappropriate affect often seen in schizophrenia. The conceptualization of the schizotypal type can, accordingly, afford a distinction with conditions of schizophrenia. It should also be noted that such schizotypal types, because of the withdrawal of affect, can, as noted above, be susceptible to the development of paranoid ideation, and can become especially sensitive to criticism. Because of this particular sensitivity, avoidant behavior is considered to be a reaction to the major problem for this type—that of intense social anxiety.

On a differential diagnostic basis, the distinction between schizotypal personality and schizophrenia provides also the essential template through which a further distinction between schizotypal and other more marginal character diagnoses can be made. These other so-called marginal character types may include the borderline personality, avoidant personality, and schizoid personality. In each of these last three types, the organization of emotion and defenses with respect to interpersonal relations tends to create isolated conditions and a paucity of primary relationships. In the schizotypal type, the basic distinction from these other types concerns the schizotypal's amalgam of cognitive constructions, such as magical thinking and the influence of correlational confusions with causations that are idiosyncratic, unusual, and problematic.

On a defense level, a combination of obsessive, paranoid, schizoid, and hysteric defenses seem most operational in this schizotypal type. The hypersensitivity and social anxiety of the schizotypal type and the resulting emotional withdrawal of such persons, along with possible ideas of reference, form a paranoid cast. In addition, the use of projection is also one way that such a person manages potential anxiety—that is, by externalizing fears and angers. The preoccupation with superstition and magical thinking and the excessive immersion in ideational content also suggests the use of intellectualization or obsessional techniques as another way to manage any kind of emotional overstimulation. The magical thinking, limited affective expression, personal isolation, and social withdrawal also suggest the inner fantasy and dulled affect associated with typical schizoid defenses. Finally, this sort of person can use hysterical denial mechanisms to screen out undesirable social interactions in order to rationalize them.

Developmental Issues

Because of the recent introduction of this schizotypal personality type in *DSM-III/III-R*, an overall consensus of etiology is not presently possible. Yet the conjecture regarding etiology could certainly include the proposition that such persons did not have stable or consistent object contact; in fact, quite the opposite would be expected. That is, relationships to parents generally lacked sufficient emotional closeness and warmth; by implication, such relations likely contained punitive features that certainly could be predicted to generate eventual social hypersensitivity. The limitations in affectional demonstrativeness by parents of children developing schizotypal dispositions is assumed as a distinct parent-child configuration. This particular family interaction is supported by the reference in *DSM-III/III-R* to the greater tendency of schizotypal persons to have a family member who is schizophrenic as compared to the general population.

In order to diagnose schizotypal personality, it is essential to rule out a diagnosis of schizophrenia in remission or a residual type of schizophrenia. Finally, an additional diagnostic indicator can be constructed by ascertaining that this schizotypal configuration is characterological and as such has been stable—that the configuration itself has been sustained in this characteristic manner over the person's life. Thus, the schizotypal organization of traits, behavior, emotion, and thinking that make up this characterological type acts to ward off sufficient stress and thereby maintains sufficient ego-integrity to insure a nonschizophrenic condition as well as a condition that prevents anxiety from flooding the personality. The defensive structure of the particular schizotypal configuration described here tends to stave off more serious pathology and permits the avoidance of the experience of emotion that would otherwise be overwhelming, and potentially threatening to the schizotypal character structure itself.

Rather than illustrating a single case of schizotypal personality, suffice it to say that clinicians as well as lay persons have in fact experienced such persons who are seriously devoted to belief in cults, seek to engage in activities that can generate fantasies regarding supernatural powers, express interest in clairvoyance, and, in an overall sense, can be fulfilled through this sort of magical and fantasy object contact rather than through actual interpersonal relations. Finally, these are also persons who do not seem to demonstrate a desire for actual affection and acceptance. They seem instead to avoid such affectional needs and emotional stimulation. This sort of style is quite different from the schizoid character who is relatively indifferent to praise or criticism. In contrast to these two styles—the schizotypal and the schizoid—is the emotion avoidant personality characterized in *DSM-III/III-R* as avoidant personality disorder. While the avoidant character is considered as an emotion avoidant type, such a character type frequently expresses a sincere desire for affection and acceptance but can only enter a social context if strong guarantees are made of the possible unconditional acceptance by others.

In the following section, this emotion avoidant disorder will be presented.

Avoidant Personality

In contrast to the schizotypal character who seeks protection in isolation, and in contrast to the schizoid character who in withdrawal radiates a distinctly remote, inaccessible quality, the avoidant character seeks to insure protection of self-esteem as a prerequisite to any attempt to attain social gratification. In fact, a yearning for interpersonal engagement is a significant wish for the avoidant character although the expression of this wish is blocked by fears of rejection and failure. Thus, this avoidant type will create distance with respect to personal attachments. Such distancing behavior reflects a desire to protect the self that overshadows the need for acceptance and affection; the avoidant personality therefore needs to perceive acceptance from others and this perception of acceptance becomes the prerequisite for entering into relationships. The avoidant personality, consequently, cannot be characterized as truly remote or isolated since relating is valued although avoided because of particular fears of rejection. In *DSM-III* and *DSM-III-R*, the avoidant personality disorder is highlighted by sensitivity to rejection, fearfulness, and distress in social circumstances. Easily hurt, the avoidant type has few friends, avoids activities that require interpersonal contact, inhibits expression to avoid appearing foolish, anxious, humiliated, or ashamed, adheres to routine to avoid risk, and needs assurances of acceptance by others before chancing the risk of interpersonal interactions.

A key dynamic that can assist in the diagnosis of the avoidant character concerns a syndrome of behavior, emotion, and fantasy regarding hypersensitivity to rejection. Sometimes this hypersensitivity to rejection can be mistakenly characterized as paranoid vigilance because the avoidant character type can perceive personal diminishment and criticism in relatively unimportant events.

In terms of differential diagnosis, this social sensitivity does not, in fact, derive from any core paranoid structure. Rather, such social sensitivity in the avoidant type seems to be a symptom of unresolved adolescent and preadolescent conflict. This conflict encompasses on the one hand, strong needs for affiliation and acceptance, reassurance and reinforcement of self-esteem, and encouragement to achieve and to feel comfortable in a given social matrix. On the other hand, the basic anxiety of the avoidant type is the intense apprehension of and sensitivity to rejection, and the protective isolation which persons with avoidant characterology attempt to neutralize by constantly seeking guarantees of unconditional acceptance. Yet, the character syndrome can be regarded as an emotion avoidant type because the person's behaviors that persist and form protracted chronic character patterns include social withdrawal, distancing in personal relations, and an overall cautious attitude with respect to any vocational involvement.

Thus, the behavioral level upon which the character label of avoidant type is based does not in any way necessarily reveal or reflect the attitudes and emotional position in the core of the character. This core configuration of attitudes and emotions, in fact, strongly contrasts with the actual behavior of the avoidant personality. These central or core attitudes and emotions include low self-esteem, personal devaluation, and social apprehension, as well as the absence of significant integration into the personality of a more mature ego, while most compellingly, there remains a resilient enough ego to contain ever-present wishes for connection with people under conditions of acceptance. It is this central social wish that generates the defining anxiety and hope for this character type. Because of the pervasiveness of this social wish and the intensity of anxiety associated with it, preoccupations concerning connections with people occur along with rationalizations for the avoidance of positive steps to accomplish the wish based on fears of rejection.

Defenses

Some flexibility is shown in the defense system of the avoidant character type in that these defenses shift between operating to protect such persons during periods of uncertainty—helping them to remain in relative isolation—and retract during periods of certainty where acceptance is predictable. Thus, during times of certainty, social exposure becomes possible and may even be rewarding.

The defense system of the avoidant character type encompasses reliance on a defensive network of repression, projection, and rationalization. The defense of repression can be strongly instituted to diminish assertive, competitive, and sexual feelings. The use of the projection defense enables feelings of assertiveness, competitiveness, and sexuality—which are considered relatively unacceptable or unsafe by the avoidant character—to be localized in others. This process of externalization can then intensify the avoidant character's fears about approaching people. Such fears materialize if others are seen—through the operation of projection—as disposed toward the expression of assertion or sexual demandingness, sensed by the avoidant character as threatening. The avoidant person is then subject to feelings of substantial vulnerability and fragility as a result of the perception of external threats that accrue from the operation of projection.

In response to such feelings of vulnerability, a wide range of social distancing, withdrawal, and isolation strategies ensue—essentially constituting a range of socially protective schizoid patterns. The defense of rationalization is employed as an additional step in promoting a sense of safety and in developing a defensive basis for the self-protective strategies of this avoidant type that contrast with the avoidant character's yearnings for interpersonal engagement and recognition. This system of rationalizations is developed to justify the avoidant character's investment in caution. Feelings of depression, frustration, and even anger during periods of aloneness can be the outcome of the self-protective purpose to the defensive network instituted in the avoidant character. Efforts at compensatory strivings can be expected to be short-lived and unsuccessful because of the potency of urges that are felt regarding social inclusion and recognition.

The use of these defensive strategies designed to calibrate the wish for closeness comprises the overall emotional regulation in this diagnosis. During periods of uncertainty, defensive strategies evoke the experience of inertia, passivity, and an underresponse to demands resembling the response of an inadequate character structure. In addition and in contrast, this defensive strategy in the avoidant personality structure reveals wishes containing needs for nurturance and acceptance. Persons of this avoidant diagnosis indeed frequently yearn for admiration. In the absence of such valuing, symptoms can develop which in behavioral terms indicate an amalgam of depressive, schizoid, and passive qualities. The basic defensive strategy that protects the essence of the avoidant character structure also implies the origins of the childhood developmental experience that could lead to the formation of this character pattern.

Developmental Issues

In the etiology of the avoidant personality type, a usually intact family or the presence of a single parent who was indeed available to the child seems to characterize a typical early context. In this hypothetical context, the parent or primary caretaker relates to the child with acceptance and even affection. Yet, it is presumed that the character of the parent is entirely colored by features of a high demand for conformity and obedience as well as a dominant nature. These features in the character of the parent can evoke an anticipation in the child of exposure regarding the child's reduced performance and accompanying feelings of deflation, shame, and humiliation. Further, the parent may use intimidation methods toward the child. This sort of conduct then becomes the child's model of interpersonal relations and such intimidation essentially prevents the child from feeling comfortable enough to be assertive in the absence of specific permission from the authority figure. The core dimension in the character pertaining to the need for approval and a corresponding fear regarding assertion may generate derivative characterological responses in the child that more or less form the outlines of this avoidant characterological configuration.

Thus, it is the need to protect oneself until some sign of acceptance is signaled that constitutes the central anxiety of such a person. In adulthood, relationships can become possible for such persons only when the partner is loving, accepting, and even adoring. Under such conditions, the isolation and deprivation that would ordinarily emerge during periods of social withdrawal can become attenuated. When avoidant personalities experience acceptance, they can, for that period, be spontaneous and gregarious. In sharp contrast to this garrulous behavior, is its opposite, the apprehension of social situations and—in the extreme form—feelings of despair in the absence of necessary signals of acceptance from others. Under conditions where this kind of person feels rejected or at least not yet accepted, behaviors of passivity, inertia, and depression can emerge. Some of the features of this kind of character configuration appear in the following clinical illustration.

Clinical Case Illustration

A 50-year-old male accountant who was a specialist in various business and financial examinations was fired from a position he held for 18 years. Apparently, he was not sufficiently credentialed to be head of his department and became embroiled in what resembled a power struggle with the new head of his division. What had actually occurred, however, was that this patient did not receive any of the necessary signals from the new chief that he was either appreciated or viewed as an important member of the staff. The patient was generally reticent and quiet, and his behavior could easily be characterized as somewhat antisocial and isolative. Actually, he was preoccupied with the fear of saying something incorrect, inappropriate, or humiliating; therefore, he avoided risks in his social behavior, which meant that he frequently only offered the minimum expected in such social contexts.

The head of the division apparently experienced monosyllabic responses from the patient and began to see the patient as oppositional, resentful, and uncooperative. Their interaction was never discussed, but it ultimately led to the patient's dismissal. In addition, his tentatively maintained relationship with his girlfriend ended. His companion complained that she could no longer accept his neglectful behavior. He would not assume responsibilities in the relationship but rather depended and waited for her to make all the plans and invite all sexual advances.

The patient found himself living alone and unemployed, and, at the age of 50, rationalized that he was permanently unemployable and not sufficiently attractive to be part of any important relationship. The psychological reality, however, was that the patient found it extremely difficult to overcome his inertia largely because of fear of rejection and became passive and somewhat depressed. Since he also could not initiate social contact, the sense that anyone could want him became an increasingly obscure idea. The memory that he

actually was capable of a relationship also increasingly became more of an abstraction and a rather remote possibility.

In this sort of emotion avoidant type, the person's current emotional state characterized by pessimism, emotional and social
avoidance, inertia and passivity, with a measure of despair, could
instantly evaporate provided some signal of interest from another
person surfaced. This reassuring expression of interest could come
from a potential partner or it could take the form of an offer of
a professional position, both of which would symbolize the establishment of a condition of acceptance. Such a potentially stark and
instantaneous reversal in attitude and feeling to sudden new and
desired circumstances is a diagnostic reflection of the avoidant
character configuration. A temporary lift to self-esteem by external
signals reduces the need for protective avoidance and softens anxiety about rejection, humiliation, embarrassment, and awkwardness.

The grouping of the emotion avoidant character disorders of this
chapter completes a more or less comprehensive overview of basic
character disorder types that reflect the cementing properties of
specific personality configurations. The first grouping, the emotion
controlled types, included the compulsive, paranoid, and schizoid
character patterns. This cluster of character patterns reflected propensities to control emotion as a way of managing anxiety. The
second grouping, the emotion dyscontrolled types, included the
hysteric, narcissistic, and psychopathic personalities. In this second
group, in contrast to the first, anxiety is managed because emotion
is not controlled. Rather, emotion can remain dyscontrolled and
the release of such emotion then becomes reassuring to the person
and helps neutralize anxiety. In the third grouping of basic character patterns, the emotion dependent types, the dependent, passive aggressive, and inadequate personalities were included. In these
characterologies anxiety was managed through the successful quest
for emotional and interpersonal dependency.
    In the final group, the emotion avoidant types, anxiety was con-
trolled by the person's search for acceptance, and, in the absence
of acceptance, by withdrawing and remaining socially distant until
such acceptance is perceived. This last group included the borderline, schizotypal, and avoidant types.
    Even though these twelve configurations can be considered a

basic complement of character types, it becomes clear from the evolution of *DSM* nosology that as syndromes and behavior are better understood and as such behaviors can also be predicted from the theoretical formulations of personality, this basic complement of character formations will evolve. The current *DSM* nosology represents only the newest approximation in the understanding of personality and its major vicissitudes—psychopathology and diagnosis.

Part 2 analyzes and distinguishes the variety of depressions and affect disorders generally considered in *DSM-III/III-R*. It also presents diagnostic considerations for these depression and affect disorders not included in *DSM-III/III-R* but still conventionally recognized by clinicians and reflected in the diagnostic statements that are naturally used by such clinicians in their everyday work.

CAPSULE CLINICAL PROFILES OF EMOTION AVOIDANT CHARACTER TYPES

Reliance on nurturant figures is prohibited and fears of interpersonal involvement are central in these diagnoses.

Borderline: The struggle to avoid emotional arousal creates a need for the use of a myriad of traits including obsessive, histrionic, paranoid, narcissistic, and schizoid. Such persons experience conflict between mood swings associated with the use of idealization and devaluation in their effort to secure identity and boundary stability. Identity confusion, emotional lability, and fears of ego fragmentation pervasively grip the personality. Ego deficiency and instability of mood also facilitate abandonment fears and an underresponse to the demands of the world. Tenuous controls are seen along with the appearance of impulsive behavior. Eruption of anger occurs. Projection and regression are typical defenses. A major dynamic concerns reliance on the defense of splitting and part-object relatedness.

Schizotypal: This nonschizophrenic pattern has the quality of a preschizophrenic or remission-like state except that characterological stability is maintained. Emotion is generally restricted but when expressed can be inappropriate. Social isolation, peculiar behavior, and paranoid ideation characterize the odd personality expression. Correlational, magical, and wishful thinking also support interest in the supernatural and there is an excessive immersion in ideational content. A wide range of defenses are used. Fear and anger are externalized.

Avoidant: A pronounced social inhibition is present largely because of fears the person has of rejection and consequent humiliation. The person needs a clear signal of acceptance from others in order to risk social interaction. Thus, the person is in continuous struggle to insure protection of self-esteem, although social relationships are indeed desired. High sensitivity to criticism and pessimism generate distancing maneuvers even though the person yearns to be involved, recognized, and admired. Behavior can contain depressive, schizoid, and passive characteristics.

PART II
Affect Disturbances

CHAPTER 6

The Depressions and Mood-Associated Disorders

A consideration of depression from a characterological point of view will be presented first in the analysis and comparisons of a variety of depressions, even though *DSM-III/III-R* does not consider depressive character disorder as a specific diagnostic entity. This analysis of the possible characterology of depression will then be followed by a consideration of diagnoses of other depressions, including the neurotic and psychotic depressions, along with a brief presentation of the use of depression as a qualifier in other disorders. In addition, elevated moods such as manic and hypomanic disorders will also be presented.

TRADITIONAL CONCEPTS IN DIAGNOSIS OF DEPRESSION

Traditionally, depressions have been broadly viewed to be either acute or chronic. The acute depressions were typically correlated to recent traumatic events in the person's life and considered reactive to these events. In contrast, the chronic depressions were considered more pathological since these conditions contained some aberrant thinking, often covered latent suicidal inclinations, and in general, reflected ties to internal processes. Such internal sources were possibly derived from constitutional factors, or, if psychologically based, then these internal processes were entrenched in a profound, intractable, developmental context.

This distinction between acute and chronic depression achieved relatively universal acceptance. The acute state became associated with a transient trauma, and therefore was considered at worst to be neurotic—while chronic depression was perceived by clinicians to reflect more serious pathology. Clinicians, therefore, assessed the chronic condition of depression as a more prognostically guarded one. This poor prognosis frequently reflected the possibility that in some cases a psychotic condition was associated with the chronic depressions. To further consolidate the distinction between acute and chronic depression, the diagnostic reference to exogenous depression was coined to describe more acute conditions in which a precipitating event in the individual's external circumstance could be related to the onset of depression. In contrast, reference to endogenous depression characterized the chronic condition and further connoted a permanently etched and fixed internal pathology.

DEPRESSIVE CHARACTER

Despite the accepted nomenclature that generated somewhat rigid assumptions regarding depression, clinicians nevertheless frequently interview and otherwise treat in psychotherapy individuals who are neither afflicted with recent depression based upon trauma of the exogenous type nor individuals who are endogenously depressed, implying a chronic or possibly psychotic diagnosis. Instead, these patients are depressed people who, with reference to object relations considerations pertaining to narcissistic and borderline diagnostic phenomena, can now be evaluated with greater clarity. Such individuals may function reasonably well, may not be psychotic, but may have experienced aspects of developmental arrest. Such early problematic experience with the primary caregiver leaves its depressive mark not necessarily as a psychosis but more on a behavioral level reflecting a depressive overlay fueled by narcissistic concerns. This depression in a narcissistic context reflects inconsistent, generally deflated self-esteem, and strong ambivalence toward that primary caretaker. Many such persons presumably received nurturant supplies but for numerous reasons, including but not limited to severe psychopathology of the caretaker, find themselves absorbed with many personal concerns. These preoccupations include the wish for special treatment, fear as well as dissatisfaction with relationships, and intense feelings of sensitivity to rejection. In addition, behavioral patterns appear in which those closest to them are attacked with frequent criticism. Finally, enough of an absence of self-assurance exists so that any close involvement with a partner is precluded.

Such a person may not be psychotically depressed with long-standing chronic, endogenous features. The all-encompassing intensity of depression, as in the endogenous form, is absent in such cases. Clinical experience also indicates that these persons, although quite self-absorbed, can by no means be classified as incipiently schizophrenic, since primary process material does not unrealistically intrude into thinking and reality contact is quite adequate.

Such persons are neither manic-depressive, cyclothymic, nor reative, since periodic fluctuations of mood do not appear to relieve the chronic depressive aspect of their functioning. They are also not dysthymic, since features of depression do not dominate but rather contribute as a distinct component of disturbance. Nor is the disorder an exogenous one, as it has not been precipitated by recent, obvious events. The question such a differential diagnostic problem raises concerns the basic nature of this sort of a depressive configuration. It can be proposed that a useful way of understanding such persons is to view this depressive configuration in essentially characterological terms. The aim of this depressive characterology is to allay anxiety specifically associated with parental caregiving figures who may be nurturant but who are also significantly inconsistent, immature, depressed, or ambivalent. This sort of etiological experience involving the ambivalent parent is one that may generate conflict for the child especially in the consolidation of the narcissistic phase of development so that a fear and premonition of impending abandonment with any primary partner becomes a palpable feeling throughout life.

Clinically, such characterologically depressed persons may, for example, be quite modest, shy, and introspective. They also may be expected to overidentify with objects of pity or those who are helpless. The overidentification with those who are helpless includes the evocation of sympathy and empathy, for example, at the sight of an animal in need. This sort of person internalizes abandonment tensions and can be self-protective through the externalization of hostility. Yet, such persons also can be frequently peace loving and noncompetitive because of their need to seek nurturance. Nevertheless, when relationships are established they can then manifest hostility, frequently as a defensive maneuver against a persistent expectation derived from early developmental experience that they will be abandoned or that the partner will in some way disappoint them or even try to control them. This type of depressive character will usually seem quite independent, and, although shy, nevertheless can reach out when conditions are interesting and nonthreatening. In terms of differential diagnosis the configuration of depressive character also differs from any of the emotion avoidant types with respect to ego strength, and is especially different as well from the borderline type. In all such comparisons, the depressive character would be expected to have a stronger ego.

This configuration of the depressive character as a likely candidate for future inclusion in the *DSM* nomenclature is added here to the other entries of depressive diagnoses considered in the present *DSM-III/III-R*. In this chapter, a further delineation of these entries will be presented in a manner that distinguishes them in terms of differential diagnostic components.

In *DSM-III/III-R* an analysis of the depressive diagnoses indicates a shift in the conception of depression as distinguished from that of *DSM-II*. As noted above, in *DSM-II*, depression was largely abstracted as psychotic versus neurotic, so that psychotic depression was clearly distinguished from neurotic or reactive depression. In *DSM-III/III-R* two main distinctions regarding diagnoses of depression concern, first of all, whether elevation of mood either in the present or past is part of the disturbance, or if only depression in the absence of any mood elevations is or has been present. The second distinction with respect to the depressive diagnosis—the presence of depression—is then further related to the severity and duration of the mood disturbance.

In the following discussion, the nosological components of the various affective or mood disorders contained in *DSM-III/III-R* are presented. The organization of this nosology comprises first the various disorders that contain elevated mood disturbances either in their current manifestation or in past episodes as a component of the disorder. Once this distinction regarding the presence of the mood elevated component has been established, divisions will then be presented reflecting the severity and duration of the episode containing the mood disturbance. If the episode is considered major—that is, a major affective disorder—then the relevant diagnostic category is bipolar, provided that a manic episode is or has been present. This bipolar state stands in contrast to a major depressive episode that would be diagnosed if only depression alone comprised the mood disturbance. On the other hand, if the episode of mood disturbance is less severe, that is, not a major affective disorder, then such a mood disturbance will be categorized as one of the other specific affective disorders: cyclothymia or dysthymia. For example, if a hypomanic episode—a milder form of elation than that present in a manic episode—is, or has been manifested, the disorder is known as cyclothymic. In contrast, if depression only appears in less severe form in comparison with a major depressive episode the syndrome is described as a dysthymic disorder. Additional minor atypical affective disorders are included for some idiosyncratic affective profiles. Finally, the diagnostic categories of bipolar or major depressive episode can each contain reference to the presence or absence of psychosis.

Table 6.1 presents this diagnostic scheme of affective disorders, so that at a glance the organization of mood disorders—especially with respect to depression and the issue of psychosis/nonpsychosis can be seen. Changes in nomenclature from *DSM-III* to *DSM-III-R* are also indicated in table 6.1 along with the various specifications that can be added to the major affective disorders to introduce refinement to diagnostic efforts within the parameters possible in the latest overall *DSM* nosology.

DEPRESSION AND DSM NOSOLOGY

In *DSM-I* and *II*, depressions were simply dichotomized. The more pathological depressions were considered psychotic along with chronic features containing symptoms such as delusions and hallucinations. In addition, psychotic depression and the depressive pole of the manic-depressive diagnosis, for all intents and purposes, were regarded as equivalent. In the manic-depressive condition, the patient typically manifested periods in one phase that alternated with periods in the other, although an emphasis on one pole rather than the other could occur. Persistent repitition of the depressive phase alone would be classified as psychotic depression. Among the nonpsychotic depressions were the reactive depressions—acute episodes based on a recent traumatic event in which the depression emerged with a purpose. The specific purpose of the depression was to allay any anxiety that was released as a re-

TABLE 6.1. Mood Disorders in *DSM-III* and *DSM-III-R* Nosology

	BIPOLAR DISORDERS	DEPRESSIVE DISORDERS
DSM-III: Major affective disorders	*DSM-III* and *DSM-III-R* Mixed Manic Depressed	*DSM-III* and *DSM-III-R* Major depression: single eposide recurrent
	(1) Mild (2) Modereate (3) Severe (4) With psychotic features: mood congruent mood incongruent (5) In partial remission (6) In full remission	
		Chronic or melancholic type may be specified
DSM-III: Other specific affective disorders	*DSM-III* Cyclothymic disorder	*DSM-III* Dysthymic disorder (or depressive neurosis)
	DSM-III-R Cyclothymia	*DSM-III-R* Dysthymia (or depressive neurosis) primary or secondary type early or late onset
DSM-III: Atypical affective disorders	*DMS-III* Atypical bipolar disorder *DMS-III-R* Bipolar disorder not otherwise specified	*DMS-III* Atypical depression *DMS-III-R* Depressive disorder not otherwise specified

sult of the trauma. In the conceptualization of reactive depression, it became clear that clinicians viewed the personality implicitly as a dynamic system that operated to protect the person. It was almost as if the phenomenon of reactive depression was conceived as an antibody to address the issue of the more important pathology of overwhelming anxiety. In this sense, depression was employed by the personality as its anesthesia against potentially debilitating, damaging, and destructive anxiety flooding. The diagnostic equation predicted that as the trauma subsided, either because the passage of time reduced the intense aspect of the trauma or because the person was able to progress in resolving or working through the crisis, then anxiety correspondingly subsided. As the anxiety subsided, the depression would begin to lift. The depression was thus, in a psychological sense, part of defense structure or an actual coping mechanism.

In *DSM-III/III-R,* the dysthymic disorder, although diagnostically more complex, is essentially equivalent to the reactive or neurotic depression of previous nosologies. This transformation of approach from *DSM-II* to *DSM-III* with respect to reactive or dysthymic depression is but one example of the nosological changes pertaining to depression that appear in *DSM-III/III-R.* Another example of a change introduced in *DSM-III/III-R* is the placement of all of the mood disturbances—whether depressive or elated— under one nosological category: affective disorder.

MAJOR AFFECTIVE DISORDERS

In *DSM-III* and *DSM-III-R* two forms of major affective disorders are considered. The first is the bipolar disorder and the second is major depressive episode.

Bipolar Disorder

The bipolar disorder is distinguished by the presence, currently or in the past, of a manic episode as a prominent and relatively persistent part of the disturbance. In determining the presence of a manic episode, an elevated or irritable mood is seen to persist even though a depressive mood may appear with this manic state. Further, during the period of this disturbed mood several manic symptoms may also emerge. These manic symptoms include increased activity, restlessness, pressured speech, flight of ideas, grandiosity, distractability, avoidance of sleep, and involvement in a variety of acting out behaviors that express grandiosity. Any cluster of these manic symptoms may occur with or without the presence of psychotic features, but the overall abnormality of mood elevation is intense enough to interfere with social or vocational activities or is likely to lead to harmful consequences.

To identify the bipolar disorder as one with psychotic features, impairment in reality testing would be evident in the form of delusions, hallucinations, catatonic excitement, or strikingly unusual, bizarre, or inappropriate behavior. These psychotic features may then be further differentiated in terms of whether they are mood congruent or mood incongruent. In the case of mood congruent psychotic features, the disturbances of thought reflected in, for example, delusions or hallucinations are consistent with a mood of grandiose euphoria. Such mood congruent disturbed thinking may be reflected by statements indicating the subject's alleged closeness with a celebrity or diety, or statements that in some other way purport to show the subject's special power or prestige. Mood incongruent psychotic features in the context of a euphoric mood would involve disturbance of thought—such as negativism or even persecutory delusions—that are inconsistent with the mood of euphoria. Thus, the mood is elevated but the thoughts are discouraging—an incongruous mixture.

Types of Bipolar Disorders

In the biopolar disorder, three essential types can be differentiated—manic, depressed, and mixed. In the manic type of this bipolar disorder, the presence of a manic episode is the defining diagnostic criterion. In the depressed type of the bipolar disorder, a major depressive episode is present, but at least one manic episode has occured in the past, reflecting conformity to the bipolar model. Finally, in the mixed type of this bipolar disorder, the patient's symptoms involve both manic and depressive features, either in mixture or frequent alternation. Considerations regarding theoretical and phenomenological aspects of the euphoria and pressure characterizing the manic mood will be presented after discussion of the affect of depression.

When signs of manic disturbance are not currently present and, in addition, have not appeared in the patient's past, the depressive mood disturbance is classified as a major depressive episode. This type will be reviewed in the following section.

Major Depressive Episode

The mood of depression that characterizes the major depressive episode chiefly involves the person's continuing inability—for at least two weeks—to experience pleasure or interest as a normal experience of everyday life. Correlated to this mood of sadness and discouragement are factors affecting appetite, sleep, energy level, and weight. In addition, an agitated or retarded level of motor activity, distractability in thinking and, of course, preoccupations involving either suicide or death may appear. The individual experiencing this major depressive episode may also show an intense sense of inadequacy reflected by concerns of worthlessness, devaluation, self-reproach, or guilt. A distinction between a psychotic and nonpsychotic major depressive episode can be drawn. In instances where the major depressive episode can be characterized as psychotic, the representation of guilt or self-devaluation incorporates delusional ideas or hallucinatory experiences. This categorization of major depressive episode as psychotic may involve either mood congruent or mood incongruent features. In the case of mood congruent disturbances in thinking, such as themes of death and punishment, the delusional thoughts clearly pertain to aspects consistent with depression since they manifest concerns regarding guilt, self-reproach, or loss. In contrast, the presence of delusions or hallucinations unrelated to the depressed content of the mood disturbance, such as a paranoid type of persecutory delusion, would qualify the episode as one with mood incongruent features.

Major Depressive Episode with Melancholia

Another discrimination that can be made involving the major depressive episode is its appearance with melancholia. In the melancholic form of the major depressive episode pleasure is absent from all activities, the depressed mood is extremely severe and usually most severe in the morning, agitation or retardation in the motor sphere is substantial, the person awakens unusually early, or phenomena involving loss of appetite, weight, or feelings of guilt are extreme.

In *DSM-III-R* an additional specification regarding chronicity can be indicated. An episode is considered chronic if the depression has continued for two years without at least a two-month interruption. Lastly, discriminations regarding severity can be encoded in the *DSM-III* and *DSM-III-R* diagnoses of the major affective disorders. The designation *mild* indicates fewer symptoms and relatively less impairment, while *severe* indicates symptoms that reflect marked interference in functioning; *moderate* places symptomatology and impairment at a level between the mild and severe positions.

Manic Episodes

An important mood disturbance within the several categories of major affective disorders is the affective condition comprising manic episodes. According to the established criteria of *DSM-III/III-R*, the manic episode is chiefly characterized as a persistently elevated, expansive, or irritable affective quality. In this manic mood, the person seems especially tuned to some private inner agenda. Clinically, this subjective agenda appears fueled by boundless energy and unusual work fervor. The person's limitless interest in a variety of projects becomes apparent, and the patient appears only superficially related in an interpersonal sense; any partner in a given interaction will experience himself as quite incidental and as replaceable.

The manic syndrome is also characterized by an expansive and pressured quality. It is this inner pressure that constitutes the clinical sense that the person is being excessive and not really authentic in the interpersonal relationship. Of clinical importance is that even when the pressured and driven quality is quite chronic, it remains out of character when the person's premorbid functioning is utilized as a frame of reference.

In view of the underlying clinical quality of pressure, it can be seen that the manic syndrome follows a consistent pattern. In *DSM-III/III-R* this pattern includes a sense of self-inflation characterized by compensatory behaviors including grandiosity, self-aggrandizement, compulsive talking, flights of ideas, acute distractability, psychomotor agitation, and increased goal activity.

From the psychological point of view, the compensatory need operating during the manic episode serves to ward off depression. This compensatory need accomplishes its mandate by providing the motivation and energy that fuels and sustains the entire manic syndrome. The person displaying this high energy profile is actually expressing a hyperutilization of compensatory defense; that is, because depressed feelings threaten to invade the entire personality—especially that part of the personality associated with the self-structure—ego functions are mobilized, drawing upon everything that can be utilized to elevate the self. It is through the establishment and maintenance of compensating ego elevation that the manic episode acquires its pressured nature. It is a nature desperate to avoid the ravages of a deteriorated self-image.

During the manic episode such compensation is infused in all the person's behaviors—for example, in pressured speech and hyperactivity; the compensatory process determines quite simply how the person engages in derivative behaviors affecting everyday living. For example, the compensatory syndrome of the manic episode can enable the person to operate with significantly reduced need for sleep, engage in inappropriate buying ventures, demonstrate grandiose planning, disregard pain, show idiosyncratic but elaborate sexual activity, and so forth. In the *DSM-III/III-R* nomenclature, this sort of manic episode can be associated with psychosis or can have a nonpsychotic manifestation. In the case where psychosis exists, diagnostic indications show an obvious deterioration in reality testing as exemplified by extremely unusual behavior, delusions or hallucinations.

In the above formulation of the *major affective disorders* including the *bipolar, major depressive episode,* and *manic episode,* the diagnostic distinctions in the *DSM-III/III-R* model relied heavily upon descriptive and empirical criteria for a differential diagnosis. However, included in the above affect formulations were some theoretical considerations that help organize the understanding of the overt mood symptomatology. In the following discussion, theoretical issues are presented as a way to further synthesize the understanding of descriptive nosology.

THE MAJOR AFFECTIVE DISORDERS: THEORETICAL CONSIDERATIONS

A reliance solely on the *DSM* model leads to elaborate description to such an extent that eventually the distinction between a symptom, a part syndrome, and a full diagnosis can be easily obscured. The introduction of a theoretical framework may promote more comprehensive understanding of symptoms so that diagnosis can be seen as a derivative shorthand for specific psychopathology, which in turn can be located in the overall domain of the personality.

Depression: The Source of All Affective Disorders

From a psychodynamic and psychoanalytic point of view, the basic theoretical understanding of depression concerns its derivation from a presumed oral conflict. This connection of depression to the oral stage of psychosexual development was discussed by psychoanalytic pioneers, such as Karl Abraham and Sigmund Freud. From this early work, depression was connected to issues of deprivation and anger. The concepts of the internalization of anger and the experience of separation from the nurturing figure that is sensed by the child as a loss could be considered theoretical precursors to the development of object-relations theory. The object representational life of the infant and phenomena of loss and mourning are therefore key theoretical concepts in the etiology of depression. Further, an analysis of the operation of coping patterns and defense mechanisms in the management of anxiety related to loss of the nurturing object is also helpful in explicating the process involved in the appearance of depression.

Defensive Operations in Affective Disorders

In depressive symptomatology, in addition to the ubiquitous repression defense, the defenses of compensation, reaction formation, and sublimation are conceived as blocking or managing the actual appearance of depression and its vicissitudes. Such vicissitudes of depression include duration of the depression, its degree of severity, and its transformation, when necessary, into equivalent expansive states such as manic or hypomanic episodes. The defense of compensation seems to be central within the depressive defense cluster and most germane to the direct avoidance or flight from depression as well as to its management.

Compensation is the defense which is utilized to promote self-esteem and to support ego functioning. For example, the compensatory mechanism begins to flower fully during adolescence. In adolescence, psychological and emotional experiences of self-doubt, worthlessness, and lowered self-esteem are deflected and neutralized, mostly through compensatory fantasy and behavior that focuses on idealizing tendencies. Through compensation, certainty replaces self-doubt, a sense of self-aggrandizement replaces feelings of worthlessness, and an inflated sense of self-assurance replaces feelings of low self-esteem. Thus, it is clear that in the adolescent stage, positive introjections and internalizations, as well as an enhanced sense of ego are further cemented through defensive patterns of compensation. This ego fortification then serves to guard against the consciousness of self-doubt, separation anxiety, and the internalization of anger—the mortar of depression. In the absence of the compensatory defense, feelings involving doubt, sadness, inadequacy, inferiority, as well as the implosive angry feelings generating helplessness—all can become more palpable and can contribute to the gradual appearance of disorganization, anxiety, and depression.

In the expansive, manic, or hypomanic phases of affective disorders, the compensatory defense operates to excess and reflects the person's desperation regarding the potential breakthrough of depressive feelings. In the manic state, for example, as well as in other expansive states, the compensatory defense is assisted in the barricade against depression by the defenses of reaction formation and sublimation. The utilization of reaction formation can be construed as preventing the person in the manic state from sexually perseverating. Sexual energy presumably then becomes transformed into work energy by the addition of the sublimation defense that now enters the process. This work energy is expressed through the initiation of multitudes of projects, compulsive talkativeness, and other such expansive symptoms comprising the manic syndrome. Thus, the excessive but threatening pleasure associated with sexual expression is transformed by the reaction formation defense to work efforts with the assistance of the operation of sublimation.

The constituent defenses of depressive symptomatology can involve etiological derivatives of all psychosexual stages; certainly with more severe depressions, such as those involving the psychoses, etiological contributions can theoretically be attributed in part to particularly chaotic or severe oral stage conflict. It seems necessary however, to see the entire depressive syndrome as it is outlined by clusters of symptoms in *DSM-III/III-R*, through the analysis of essential defenses. This understanding of defense with respect to depression can provide a more lucid distinction between the categories of depression and affective disorders presented in table 6.1. Especially important to note with respect to such distinctions of differential diagnosis is that the operation of compensation, along with reaction formation and sublimation, in most cases seems to account for bipolar affective disorder including manic episodes, while the major depressive episode including solely depression reflects a massive degeneration of the compensatory defense itself.

With reference to other specific affective disorders, such as the cyclothymic, deterioration of compensation, reaction formation, and sublimation would be theoretically less severe and therefore account for a less severe diagnostic state. In terms of such severity of diagnosis, the dysthymic disorder also referred to in table 6.1 is a diagnostic state in which the defensive effects of compensation have been reduced but not obliterated.

In the following sections, the diagnoses of cyclothymic, dysthymic, and atypical affective disorder will be reviewed in terms of their syndromal formulations. This presentation emphasizes the vital part played by theory in connecting the various denotative references to affective disorders and depression so that the distinction between psychopathology and diagnosis and its relation to the fabric of personality can remain clear.

OTHER SPECIFIC AFFECTIVE DISORDERS

Table 6.1 identifies the cyclothymic and dysthymic disorders as less severe than the major affective disorders of bipolar and major depressive episode. These less intense but still relatively distinct diagnoses are both qualitatively and quantitatively different from the more severe types of affective disorders and are classified together in table 6.1 as other specific affective disorders.

Cyclothymic Disorder or Cyclothymia

In the cyclothymic disorder, or simply cyclothymia as it is relabeled in *DSM-III-R*, components both of depressed mood and of affective excitement appear for periods of time. In between the episodes of such disordered or idiosyncratic affect there may be periods during which the individual's normal mood predominates. During the occasions when disturbance is present, both hypomanic and depressive affect may appear more or less simultaneously, or alternations in the sequence in which these moods appear may occur. Thus, in the cyclothymic disorder, both severity and duration of symptoms are less forceful, since the individual experiences hypomanic rather than manic states. It is the presence of this frequently relatively brief but repeated hypomanic state, on the expansive side of the affective pathology, that most pointedly characterizes this cyclothymic disorder.

By hypomanic episode is meant that a period of excitement, high energy, and elation occurs, but this state is qualitatively less intense than in a full-blown typical manic episode. Hypomanic states are differentiated from manic episodes by the fact that hypomanic excitement does not interfere severely in vocational or social functioning and is not sufficiently intense to place the individual in obvious danger. Therefore, there is a difference of degree between manic episodes and hypomanic episodes, with the manic episodes reflecting considerably more severe pathology in the nature of the mood disturbance itself. Similarly, regarding the depressive aspects of cyclothymic pathology, the degree of depression does not reach the qualitative intensity and consequent impairment of living that characterizes the major depressive disorder.

Dysthymic Disorder or Dysthymia

The dysthymic disorder, or simply dysthymia as it is relabeled in *DSM-III-R,* is also less severe than the major depressive episode and is distinguished from its cyclothymic counterpart by the absence of any expansive qualities or high energy periods. Dysthymic disorder corresponds to the diagnosis variably referred to in earlier nomenclatures as depressive neurosis, depressive reaction, or exogenous depression, and is still assigned the alternate designation of depressive neurosis in *DSM-III* and *DSM-III-R*.

An innovation introduced in *DSM-III-R* allows the clinician to specify whether dysthymia is a primary or secondary type, as well as containing the property of early or late onset. The primary type of dysthymia is not related to other disorders—either those that are psychologically based such as an anxiety disorder, or those that show physical manifestations, such as arthritis. A secondary type of dysthymia, in contrast, indeed would be associated with another chronic disorder either of psychological or somatic origin. Early as opposed to late onset simply refers to the depression occurring before or after the age of 21.

In descriptive terms, the dysthymic or depressive neurosis diagnosis of *DSM-III-R* comprises a mood of depression that appears quantitatively more often than any periods during which depression is absent and persists for a minimum duration of two years. Among the symptoms characteristic of depression, those affecting appetite, sleep, and level of energy may appear along with reduced self-esteem, a sense of hopelessness and impaired concentration or decisiveness.

The disorders comprising the diagnostic level of the category *other specific affective disorders*—with its two divisions, the cyclothymic and dysthymic—can appear with a gradual onset and then follow a slow and insidious course. This quality of gradualness, when it occurs, stands in contrast with the major affective disorders in which symptomatology may develop more suddenly and more flamboyantly. Such differences which can appear in onset and cause of other specific affective disorders on the one hand and that of major affective disorder on the other, is an additional qualitative distinction between the two. Because of the difference in severity of symptomatology, this distinction between the broad categories of major affective disorder, and that of other specific affective disorder, reflects the fact that the major affective disorder can be considered a major syndrome, while the other specific affective disorders are relatively less intense in terms of the severity of pathology present although also quite problematic. For example, other specific affective disorders of cyclothymia and dysthymia would not include psychotic symptomatology, while the major affective disorders of bipolar and major depression can indeed appear with psychotic features.

Differential Symptoms: Hypomanic and Dysthymic Elements of Cyclothymia

There are a number of symptoms that are compared in *DSM-III/III-R* distinguishing and creating a differential profile between the depressive and hypomanic periods of the cyclothymic condition. These differential symptoms are clearly suggestive of a mood disturbance but express distinct aspects of affective pathology correlated either with a definite mood of depression or a state of expansiveness. These differentiating symptoms can be roughly divided into a few categories.

DISTURBANCES OF PLEASURE

The category that involves symptoms most directly relating to mood impairment contains features composed of loss of enjoyment for the dysthymic person on the one hand and, on the other, excessive efforts to achieve pleasure for the person in the hypomanic phase of the cyclothymic condition. More specifically, in the dysthymic person, a decrease in sexual activity that corresponds to a loss of interest in sex is frequently reported while, in contrast, in the hypomanic person sexual activity can be heightened. Generally, in the cyclothymic condition there is a contrasting avoidance or attraction displayed to all involvements related to pleasure correlated with the appearance of the dysthymic or hypomanic aspect of the disorder. Further, in the contrasting clyclothymic episodes, tearyness as opposed to joking, punning, and even inappropriate laughing can distinguish between depressive and hypomanic periods.

IMPAIRMENTS OF ENERGY

In a general manner, level of energy appears in a maladaptive form in the depressive or hypomanic phases as exemplified by a number of specific disturbances. These manifestations of disordered energy include, for the depressive and hypomanic, respectively, the contrast between low and high activation level, feelings of lethargy as opposed to restlessness, and the presence of periods of silence in contrast to unusual talkativeness.

DISORDERS OF ESTEEM

Another category that encompasses several symptoms in which disordered functioning appears that is differentially expressed by patients in depressive and hypomanic phases is that related to self-esteem. In the dysthymic person a sense of inadequacy and pessimism is present, along with an avoidance of social interactions. In contrast, for the hypomanic person, self-esteem is expressed in the form of grandiosity. In addition, optimism is typical for the hypomanic and includes boasting and ventilation of expansiveness.

PERSONALITY INTEGRATION

The final grouping of symptoms by which depressive and hypomanic phases differentially express pathology relates to general personality coherence. This personal sense of organization affects the quality of sleep, for example, in that the depressed person either sleeps excessively or cannot sleep as much as desired. On the other hand, in the hypomanic phase there is a consistent need for less sleep. Further, in the depressive period, limitations appear in capacities for attention, concentration, and application of cognitive abilities; in contrast, in the hypomanic period, creativity appears in thought and cognitive processes may be quite sharp rather than unclear. Accordingly, in the depressed person, the ability to apply himself is diminished, while the involvement for the hypomanic person invariably reflects expansiveness.

These differential diagnostic considerations regarding affect disturbances are among those that clinically can be useful in differentiating depressive from hypomanic phenomena. Such findings can be applied to the contrasting extremes of cyclothymia, that is, the hypomanic and dysthymic episodes that comprise the disorder. The remaining affect disorders considered in *DSM-III* are called atypical bipolar disorder and atypical depression—relabeled in *DSM-III-R* as bipolar disorder not otherwise specified, and depressive disorder not otherwise specified, respectively. These diagnostic entities will be presented in the following section along with a final discussion of a disorder outside of *DSM* nomenclature that clinicians refer to as agitated depression.

ATYPICAL AFFECTIVE DISORDERS

The remaining *DSM-III/III-R* categories of affective dysfunction concern affective disorders that are considered atypical. In the bipolar domain of the *DSM-III* category of *atypical affective disorders,* the conditions included are those in which some manic or hypomanic features appear. However, these characteristics are not pervasive enough to qualify as a genuine cyclothymic or bipolar disturbance. *DSM-III* classifies such atypical affective disturbances as *atypical bipolar disorder.* As another example of disturbance in the atypical affective disorder category, a hypomanic episode may appear but without the phenomenon of depression or a phase of depression that characterizes the cyclothymic disorder. In *DSM-III-R* this atypical affective disorder is known as *bipolar disorder not otherwise specified* and includes the disorder often called *bipolar II*: a condition in which a hypomanic episode appears as well as an episode of major depression rather than the more minor depression of dysthymia. This type of major depression is usually associated with manic episodes as in manic-depressive psychosis— that is, bipolar I. Thus, in bipolar II the major depression appears instead of the less severe depression usually associated with cyclothymia.

Further, in the *DSM-III* category of *atypical depression,* features of depression occur, but the depression does not qualify as a diagnosis of either major or dysthymic affective disorder. For example, symptoms characteristic of dysthymic disorder may appear, but these are relatively briefly experienced. In this atypical depression, a nondepressed mood typically occurs more than sustained depressive periods. One of the most important usages appropriate for this diagnostic category is to classify the appearance of depressed mood that has not yet been sustained for the two-year period required for dysthymia.

According to current *DSM* criteria, this atypical depression can also occur in an individual diagnosed as schizophrenic, where the schizophrenic process is in remission and depressive affect surfaces in the absence of schizophrenic symptoms. In *DSM-III-R* the category of atypical depression has been renamed *depressive disorder not otherwise specified.* Table 6.1 indicates the various labeling of these atypical depressions in both *DSM-III* and *DSM-III-R* as well as their relation to the current *DSM* division of affective disturbances into bipolar and unipolar types of mood disorders. The agitated depression that combines features of both divisions in a somewhat unique manner will be considered next. Although this diagnosis of agitated depression is outside of the *DSM* system, it is presented here because of its traditional clinical usage.

AGITATED DEPRESSION

In addition to the *DSM-III/III-R* nosological categories of mood and depressive syndromes, clinicians frequently refer to the diagnosis of agitated depression. Agitated depression involves a mood of sadness or regret that contains elements of irritability, impatience, restlessness, insomnia, and considerable covert, although transparent, hostility. The ubiquitous appearance of this kind of agitated depression strongly suggests that it needs to be distinguished from the form of cyclothymic disorder in which both depressive and hypomanic elements are intermixed. Although the mixed type of cyclothymia conveys a quality of agitation, the agitated depression is quite different from the cyclothymic disorder. The agitated depression is mainly focused on the agitation and covert hostility in the absence of an energized manic or hypomanic process. Further, agitated depression seems to have two distinct forms, a chronic type, and an episodic and impermanent type. The main difference between the chronic and acute type of this agitated form of depression is that in the chronic condition, because of the person's moralizing predisposition, there is a long-standing difficulty in allowing the emergence of hostile expression. Generally, in the face of feelings of loss that can induce depressive affect, the agitated state serves to defensively ward off such depressed feelings while simultaneously enabling the transformation of angry emotion into motoric agitation.

Involutional melancholia can be considered one form of this chronic type of agitated depression occurring in reaction to losses experienced or anticipated in mid-life, that is, the involutional period. This disturbance of agitation tends to occur among middle-aged people who demonstrate the trait of impatience and reduced frustration tolerance and also display a perfectionistic and obsessional premorbid character structure which tends to constrict overt expressions of anger. Premenstrual syndrome or P.M.S. is an example of the acute form of agitated depression. Hostility, anger, impatience, and petulance become palpable in this syndrome. During such episodes, the acute form of agitated depression appears and just as suddenly recedes after menstruation occurs. In addition, an acute form of agitated depression is frequently observed in persons who express feeling burdened or pressured. A sense of being overextended and the presence of symptoms of over-sensitivity to noise or to distractions are also reported.

In this chapter on affect disorders and the variety of depressions including both the diagnoses in *DSM-III/III-R* as well as some outside of the *DSM* nomenclature, a body of clinical data has been sorted to help clinicians discern important differences in symptomatology. The diagnostic complexity that emerges stems from the fact that depression is more than a manifestation of various symptom features. While it is true that the depressive experience can be either major or minor in its quality, depression can also be a component of different diagnostic states both within the domain of affect disorders and outside of them, as for example in various character disorders. Within the domain of the affect disorders, the experience of discomfort associated with the sense of lost opportunities, lost youth, and lost anticipation of rewards for good conduct—which characterize an involutional depression—is an entirely different experience from the sadness that insidiously develops at a younger age.

The qualities that various depressions have in common relate to experiencing a pressed down feeling and the sense of a heavy burden inherent in the composition of the word "depression" itself. The experience of time is slowed down and hopeful possibilities dashed. Consequently, it is possible to understand that the manic and hypomanic flight to a more elevated position characterized by an accelerated time sense and optimistic perspective in order to defensively deny the experience of being pressed down is an understandable psychic strategy for managing the pain of depression. The particular form any depressive experience takes—whether bipolar, major affective, agitated, reactive, or chronic—depends largely on an amalgam of factors. These include ego development, the relative strength and nature of ego functioning, adaptational formations of character structure, the quantity and press of impulses based on inherent constitutional and dispositional features, historical experience of loss, neglect, disappointment, and anger, reactive responses to current events, and the overall presence of current stressors.

DEPRESSION AS A SECONDARY DIAGNOSTIC CONSIDERATION

Feelings of depression also can accompany several diagnostic configurations as a collateral feature. For example, in the characterology associated with the emotion controlled personality disorders of compulsive, paranoid, and schizoid types, satisfactions and gratifications are exceedingly difficult to attain except in fantasy. This difficulty in the experience of gratification can generate a state of dissatisfaction sometimes bordering on depression. For example, the compulsive character who is under pressure from superego imperatives is disposed to strive for perfection, closure, and a sense of moral superiority and propriety. Under such superego pressure, impulses are not entirely free. Rather, these impulses are directed more readily to the achievement of work goals. The chronic continuation of this sort of controlled style can gradually induce a sense of staleness and depression as the spirit of life becomes imperceptibly but steadily diminished. Such a state, controlled and devoid of joy, not only affects the subject but those with whom the subject is intimately involved as well. The deleterious effect on others occurs because these partners also become deprived of pleasure as life is subverted to rigid routine. In marital or sexual intimacy repetitious and controlled patterns of behavior or habitual sexual avoidance may take the place of opportunities for pleasure, so that dissatisfaction can spread to family life.

The variety of phenomenological factors involved in depression and the array of character structures that can contribute to the appearance of depression suggest that depression itself is hardly a unitary phenomenon. When anger is an important element in the depressive syndrome, agitation, restlessness, and motoric complications can be experienced. Another way in which the emotion of anger can be encompassed in depression in a manner that invests the depression with a distinct cast involves the mechanism of turning the anger against the self. Such a clinical phenomenon of the turning of anger against the self may involve pathology of anger rather than depression although the personal experience of suffering is likely to be that of depressed affect. The person's feelings manifested in this type of depression can include experiences of guilt, self-reproach, and even an array of masochistic self-punishing patterns. Turning anger against the self as a source of depression is a particular mode of depression that will also drastically affect others in the interpersonal context.

In sharp distinction to the depressions so far discussed is the depressive feeling based upon experiences of loss. The particular feeling of loss derived either from infantile deprivation, an actual lost opportunity, the loss of a loved one, or the loss of a position of importance can make a difference in the kind of depression experienced.

Finally, consistent with the specific nature of the way in which depression arises and how it is managed by the individual is the clinical phenomenon of the presence of a depressive condition that is not consciously experienced. In such cases, the person develops behavior and symptoms that are clinically considered to be depressive equivalents. For example, overeating can be an expression of depression. Fatigue or an excessive need for sleep may also mask feelings of loss and depression. A multitude of such depressive equivalent features can appear despite the patient's disclaimer regarding the experience of the actual depression itself. The phenomenon of depressive equivalents suggests that depression is invariably embedded in a personality network consisting of defenses, emotions, fantasies, and psychic strategies designed always to manage the feeling of the depression itself. In the following section some of these considerations regarding this personality network surrounding the depressive phenomenon will be discussed.

THE DEPRESSIVE NETWORK

It has been pointed out throughout this chapter, that depression in the personality affects and is affected by several other personality domains. For example, the diagnosis of reactive depression is understood to be a response to recent trauma where the chief function of the depression serves to allay intense anxiety. Thus, in circumstances of trauma, depression and anxiety are observed to be inextricably connected. In such an instance, the depression serves a defensive function as an insulator against potentially more damaging pathology or more distressing feelings that would otherwise surface in the form of overwhelming anxiety or panic. In other cases it is the overall tension that is experienced while depression is suppressed. Under these conditions in which tension is indeed experienced, the emotions of sorrow, grief, loss, discouragement, and despair are suppressed and the person is thereby shielded from such intense feelings. Thus, in terms of personality functioning, depression either surfaces or recedes depending upon psychic strategies designed and utilized in the protection of the person's fundamental needs for the cohesion and overall integrity of the ego. In the case of reactive depression, the experience of depression insures that the effects of trauma are slowed down, allowing a process of recovery to occur. This process of recovery is based on the increased insulation and fortification enabled by the reduction in anxiety implemented by reactive depression. Emotional, psychological, and even physical preparedness are then available to promote reintegration. That depression is indeed embedded in a personality network is thus suggested by the implicit relation between defenses, emotions, and clinical states.

In terms of coping and managing the stressors of life, there is an adaptive component to reactive depressions especially when the state of depression inhibits the full impact of feelings associated with profound despair, suicidal ideation, and hopelessness. In this sense of experiencing severe despair or severe depression, the issue of suicidal potential becomes a glaring clinical concern.

DEPRESSION AND SUICIDE

In terms of diagnostic considerations, suicidal possibilities can exist in practically any of the depressive diagnostic states. The issue of the probability of suicidal acting out depends in large measure upon the resilience of the subject's inner resources. In addition, from a diagnostic point of view, the clinician needs to understand the various risk points in the depressive process. For example, suicidal acting out possibilities occur both with the presence of conscious fantasy as well as in the absence of fantasy. In the presence of fantasy, suicidal rumination can persist not only in chronic states of depression but also, and especially, in acute depressions. The presence of fantasy and rumination that can include themes of abandonment, loss, hopelessness, intense anger toward the self, and, finally, unendurable psychic pain also can be precursors to suicidal acting out. The act of suicide is perhaps then perceived by the depressed person as a resolution to this confluence of disturbing preoccupations, either as an acting out against the self or as an acting out against others. The suicidal act itself may be driven by underlying and powerful feelings of guilt or worthlessness that may be compatible with the basic character needs of the personality. In a psychoanalytic or dynamic context the clinician may understand acts against the self to be based upon the presence of primitive and severe superego imperatives. At such a self-destructive point, it may be said that the person essentially abandons the self.

From another vantage point, the suicidal act can be a result of the wish to eliminate current emotional pain, to form oneself anew, and to enact a fantasied sequence of death followed by rebirth with new possibilities. Another sequence enabling suicidal acting out can occur in the absence of conscious fantasy or rumination. In fact, the experience of conscious reflection is usually diminished when the person embraces an acting out strategy. In such cases, suicidal acting out exists at the level of character where behavior becomes instrumental to the person's need system. Such acting out therefore can be automatic or reflexive and is substituted for the temporization usually achieved by thoughtfulness and introspection, as well as by involvement in fantasy.

The condition in which suicidal acting out takes place in the absence of rumination frequently occurs when, after some period of time in which depression has prevailed, the depression suddenly lifts and the person reports feeling euphoric, settled, relieved, and unusually optimistic. This point in the depressive process should in all cases be regarded as a critical suicidal signal. The defensive mechanism that is instrumental is the obsessional component referred to as compartmentalization. In one compartment of thinking is contained material screened free of depressive contamination so that the person is depression free. In the other compartment is contained the most succinct and derivative thought of the depression—that of suicide. This kind of suicidal thought is a simple thought of certainty and is cleansed of any ambivalence. Both compartments—that of the feeling of well-being, and that of the certainty of suicidal intent—do not in any way modify one another. Rather, the compartmentalization resembles independent thought processes without linkage. When the patient's expression of well-being generates a sense of confidence on the part of others so that supervision is relaxed, then the compartment embodying the despairing final solution of depression can be asserted and suicidal acting out may just as suddenly prevail. Clinically, such a process shows that in depression a sudden lifting of the depressive feelings and a corresponding expression of well-being—a flight into health—is a clear suicidal indicator and cuts across all of the various affect disorders whenever depression is the clinical focus.

Even without the mobilization of compartmentalization the development of signs of improved feelings or liveliness in the context of a depressive disorder can be an occasion for potential suicidal danger. As the process of recovery emerges, depressive ideation and rumination may be eclipsed by the release through treatment, for example, of renewed energy. This increase in energy paradoxically provides the means to act upon depressive, suicidal fantasy that was previously dissociated from energy and therefore inert. The emergence of this energy masks the fantasies, imparts a facade of recovery, but can potentially fuel enactment of depressive, self-destructive ideation.

Other more typical indicators of suicidal possibilities include the giving away of one's possessions. Such behavior symbolically conveys conscious or quasi-conscious preparation for leaving life by dispersing formerly valued possessions. In psychoanalytic terms, this kind of comprehensive disposing phenomenon is referred to as decathecting. One is disposing of everything that has had a cathexis or bond of interest, including, finally, the self.

In the acting out of depression, it can be assumed that the essential purpose of the psychic strategy is to achieve an improved sense of the self by expiating guilt and eliminating self-reproach. The loss of reflection and introspection implied by acting out limits the individual's understanding that perhaps the better state of affairs is ultimately not attained by acting out. The pressure to feel better as a result of the acting out becomes the person's essential goal, distorting the conceptual implications of the loss of the self. In addition, fantasies of transformation toward improvement through death, often at unconscious levels, further aid the implementation of the apparent paradox of embracing suicide to seek a more satisfying state.

The alleviation of depression by action rather than by a process of painstaking planning and the sequence of necessary but difficult steps that such planning requires is comparable also to the avoidance of disturbing anxiety through the expression of impulse. The use of impulse that enables acting out is clinically well known as a coping strategy for anxiety. The acting out takes place when repression neutralizes both insight and the experience of feelings so that the action constitutes the major pattern in the minimization of anxiety. For example, in the development of the various character or personality disorders, the particular structure of the character is chiefly determined by the style and manner in which anxiety is managed and allayed. This motive of the person to avoid anxiety is extremely compelling and is implicated both in the formation of depression and in the development of acting out patterns. Experiencing both anxiety and depression can be extremely painful and disruptive, so that the condition of acting out, although usually a self-defeating strategy, nevertheless seems to help in the temporary suppression of intense psychological and emotional discomfort.

The discussion of depression in this chapter along with its diagnostic states and vicissitudes, also reflects commonalities between the process involved in acting out and the experience and management of anxiety. In the following chapter the various diagnostic states that constitute the complement of such anxiety states or disorders included in *DSM-III/III-R* and previously known as neuroses, will be presented.

CAPSULE CLINICAL PROFILES OF AFFECT DISTURBANCE DISORDERS

The particular form of any depressive experience—whether bipolar, major affective, agitated, chronic, or characterological—depends on a variety of conditions. These conditions or determinants include developmental experiences, the relative strength and nature of ego functioning, adaptational formations of character, the nature of impulses, environmental conditions, stressors, and, of course, constitutional and dispositional factors. Emotions of anger, sorrow, grief, loss, discouragement, despair, and a demoralized quality constitute a depressive cluster or experience. Manic or the less euphoric hypomanic dispositions are understood as expansive defensive states that distance the depressive feelings. Act-

ing out and anxiety are also central collateral concepts in the entire
context of the depressive dynamic.

Depressive Character: The emotional stance of this characterological position is one of the projection of hostility as a defense
against feelings of vulnerability. Yet such persons can reach out
when conditions are nonthreatening. Traits can include mod-
esty, shyness, a tendency toward introspection, and an overidentification with helpless victims or objects of pity. Such persons function reasonably well and are nonpsychotic. The
depressive overlay seems fueled by narcissistic concerns that lead
the person to feel emotionally deflated. Low self-esteem and
ambivalence toward primary caretakers are characteristic of depressive character dispositions with the perception that the caretaker is inconsistent, ambivalent, immature or severe, and even
depressed. Fears of abandonment seem prevalent.

Bipolar Disorder: This disorder may exist within a psychotic
or nonpsychotic context. In its psychotic form, the disorder is
consistent with the traditional diagnosis of manic-depressive
psychosis. Manic episodes are the prerequisite condition usually
alternating with periods of depression. The manic trait cluster
includes increased activity, excitement, sleeplessness, euphoria,
grandiosity, or irritability, all of which interfere with vocational
or social functioning. The depressive episodes, when present,
are major in scope. Three types of the bipolar disorder can be
diagnostically identified:

1. Manic type: The criterion is a manic episode including a
full display of euphoric, expansive, grandiose, or irritable overall functioning without episodes of major depression.

2. Depressed type: Major depression occurs, but history
shows at least one manic episode.

3. Mixed type: Manic and depressed features occur in frequent alternation or appear together.

Major Depressive Episode or Major Depression: Persons with
this condition are unable to experience pleasure. Their sad mood
affects sleep, appetite, weight, and overall energy level. Distractability, suicidal thoughts, feelings of inadequacy, devaluation, and guilt characterize the syndrome. In the psychotic state,
delusions are likely to emerge that may or may not be congruent
with the depressed mood. With melancholia, the depression is

especially severe in the mornings along with the appearance of psychomotor retardation or agitation and an overall loss of appetite or weight. Degeneration of the compensation defense is central in the emergence of depression signified by loss of hope, anticipation, pleasure, and self-esteem.

Manic Episodes: Persons exhibit persistently elevated, or irritable affective quality along with boundless energy and an unusual work fervor. Interpersonal responses are superficial. A pressured quality exists and the person shifts from idea to idea. Qualities of self-aggrandizement, compensations, and compulsive talking are typical in the person's behavioral repertoire. The compensations are designed to ward off depression. Hallucinations and delusions may appear when the manic episode exists within a psychotic context. Sexual preoccupations and inappropriate buying ventures may appear and disruptions to vocational or social functioning occur. Included in the defense cluster is reaction formation and sublimation which transform sexual excitement to work efforts, and compensation, which engenders expansive strivings.

Cyclothymic Disorder or Cyclothymia: Depression and excitement appear for periods of time with relatively brief periods without symptoms possible in between. Severity of symptoms are less forceful than in the bipolar disorder in both excited and depressed phases. Hypomanic states—that is, attenuated moods of excitement—rather than full manic periods appear with some grandiosity, optimism, euphoria, and expansion. The excitement is not significantly disruptive to vocational or social functioning, a major contrast with manic episodes. Psychosis is absent. Excessive effort to achieve pleasure during the hypomanic phase and heightened sexuality are seen. A disordered energy level is also evident, and attention and concentration are negatively affected.

Dysthymic Disorder, Dysthymia, or Depressive Neurosis: This disorder is less severe than the major depressive episode although the depressed mood exists more often than not for a period of two years without potential for psychosis. A loss of pleasure and, typically, a decrease in sexual activity is seen. A sense of inadequacy and a pervasive pessimism characterize the personality. Avoidance of social interaction is also evident. Disturbances related to appetite, sleep, energy level, and concentration may occur.

Atypical Bipolar Disorder (Bipolar Disorder Not Otherwise Specified in *DSM-III-R*): In this disorder, there may be hypomanic episodes without past manic states or cyclothymic phenomena. A major depressive episode may or may not have occurred but the milder depression associated with cyclothymia is absent.

Atypical Depression (Depressive Disorder Not Otherwise Specified in *DSM-III-R*): Features of depression occur, but these are not sufficient to qualify either as a major depression or as dysthymia. The scope of the depressed mood is less encompassing than other depression diagnoses and persistence of depressive features endures less than two years.

Agitated Depression: Irritability, impatience, insomnia, restlessness, and covert hostility comprise typical traits of this disorder. There is an absence of any cyclothymic profile. This disorder may exist either in the chronic or transitory state, often occuring in the context of an obsessional premorbid structure. In the chronic state, a position of moralizing prevents hostility from emerging directly. In reaction to mid-life pressure in which losses are experienced or anticipated, an agitated depression may emerge as involutional melancholia.

PART III
Neurotic Phenomena

CHAPTER 7

Anxiety Disorders or Anxiety and Phobic Neuroses

In volume 1, *History of Psychopathology,* the emotional experiences of depression and anxiety were identified as key components of psychopathology, referred to by the earliest researchers of aberrant behavior. These personality components of depression and anxiety have thus, from the first conceptions of psychopathology, been recognized as indicators of strains in adjustment. Correspondingly, efforts towards diagnosis have gradually been refined in order to relate these pervasive dysphoric affects to appropriate entities in the nomenclature. In the previous chapter on depression and affect disorders, disturbances related to depression were surveyed and the current diagnostic classifications were discussed. In addition, several nuances of depressive affect were considered in order to enrich the clinical appreciation of the stresses involved in depressive experience.

The present chapter examines the phenomenon of anxiety as it is central to various personality impairments and stresses manifested in the person's experience. As in depression, anxiety has historically been central in the understanding of psychopathology and its etiology, presumably because the experience of anxiety is a frequent component in a variety of pathological conditions. Further, the importance of anxiety as a pivotal force of psychopathology is reflected in the *DSM-III/III-R* grouping called anxiety disorders. In historical terms, these anxiety related psychopathological entities were known as neuroses. The work of psychopathologists and clinicians has been to distinguish the various types of neuroses from one another and to determine and identify distinctions in etiology. Although the term neurosis implied neurological underpinnings to these disturbances, important historical developments made clear that major contributions to the formation of such neurotic disturbances concerned the interpersonal and intrapsychic development of the individual who suffered with anxiety as a central symptom. Thus, while inherent proclivities, biological inclinations, and even oblique neurological factors have been applied in the formation of the neuroses, the effect of pressures of living on the individual that interfere with the development of adaptive behaviors can be proposed to be most crucial in the etiology of virtually all of the anxiety disorders.

On a descriptive level, perhaps the major feature to be recognized about neurotic functioning is that an experience of severe apprehension, dread, or even agony is sustained as part of the symptomatology. Yet, there are times when neurotic symptoms are clustered in such a way as to reduce or avoid the disorganizing effects of the anxiety. Nevertheless, such anxiety remains central as the driving force of these neurotic disorders, even when neurotic symptoms develop that obliterate the conscious experience of the anxiety. Thus, hysterical, conversion, dissociative, and somatization disorders can all be encompassed within the range of neurotic functioning. In all such disorders, symptomatology can be viewed to exist, theoretically, in order to manage anxiety. It is proposed, therefore, that both the palpable presence of anxiety as well as the presence of alien hysterical symptoms are developed in connection with this anxiety. Since anxiety plays such a central role in all neurotic phenomena, aspects of anxiety in psychopathology will next be considered followed by a survey of those neuroses in which overt, manifest anxiety predominates: phobic disorders and anxiety states.

DEPRESSION, ANXIETY, AND CHARACTER FORMATION

The diagnostic understanding of anxiety can be appreciated by observing the relationship between the disorders in which: (1) anxiety is clear and palpable, the anxiety disorders; (2) disorders where the anxiety is neutralized as in the depressive disorders; and, (3) syndromes in which entire personality configurations develop out of a need to regulate the anxiety through the fabric of characteristic functioning, so that the anxiety is effectively eliminated. This last phenomenon has been discussed in part 1, where personality or character disorders were considered.

In the personality disorders, various enduring character traits are developed that regulate the anxiety in a relatively stable manner by externalizing the source of conflict and disturbance. In the anxiety disorders of *DSM-III/III-R*—or formerly, the neuroses—the experience of anxiety remains conscious and disturbing rather than neutralized through depression or absorbed into the character patterns of the character or personality disorders.

The formation of character structure to regulate anxiety allows the personality disorders to be contrasted with the neuroses in several dramatic ways, enabling diagnostic clarity. First, the development of stable characterology, to externalize anxiety, means that disorders of character involve the entire fabric of personality functioning. As such, disturbed aspects of functioning are not experienced as alien or dystonic. Instead, these long-term disturbed patterns of characterology are experienced as a part of the self, that is, in ego syntonic terms.

With regard to the neuroses or anxiety disorders, apprehension that is experienced and symptoms associated with such fears are themselves experienced as foreign, ego alien, or ego dystonic. A person suffering with an anxiety disorder or neurotic disturbance can therefore bring focus to both the anxiety and the associated symptoms as discrete and conscious sources of disturbance and discomfort. Since symptoms become the focus of disorder in neurotic functioning, other aspects of the personality can retain coherence and remain uncontaminated by the process of externalization that characterizes the personality disorders. This component of coherent functioning, however, is experienced as an aspect of personality that is in conflict with another part of the personality largely represented by neurotic functioning.

The element of an individual in conflict with himself has more or less shaped our understanding of psychopathology. This understanding considers that personal conflict with its roots in individual early development reflects the core nature of psychopathology. Clarification of the various neurotic entities in historical terms helped rescue the understanding of psychopathology from the belief that external, concrete, or supernatural agents were primary causes of such disorders. The next section presents the various neuroses or anxiety disorders of *DSM-III/III-R* as well as other clinical observations of anxiety states not listed in *DSM* nomenclature.

ANXIETY DISORDERS

In *DSM-III,* the anxiety disorders are divided into two main classes: phobic disorders (or phobic neuroses), on the one hand, and anxiety states (or anxiety neuroses), on the other. This distinction is based essentially on the functional role of symptomatology in relation to anxiety. Is symptomatology developed with an aim toward avoiding or reducing the anxiety, as in the phobic disorders, or is symptomatology involved in the sustained experience of anxiety itself, as in some of the anxiety states? In the remaining anxiety states, are behaviors utilized in an effort to bind the anxiety, as in compulsions, or is symptomatology designed as an attempt to master the anxiety, as in the traumatic disorders? Thus, it may be proposed that symptomatology serves the purpose of either reducing, sustaining, binding, or mastering anxiety.

Table 7.1 presents the diagnostic entities comprising the anxiety

TABLE 7.1. Anxiety Disorders of *DSM-III* and the Role of
Symptomatology in Managing Anxiety

Phobic Disorders	*Function of Symptomatology*

Agoraphobia
  with panic attacks
  without panic attacks
	Avoid anxiety

Social phobia	Avoid anxiety
Simple phobia	Avoid anxiety
Anxiety States	*Function of Symptomatology*
Panic disorders	Sustain anxiety
Generalized anxiety disorder	Sustain anxiety
Obsessive compulsive disorder (or obsessive compulsive neurosis)	Bind anxiety

Post-traumatic stress disorder
  acute state
  chronic or delayed state
	Master anxiety

Atypical anxiety disorder	Mixed

disorders of *DSM-III* and the role of symptomatology in managing anxiety. In addition, table 7.2 presents the *DSM-III-R* reordering of the diagnostic entities considered. Table 7.2 is introduced so that the reader can appreciate the trends of classification and difficulties classifiers are confronting in trying to arrive at diagnostic parsimony. Since table 7.2 is the newest *DSM* version and therefore perhaps still in the process of change, the discussion in this chapter will focus on the basic *DSM-III* classification system with discussion of the *DSM-III-R* version whenever it is relevant. In *DSM-III-R,* anxiety states and phobic disorders have been combined into one grouping: anxiety disorders, or anxiety and phobic neuroses. Nevertheless, because the distinction between the two major neurotic classes encompassed by the term anxiety disorder has meaningful differentiating features in terms of diagnosis, etiology, and the subjective experience of anxiety, the division between the anxiety states and phobic disorders of *DSM-III* will be retained in the organization of the present discussion.

PHOBIC DISORDERS

In the clinical setting, phobias are indicated by an unusual or intense apprehension focused on a relatively specific object or situation. While the object of the phobia may range from the narrow to the more general, the individual experiences intense anxiety regarding this object and seeks to avoid any encounter with the object, while simultaneously recognizing that it is unreasonable to be preoccupied in such an intensely fearful manner.

TABLE 7.2. Anxiety Disorders of *DSM-III-R*, or Anxiety and Phobic Neuroses

Panic disorder:
    with agoraphobia
    without agoraphobia
Agorophobia without history of panic disorder
Social phobia
Simple phobia
Obsessive compulsive disorder or obsessive compulsive neurosis
Post-traumatic stress disorder
Generalized anxiety disorder
Anxiety disorder not otherwise specified

From a psychoanalytic and general psychodynamic point of view, an intense internal fear is displaced onto an external object or situation in the formation of phobias. This displacement of the focus of concern and the accompanying fear shifts the individual's attention from a disturbing inner impulse, often actually a wish, to a safer outside location. Thus, presumably, a stronger internal fear usually involving a wish is thought to lurk behind the phobic target. This defensive displacement maneuver, in spite of the intense apprehension it generates, nevertheless presumably allows the individual greater security. Efforts toward mastery are therefore implemented by the concentration on and avoidance of external circumstances created by displacement, rather than on the recognition of an internal conflict. Yet, the person remains in conflict even after the displacement is made from internal impulse to external object. The conflict remains because the unconscious nature of this defensive displacement process disguises the conscious focus of conflict without eliminating its hidden source; thus, the actual source of internal apprehension is unrecognized. The displacement of the central conflict evokes the individual's view of himself as unreasonable, since he now fears what he understands to be innocuous objects. Thus, the person strongly feels the irrational aspect of his phobia. As noted above, phobic disorders listed in *DSM-III* imply that an effort is mobilized by phobic individuals to avoid or diminish anxiety by limiting exposure to specific objects or circumstances that tend to generate such anxiety.

Agoraphobia

In its most broad appearance, the phobic disorder takes the form of the diagnostic entity known as agoraphobia. In agoraphobia the object of fear is not a narrow and highly specific object or situation. Rather, a broader condition involving public or open places becomes the circumstances to which the individual develops a specific, intense, and compelling fear. The scope of the agoraphobic disorder can be appreciated by considering the root words encompassed in the diagnostic term. *Phobia* derives from the Greek *phobos*, meaning fear, and the Greek word *agora* literally means marketplace. Thus, agoraphobia is the fear of an open, public area where people commingle and correspondingly, where secure, tan-

gible boundaries are absent. Further, the crowd that can gather in
such an open space could tend to obscure exit pathways.

Historically, the marketplace was the original open public setting where people congregated. By transposition, the various public settings where people currently can meet or pass through can
determine the specifics in the way agoraphobia is manifested. Thus,
the individual suffering from the agoraphobic anxiety disorder experiences symptoms of overwhelming apprehension and an intense
urgency toward avoidance or escape when in public places. In such
open boundaryless conditions defining properties that the individual ordinarily associates with home and the familiar are absent.
Familiarity of home offers refuge, solace, safety, and mastery to
such people—essentially an externalization of the need for ego
support and security. Such a need for reminders of the familiar—
also serving as ego support—can develop out of difficulties and
self-doubt involved in everyday life over which the individual does
not feel a sense of mastery. The phobia refers then to facing the
outer, public world devoid of familiar safety features associated
with home. The psychological core of such fear is thought to reflect the need to adopt a pervasive position of dependency—therefore the fear of losing sight of the route to the familiar. The pressure of such dependency needs presumably limits the individual's
propensity for growth, expansion, the acceptance of challenges and
risks, and willingness to explore new things. Further, the emphasis
on dependency preoccupations may mask deeper fears; that is, in
an open space, without boundaries or a friendly, reliable companion, various unacceptable urges or impulses can have a greater
likelihood of surfacing. Such impulses can be identified as sexual
or aggressive and may be experienced as tendencies which the dependently oriented agoraphobic person feels terrified about, and
inadequate to contain, control, or master. It is likely that this level
of terror generates the pressure that makes the agoraphobic pattern so intense and encompassing.

In terms of additional diagnostic indications, the agoraphobic
person also can anticipate intense distress in circumstances that
may involve crowds, open stadiums, vehicles, elevators, bridges,
or tunnels in which egress is not completely assured. Thus, the
agoraphobic experience includes not only the original denotation
of open spaces but also encompasses feared circumstances that have
often been classified as claustrophobic—fear of closed spaces.

In circumstances where safety precautions for the severely dependent person are absent, feelings of dread and terror develop in anticipation of the target situation. This anticipatory fear or the intensification of the terror usually precipitates avoidance strategies that are rapidly learned. Such avoidance strategies also become deeply etched in the person's behavioral repertoire. These avoidance behaviors form a pattern that clearly introduces limitations and constrictions over the agoraphobic's participation and exposure to the everyday events of life. In milder cases of agoraphobia, the individual can successfully limit participation to familiar places and simply avoid the few circumstances that evoke the paralyzing fear. Correspondingly, in more severe cases of agoraphobia, the need for security through continuous contact with the familiar creates an exceedingly constricted existence. In these extreme cases the individual may not be able to leave home, or, may only be able to do so in the presence of a trusted companion, and perhaps only for circumscribed excursions. It should be noted that some agoraphobic symptoms may be amenable to alleviation by new psychotropic agents in the same way that panic attacks and obsessional symptoms can now be managed with the help of pharmacological advances.

Agoraphobia and Its Relation to Panic Attacks

The disorder of agoraphobia can be further distinguished by the presence or absence of attacks of panic that occur in conjunction with the phobia. Such panic attacks are the most severe form of anxiety-terror reactions and are accompanied by a host of physical sensations precipitated by the attack. If these panic attacks are present in the context of the agoraphobia, several symptoms of especially intense apprehension may be evident. Such symptoms may occur at the physical level, or may include experiences of unreality and concern about loss of control. In addition, features accompanying the agoraphobic syndrome can include feelings of depression and discouragement and a sense of anxiety regarding opportunities that are missed because of the constrictions that, as a result of this phobia, become part of life. Further, ruminations can extend to carefully reviewing in one's mind the components of proposed expeditions in a typically obsessional manner. For example, even the prospect of a simple shopping expedition can induce prolonged obsessional rumination about the shopping route, the reliability of the accompanying companion, and all the un-expected dangers that could possibly arise. As discussed in the chapter on obsessive characterology, the particular fear is likely to concern a loss of control, the appearance of the unexpected, and, therefore, unmanageable, all largely related to the surfacing of emotion or impulse as an unexpected, uncontrollable event. In the form of agoraphobia with panic attacks, either the presence of a destructive impulse or the sense of a total loss of boundaries is understood to be the source of panic. While the individual is in-tensely frightened, the source of fear usually cannot be specified but can best be viewed as any opening that may allow terrify-ing feelings to emerge in an uncontrollable circumstance. Such an uncontrollable circumstance may be symbolized by the open, unstructured, unbounded place.

One of the major differential diagnostic difficulties encountered when considering an agoraphobic syndrome is in distinguishing between the individual with agoraphobic symptoms based on neu-rotic and intense dependency needs on the one hand, and the per-son who is not capable of functioning autonomously because of deficiencies in the integrity of the ego on the other. In the instance of the person who is ego-deficient, the reassurance that is expe-rienced by the presence of a familiar companion and recognition of familiar surroundings becomes a social imperative that enables more adequate functioning. In this clinical form of ego-deficiency, the agoraphobic condition can be better understood in diagnostic terms as a reflection of more severe pathology although, perhaps in latent, incipient, or prepsychotic form.

In the phobic condition itself, it is likely that the essential fear dominating the individual is in the experience of impulses or emo-tions sensed by the person as those that cannot be mastered, tol-erated, or controlled. Thus, the fear of such internal conditions containing the possibility of the existence of threatening emotions and impulses can become displaced and externalized onto general targets outside the individual. By externalizing such threatening feelings, the person gains greater reassurance of perhaps more readily controlling and avoiding them.

In the phobia to be considered next, the target of fear is limited to social situations in which the individual feels scrutinized by oth-ers and develops anxiety regarding humiliating or embarrassing aspects of himself that he believes may be exposed.

Social Phobia

In social phobias, the phobic focus that generates an intense experience of anxiety is on the possibility that the individual may unwittingly do something visible that reflects poorly on himself. Thus, such persons learn to manage this sort of anxiety by developing patterns of avoidance in relation to specific social situations. These situations may include meeting new people, public speaking, or even dining alone. The manifest fear usually concerns an expectation that some event will occur to create acute embarrassment or humiliation. Such fear is intense enough to cause substantial distress although patterns of avoidance that are formed may be relied on to a degree that cause interference with effective work or social engagement.

As in agoraphobic conditions, it is likely that in social phobia a sense of self-deficiency exists and a specific emotional constellation involving the person's impulses has not been comfortably integrated into functioning. The lack of insight into these underlying factors makes it impossible for the nature of the troublesome impulses to be directly acknowledged. Therefore, inner conflict is expressed in externalized form where the personal sense of diminishment, displaced onto a circumstance with an audience, can be more readily controlled and avoided. Whereas in the agoraphobic condition, personal wishes and impulses may relate to aggression in the social phobias, the fear of embarrassment or humiliation regarding personal exposure suggests that the impulse to be avoided may relate to sexuality. In this sense the individual with social phobia acts as though the social situation is one where exposure regarding personal sexual proclivities, or even the existence of sexuality, may somehow become visible and cause rejection, embarrassment, and isolation.

Nevertheless, the major fear sequence that characterizes social phobia includes: appearing inadequate in relation to the expectations of the situation; feeling scrutinized and rejected; and experiencing humiliation and isolation. The urgency devoted to protecting the individual from exposure of inadequacies and the anticipation of rejection and isolation suggests that there are likely to be underlying dependency inclinations present that act as important contributions to the basic formation of social phobias. Such dependency characterology inherently diminishes the individual's sense of control regarding regulation of impulses associated with adult functioning. Social functioning and situations in which competence is expected can then be avoided by the behavioral patterns associated with social phobia allowing the social phobic to adopt a more childlike stance of safety. This protected stance involves the fortification of limitations that accrue from the development of strategies designed to risk fewer public activities. Thus, the need for dependency may be viewed as serving the purpose of avoiding the risks inherent in attempting more mature challenges.

Social phobia has only recently become a diagnostic entity in the *DSM* nomenclature. It encompasses the fear of specific situations in which scrutiny can lead to embarrassment that the individual recognizes as unrealistic. This fear needs to be differentiated from the broader fear of rejection along with timidity and social discomfort characterologically involved in avoidant personality disorder. Further diagnostic differentiations concern the terror of being alone in agoraphobia and the nonspecific fear that develops in generalized anxiety disorder.

The next diagnostic consideration, simple phobia, will present disturbances embodying various specific and narrow phobias.

Simple Phobia

The description of simple phobia is generally one that corresponds to the traditional understanding of a specific irrational fear. In addition to the simple irrational fear—which is sustained over a period of time toward a narrowly defined object or condition—an overwhelming need to avoid the feared circumstance accompanies the phobia. These simple phobias can involve a variety of objects or situations, that have to some degree become commonplace as suggested by their usage in everyday language and of their universal interest; for example, acrophobia is the fear of heights and claustrophobia is the fear of enclosed spaces. In addition, phobias pertaining to specific animals are also often seen as are phobias involving inanimate objects or abstractions such as in the fear of the number 13—triskaidekaphobia.

In contrast to the social phobias and agoraphobia, the simple phobias such as acrophobia—fear of heights—are relatively of less clinical concern and generate fewer problems for the person. The simple phobia is usually sufficiently narrow to enable managing any tension regarding the object of the fear by successfully avoiding the over-determined phobic condition. For example, the person with acrophobia can usually avoid the phobic tension evoked when ascending to a high point of a building or landscape by consciously deciding not to look down. Such a strategy is not as possible in terms of a social phobia or especially with respect to agoraphobia. Nevertheless, in the clinical condition of any simple phobia, either the fear involved or the avoidance of the phobic object interferes in substantial ways with normal routine, social activities and personal relationships. Usually in simple phobias a recognition of the irrational nature of the fear is acknowledged.

One of the problems for an individual who suffers from a simple phobia is that the assumed underlying and significant conflict expressed by this simple phobia can broaden as when a simple phobia gradually develops into agoraphobia. Often this underlying conflict can be symbolized by the nature of the simple phobia. For example, acrophobia may symbolize a conflict involving wishes versus fears regarding success or achievement in which the fearful aspect of the conflict is conveniently displaced to anxiety about physically elevated circumstances and their avoidance.

In the preceding example of acrophobia, it is apparent that the emotions of fear, dread, and apprehension persistently experienced by the phobic individual are only part of a deeper and wider emotional complex. For example, the striving for success or achievement, that can be the underlying issue eliciting fear and therefore to be avoided, may be inextricably associated by the phobic person with the generally correct assumption that aggression and assertion are necessary to express in connection with the drive to accomplish. The reaction to the affect of aggression or anger that the individual believes characterizes assertion, self-promotion, or ego aggrandizement can be theoretically viewed as having determined the clinical problem of the fear and anxiety to be avoided in the first place. This emotion complex of fear, anger, aggression, assertion, and striving also reflects the operation of a corresponding cluster of defense patterns that are mobilized by this compelling array of emotions.

Defense Patterns in Phobias

In addition to the defensive patterns of displacement and avoidance—central to the operation of phobias—the presence of the state of anger reflects a possible central emotional core in the entire phobic syndrome. The presence of anger also reveals that the defense of reaction formation can be the major hidden variable of the phobic defense fabric. In addition to the avoidance and displacement of inner conflicts or emotions in the particular phobia, the role played by reaction formation reveals a concealed attraction to the feared circumstance. For example, the phobia of heights—acrophobia—can be hypothesized as cited above, to be a displacement for a fear of success or elevated status. Yet, the impulse usually associated with striving and asserting ones wishes is also frequently mixed with the aggressive impulse. In people who cannot acknowledge these aggressive and assertive impulses, the defense of reaction formation is usually utilized so that the person is able to deny and avoid any hint that the anger, aggression, success, striving, or elevated status is, in fact, attractive. Thus, with reaction formation—a defense that is here conceived as primarily used to neutralize pleasure responses—the object of attraction is turned to its opposite and thereby, in a general sense, rendered unimportant, or even entirely devalued, and in its intense form becomes an object of fear or revulsion. Following this paradigm, transformations are made in the personality based upon such reaction formation: anger is transformed to fear and pleasure is transformed to displeasure, forming the phobic configuration. What remains constant however, is the focus on and interest in the object, albeit a fearful or phobic one, which in a psychological sense, therefore, represents a distorted attraction.

In *DSM-III/III-R* the retained interest in and focus on the object is considered important enough to raise the differential diagnostic question of whether such symptoms are truly phobic, or, instead, if they should be understood within the dynamics of obsession. Generally, the distinction between the obsessional and the phobic lies in the manner in which the component of fear or apprehension is managed. In the obsessional individual, circumstances are carefully checked in order to determine if the feared objects are present or not. Thus, there is careful and active scrutiny with attempts to uncover the presence of a dangerous situation. On the other hand, the individual with a circumscribed phobia is not usually apprehensive unless the target of that person's phobia manifests itself. Because of the unique operation of the reaction formation defense, it becomes apparent that for the individual with a specific phobia the following principle applies: behind the fear is the wish. The wish however, is unacceptable and frightening, and so is transformed through displacement onto an external symbol that is also feared, but, by virtue of its external locus, can now be avoided and therefore mastered in the pathological manner of avoidance.

In the following section, neurotic disorders are considered in which anxiety is experienced in a more general sense and not limited to target situations or objects. These include panic disorders, generalized anxiety disorders, obsessive compulsive disorders, and traumatic stress disorders. These neurotic disorders are also referred to in *DSM-III* as anxiety states, and are listed in table 7.1 along with the phobic disorders.

ANXIETY STATES OR ANXIETY NEUROSES

In the anxiety states or anxiety neuroses, in contrast with the phobic disorders, the distress of anxiety occurs in a more sustained and pervasive manner not related to a narrow object or circumstance. Therefore, this anxiety encompasses a considerably greater segment of the personality and it is consciously experienced. These neuroses form part of an overall complement of neuroses as described earlier in this chapter. The neuroses discussed here, however, are distinctive because the experience of anxiety is central, palpable, and sustained. Therefore, the anxiety is not limited to specific target situations as in phobias, nor is it converted into bodily equivalents as in somatoform states. In addition, neither is there a dissociation that is present involving bodily functioning as in the hysterias. The first of these anxiety states to be considered is that of panic disorder.

Panic Disorder

Of all the anxiety states, panic disorders have the closest resemblance to phobic disorders. This similarity of panic and phobia is composed of elements such as frequent periods of intense dread and apprehension amounting to intense distress. Unlike phobic disorders, however, the panic attack is not usually directly linked to a specific object or circumstance. Thus, the panic attack is subjectively experienced as a feeling of agony that suddenly arises leading to a frightening and sustained crescendo. In the period during which the panic attack occurs a variety of specific symptoms can become manifest in association with the disorder. Many of these symptoms are clearly physical manifestations of the emotion of anxiety exercised to heightened intensity.

This group of physical symptoms that may accompany panic disorder usually begins to surface in a way that signals the person on the level of sensation. For example, the person may sense an unsteadiness. This sensation can then suddenly crystalize into symptoms such as dizziness or lightheadedness. In addition, at the physical level the person may experience heart palpitations, pain or tightness in the chest, a loss of comfortable breathing, sweating, hot and cold flashes, and numbness or tingling of the extremeties. A further escalation of physical symptoms may include nausea, chest pains, sweating, or choking. Hot flashes, chills, or shaking may be additional physical symptoms.

A deepening of symptoms may occur independently or together with the physical manifestations of anxiety. This deepening of symptoms can include the sensation of an impending fainting spell, a sense of unreality or depersonalization, and perhaps most distressing of all, a pronounced fear of incipient or imminent loss of control. The sensation of loss of control can in turn involve the fear of becoming crazy, or even the anticipation of dying.

Within the context of the neurosis of panic disorder, the various symptoms, whether involving sensations, physical manifestations of anxiety, or fears of death are not based upon the presence of any actual physical or organic impairment. In the *DSM-III-R* classification, if the panic disorder is associated with agoraphobia— in that there is any history involving fear of being alone in open spaces or in situations where escape could be difficult—then the condition is diagnosed as one of *panic disorder with agoraphobia.* If, in contrast, the panic disorder occurs without a history of agoraphobia, then it is classified as *panic disorder without agoraphobia.* This classification differs from that of *DSM-III* in which it is agoraphobia that is further subdivided into types with or without panic attacks. In addition, in *DSM-III-R,* if the panic disorder appears with fewer than four of the symptoms described, the condition is known as a limited-symptom attack.

It should be noted that current research tends to relate the symptoms of panic disorder to a biochemical condition treatable with pharmacological agents. Yet, psychological factors in the etiology of panic disorder remain meaningful in appreciating the particular terror and intense anxiety symptoms comprising the experience of panic. For example, the fearful apprehension that periodically escalates into a panic regarding an anticipation of personal disorganization in the sense of an explosive sensation of fragmentation suggests an underlying fear. This underlying fear appears to relate to any possibility of the loss of control over aggressive and destructive feelings. Such an intense fear, experienced in terms of panic, suggests the possibility that the person vaguely recognizes this same feared aggressive process—although it remains one that is persistently denied. As controls naturally fluctuate between rigid and somewhat more relaxed, the threat that leakage of anger may penetrate the control network becomes a major concern for the person. This process of the possible display of anger is abetted by the fact that controls seem almost never to be accepted as totally reliable. Therefore, such controls are continually reinforced along with preoccupations about their sufficiency. This focus on control reflects the awareness of mildly perceptible anxiety regarding the undesired emotion of anger that the person fears may penetrate to the surface.

Generalized Anxiety Disorder

In many ways, the diagnosis of generalized anxiety disorder—referred to in *DSM-II* as anxiety neurosis—can be considered the classic neurotic disorder insofar as the experience of distressing anxiety defines the syndrome. In this sense, the individual suffering with the generalized anxiety disorder presents the complaint of general, persistent, or free-floating anxiety.

In more specific terms, the experience of anxiety has been grouped in *DSM-III/III-R* into several types of manifestations and the diagnosis is made when symptoms from these groups occur. These kinds of anxiety manifestations include fearful anticipations, vigilance, symptoms of motoric anxiety, and autonomic hyperactivity. In *DSM-III-R,* the person's unrealistic worry about possibilities in two areas of life for six months or more is the central diagnostic criterion of generalized anxiety disorder. In addition, the accrual of 6 out of 18 symptoms from the remaining three types of anxiety manifestations are necessary. These anxiety manifestations are designated as the areas involving motoric, autonomic, and vigilance symptoms.

The cluster of symptom manifestations most central to the clinical appreciation and diagnosis of generalized anxiety disorder involves fearful anticipations. In addition to the dread of a usually unnamed calamity that is expected, the person may experience free-floating anxiety along with worry and rumination. Such a constellation of manifest anxiety often brings into play symptoms associated with the grouping referred to as vigilance that can contribute to the generalized anxiety disorder. In the grouping of vigilance, fearful expectations are managed by a narrowing process in which the individual may become overly attentive in focusing on possibilities of disaster. Such vigilance can bring to the surface a series of symptoms that are troublesome, including distractability, inability to sustain concentration, interrupted sleep, irritable and impatient reactions, or a general feeling of edginess.

The persistent intense anxiety that essentially defines the generalized anxiety disorder can also involve a series of motoric tension or anxiety outlets. These motoric anxiety symptoms include such reactions as trembling, twitching, fidgeting, and the specific symptom known as the "startle response." Such motoric symptoms of anxiety can further lead to muscle ache, fatigue, inability to relax, and the appearance of facial strain. Finally, at a deeper level of sensation, and deriving from the reference in *DSM-III* and *DSM-III-R* to autonomic hyperactivity, is a wide range of symptoms. These include pounding or racing of the heart, dryness of the mouth, clammy hands, feelings of dizziness, and a host of tension related symptoms of the stomach, digestion, and breathing.

Causative Factors

The anxiety felt in generalized anxiety disorder may be experienced as occurring in attacks or waves, or as free-floating. The surfacing of the anxiety is likely to relate to concerns that the person has regarding inner impulses. For example, if an impulse has been acted upon, or if the individual either overtly or covertly experiences the need to enact such an impulse, then any of these instances can produce a release of anxiety symptoms.

Such anxiety symptoms occur in response to objects and events in which impulses become aroused, although the trigger mechanisms or precipitators of the anxiety cannot usually be identified or specified. More specifically, the sufferer of an anxiety experience is involved in a sequence of events. An impending encounter with another person or the prospect of leaving a familiar place in order to begin a new phase of life are examples of events that can precipitate such symptoms. Sexual encounters or apprehension of such encounters or any circumstance viewed as requiring assertion or aggression can also qualify as conditions that bring the symptoms of these anxiety states to the surface.

The personality context that allows for the manifestation of anxiety symptoms related to these neurotic or anxiety disorders seems to be one in which a constraint against the expression of certain impulses becomes necessary. This constraint is, however, usually only tenuously maintained. Therefore, the individual may have an underlying fear that feelings, actions, or thoughts that are not permissible or appropriate can involuntarily surface, and this sort of anticipation then becomes the necessary condition for the appearance of anxiety.

Defenses and Dynamics

Repression is generally the major defense mechanism relied upon to maintain steady control over emotions viewed as unacceptable or inappropriate. Because repression must be maintained in a continuous and active manner, the threat usually exists that repression may become ineffective so that the emotional material denied to consciousness may break through with corresponding unexpected immediacy and possible dire consequences. It is this distinct possibility of the unexpected that mobilizes the clinically apprehensive quality of anxiety states and panic disorders.

Theoretically, central underlying dynamic factors contributing to the sense of fear that characterize both the generalized anxiety disorder and panic state involve the vicissitudes of dependency and separation and needs for approval and acceptance. The dynamic context for the crisis centering on independence and separateness involves the individual's fear and sense of inadequacy about meeting the expectations of mature functioning. In addition, the need for approval underlies the reluctance to take risks. The need to incorporate emotions involving assertion, competitiveness, and sexuality in adult life can also evoke anxiety regarding the expression of the feelings and impulses associated with adult strivings and expectations. Feelings of threat and danger associated with the aggressive, assertive, competitive, and sexual expansion appropriate to adulthood may etiologically be connected to early childhood limitations, discouragement, and complexes. Such etiological limitations then emerge as a residual sense of danger about these assertive impulses in adulthood. As an adult, then, the individual presumably becomes persistently anxious because of the many circumstances in which the prohibited assertive impulses and feelings are called upon. The person's persistent anxiety then results in a retreat to dependency in order to avoid the expression of these more mature impulses and the risk that such expression would evoke disapproval. Thus, the feelings associated with threat and danger will most likely be elicited at times when emphasis is placed on separation, independence, or autonomy. During such challenging times, the pervasive anxiety characterized as fearful anticipations can be triggered. The person then expects that something dreadful, yet somewhat indefinable, may occur.

In terms of differential diagnosis, it can be proposed that less plasticity and reduced strength of the ego exists in panic states in contrast with the ego functioning occurring in the generalized anxiety disorder. In either case, the presence of conscious fear and suppressed anger along with uncertainty regarding sexual expectations can generate overwhelming cumulative stimuli that begin to bombard the person in the form of tension and anxiety. Consequently, the person begins to feel unable to cope, leading inexorably to a sense of dread.

In the following section the syndrome of obsessive compulsive disorder will be described in which symptoms bind anxiety to prevent disruptive or panicky intrusions of such anxiety. This disorder is contained within the category of anxiety disorders of both *DSM-III* and *DSM-III-R*.

Obsessive Compulsive Disorder
(or Obsessive Compulsive Neurosis)

Not only is the obsessive compulsive disorder or neurosis a ubiquitous entity in modern diagnostic nomenclatures, but it is one of the earliest of the neurotic syndromes to be isolated and defined. In the current *DSM* nomenclature, a distinction is made between obsessive compulsive character structure in contrast to obsessive compulsive neurosis. Essentially the pathology that is considered obsessive compulsive character is labeled obsessive compulsive personality disorder and listed and defined under the category of character or personality disorders. These are disorders of obsessions and compulsions that act to control emotion. By comparison, the obsessive compulsive disorder or neurosis discussed in this section is listed and defined in the category of anxiety disorders and has a neurotic cast. Within this neurotic diagnosis, obsessive or compulsive symptoms appear because controls are insufficient to contain emotion which then is experienced in palpable terms as anxiety. In response to this experience of anxiety, these obsessions and compulsions are employed in an attempt to extinguish this tension. Thus, in the obsessive compulsive character or personality disorder, the obsessions and compulsions are implemented in a way that precludes the experience of anxiety while in the obsessive compulsive neurosis the obsessions and compulsions are mobilized in response to anxiety that has already surfaced.

The major distinction between the obsessive compulsive neurosis and the obsessive compulsive personality disorder is that in the compulsive personality or character, the obsessive compulsive style corresponds with the major part of personality functioning through its domination of the fabric of the character structure. In addition, since the compulsive configuration essentially encompasses the character structure, the obsessive thoughts or compulsive behaviors associated with this character structure generally have an ego syntonic quality. Therefore, the possibility for the appearance of palpable anxiety or tension within the expression of symptoms in the obsessive compulsive personality disorder or character is limited. Any anxiety or tension that does appear in the obsessive compulsive personality disorder is generated by a failure of the character structure to achieve externalization of the source of difficulty.

On the other hand, in the diagnosis of obsessive compulsive neurosis or obsessive compulsive disorder, symptoms involve repetitious thought or behavior experienced as ego alien or ego dystonic. This dystonic experience means that the individual with such neurotic symptoms experiences an immediate sense of tension and conflict regarding the pressure inherent in the symptoms being expressed. It is this quality of alien pressure associated with the obsessive compulsive symptoms that defines the ego dystonic state. Further, this symptomatic pressure which is sensed as foreign stimulates concern in the person that something is wrong. An awareness emerges that personality functioning itself is impaired. Thus, the major qualities defining the obsessive compulsive neurotic disorder involve repetition, distress, and the sense of an alien presence in the personality or in the behavior of daily functioning.

Nature of Obsessive Compulsive Distress

The obsessive compulsive neurosis may appear symptomatically in the form of obsessions or compulsions—depending on whether an ideational or motoric form of the underlying conflict is expressed. These symptoms relentlessly strive for expression, clashing vividly with the individual's desire for personal control. Since the symptoms relate to the pressure of underlying impulses, the core conflict of the obsessive compulsive neurosis concerns the presence of impulses striving for expression against control elements in the personality related to order and conscience.

With regard to obsessions, particular ideas, feelings, fantasies, and especially thoughts, continuously intrude into consciousness. These repeating thoughts are sensed as involuntary and ego dystonic and may appear pointless or even repellant to the subject. If symptomatic thoughts appear pointless, the distress for the individual is largely a sense that something foreign, not accessible to understanding, and not under personal control is conflicting with the individual's desire for personal integrity. If, on the other hand, the symptomatic thoughts are experienced aversively, then very often the obsessive thoughts stand in conflict with moral standards of conscience that the individual strongly desires to maintain. Such standards may involve principles regarding religion, sexuality, or matters of aggression that relate to the individual's strongly held moral scruples.

Obsessive thoughts result in suffering for the individual, not only because they appear clearly embedded in a sense of conflict, but also because such thoughts impair the individual's efficiency in carrying out responsibilities. This sense of conflict is reinforced by the recognition that the obsessional material arises from the subject's own processes and is clearly not intruding from the outside or being externally imposed. Further, the person undertakes efforts and strategies to rid his thinking of the obsessions, to ignore them, or to neutralize them.

While obsessions involve a cognitive expression of symptomatology and conflict, compulsions are the motoric or behavioral counterpart of this syndrome; that is, in compulsions, the personality becomes pressured to yield to specific behaviors that are basically not consciously desired. The compulsive behavior may occur excessively or even apparently senselessly and thereby generates distress. Such compulsive behavior may also emerge from the feeling that some aversive future occurrence can be deflected by employing the usual stereotyped action, that is, by pursuing a compulsive ritual. Compulsive ritual contains an inherent magical wish fulfillment element and therefore, compulsive ritualistic behavior is always an irrational attempt to prevent future difficulty.

A typical compulsion may, for example, involve the need to repeatedly engage in hand washing to avoid such a vague future calamity. Compulsive neurotic individuals may check and double check that a stove is turned off, that windows are locked, or that a door is locked, in order to secure feelings of safety. In more severe instances of compulsive behavior, the symptomatic individual may need to return home in order to recheck even after having traveled a distance. The manner in which this rechecking occurs illustrates the interference that the symptoms create in the individual's carrying out of responsibilities. As noted in *DSM-III-R,* the compulsive behaviors are, in addition, viewed by the sufferer as illogical and excessive, and both obsessions and compulsions interfere with routine, with vocational and social activities, and with relationships, causing significant personal distress.

The nature of the underlying conflicts involved in obsessive compulsive symptomatology can often be understood through the prevailing invasive thoughts or behaviors. If the symptom involves checking locks because of a vague fear of uninvited entry, or if the stove is checked for purposes that are ultimately explained as avoiding a potential explosion, then the role of managing angry feelings and the issue of anxiety associated with the potential loss of control over anger may be suggested.

Obsessive thoughts that involve sexual imagery may similarly suggest the individual's struggle to manage sexual emotions and the underlying conflict involving sexuality as it is opposed by conscious moral persuasion. It is the individual's characteristic striving to be correct, proper, moral, and good that contributes to a heightened conscientiousness and a central difficulty managing feelings and impulses such as aggression and sexuality. These feelings of anger or sexuality are viewed therefore as inconsistent with strivings of morality and conscience. Thus, the underlying conflict in obsessive compulsive neurosis generates intense anxiety based upon the difficulty in integrating emotional and impulse functioning into everyday life. The purpose of the obsessive compulsive symptoms, then, is to bind the anxiety produced by such conflicts.

Consistent feelings of discouragement naturally occur when the obsessive compulsive symptoms repeat in a ritualistic way and when the syndrome gains an acute grip on the person's cognitive or behavioral functioning. The individual feels overwhelmed by these alien symptoms—thoughts or behaviors that are not under voluntary control—and consequently may experience depression. Such a depressive experience may appear either symptomatically, or the diagnostic condition can become complicated so that the primary diagnosis of obsessive compulsive neurosis may have added to it that of dysthymia.

Ambivalence and Developmental Factors

In the dynamic formation of obsessive compulsive neurosis, the phenomenon of ambivalence is a trenchant reflection of the powerful influence of the underlying conflict. This central conflict is characterized by the desire to yield to an emotionally based wish or temptation that is related to an impulse on the one hand, which is opposed by scruples of conscience, morality, or propriety, on the other. Since the individual's sense of self is presumably integrated around correctness and order, then yielding to temptations and any threat of loss of control over emotions can generate significant anxiety. This anxiety originating from conflicts between different parts or agencies of the personality represents an exemplification of neurotic functioning. Obsessive and compulsive symptoms that are subsequently produced actually serve to bind or restrict anxiety by allowing partial expression as well as denial of the disguised impulses that can then remain hidden. These symptoms also limit conscious access to the nature of the underlying conflict. However, symptomatic ambivalence appears as pressure to entertain an idea or to perform an activity, while such pressure is simultaneously opposed by the feeling of not at all wanting to think such ideas or perform such acts. Thus, the approach-avoidance ambivalence seems to be a transformation of the conflict between yielding and stopping. In this transformation, the neurotically obsessional individual may say, "I must wash my hands, but I don't want to." In symbolic unconscious terms the individual may actually feel guilty about sexual thoughts or feelings that on the conscious level would appear improper. The person therefore needs a displaced or symbolized manner of cleansing the taint of the so-called improper impulse. Yet no matter how often obsessive or compulsive efforts are made to suppress the impulse, its strength is always rejuvenated and reappears; the obsession or compulsion must be repetitively reinstituted in order to repress the impulse once again.

In psychoanalytic developmental terms, the obsessive compulsive neurosis is attributed to issues of early toilet training considered the anal phase of psychosexual development. Theoretically, conflicts at this stage remain salient either because of fixation, sternness of toilet training, or because of a regressive retreat based upon the difficulty in mastering later oedipal anxieties. The power struggle that accompanies stern toilet training concerns the child's decision whether "to do or not to do," or the decision either to follow the parental dictate conscientiously or to follow personal inclinations. Such ambivalence becomes internalized as the central conflict about whether to yield or to stop. Because the obsessive compulsive neurosis is thought to reflect anal stage derivatives, the character style associated with such neurotic conflict often involves preoccupations with being good, doing the right thing, and orderliness. Since a retreat or regression from oedipal anxiety is presumed to contribute to the development of obsessive compulsive neurosis, anxiety regarding competitive and sexual feelings is thought to be inhibited by the binding effect of the repetitive symptomatology.

The Obsessive Defense Cluster

In terms of defensive structure, reaction formation, isolation, and undoing are considered to be the main defense mechanisms typically utilized in obsessive compulsive neurosis. Reaction formation can assist repression of impulses and unacceptable wishes so that in the obsessive compulsive neurosis, any yearnings for disorder, rebellious aggression, and free amoral expression of impulse can be converted to an opposite disposition toward order, conformity, emotional control, and propriety. Although rebellious, hostile, and sexual thoughts can indeed repeatedly intrude into consciousness, nevertheless, because of the use of the defense of isolation these thoughts intrude without the experience of affect appropriate to them. In the case of obsessional ideas, such isolation of the ideas from the corresponding emotion can prevent the likelihood of action based on any present antisocial or rebellious ideation. This isolation of thought from affect has at least two effects. First, the isolation of thought and affect makes the persisting ideas safer through their distance from potential or actual action. Second, the thought-action split also makes the persisting ideas distressingly uncomfortable since the loss of affect prevents understanding of the meaning and intent of the obsession. This distress—related to the unclarity of the affectless idea—is amplified by the underlying threatening emotion, such as anger or sexuality, that unconsciously generates anxiety. Finally, the defense mechanism of undoing is thought to permit symbolic assertions of such threatening aggressive or sexual impulses, such as the intrusive thought of the possibility of fire; this symbolic assertion of impulse is then usually followed by a second stage in which the symbolically expressed thought is undone or reversed—for example, through checking that the stove is not on.

The defense triad of reaction formation, isolation, and undoing operate together to remove emotional potency from the intrusive thoughts and behavior characterizing obsessive compulsive symptoms. These defenses generally are supported by an intellectualized and highly ideational approach that also serves to bolster or insure a sense of control. The emphasis on control derives from an underlying sense of threat regarding the appearance of anything unexpected or surprising. This threat about the unexpected reflects the presence of anxiety associated with the possibility of impulsive emotional expression and especially loss of control over such emotionality.

Consideration of the developmental derivatives, defenses, and dynamic formulations of the obsessive compulsive neurosis illuminates the central role of anxiety in this neurosis—anxiety engendered by the presence of impulses that defy standards of morality and conscience. The role of anxiety as the definitional quality of neurosis can also be seen in the presentation of the post-traumatic stress disorder in the next section.

Post-Traumatic Stress Disorder

The post-traumatic stress disorder is of particular interest to clinicians because of two salient historical factors. The sudden appearance of repetitious trauma stimulated by battle conditions during World War I enabled Freud to further elaborate his psychoanalytic conceptualizations in both theoretical and practical terms. These battle crises had a dramatic impact on progress in understanding neurotic functioning and consequently broadened the clinical outlook of the etiology and treatment of neurosis. More recently the social implications related to poignant and frequent occurrences of traumatic stress syndrome in veterans of the Vietnam War have revived special interest in traumatic disorders.

The psychological casualties of war that contribute to the appearance of post-traumatic stress disorders are based strongly on empirical findings. Thus, the trauma presented by so many casualties who are impaired on their return to society has underscored the need to include this type of disorder in overall clinical nomenclature. As seen in table 7.1, *DSM-III* recognizes two distinct types of post-traumatic disorder. The first, an acute type, is characterized by symptoms that develop relatively closely in time to the traumatic event; the duration of this type of reaction to trauma is less than six months. The second type is considered chronic as symptoms last more than six months, or first appear six months or later after the traumatic event. In contrast, in *DSM-III-R*, the diagnostic entity is designated simply as post-traumatic stress disorder and if symptoms first appear six months or more after the traumatic experience, delayed onset is specified as part of the diagnosis.

Post-traumatic stress disorder is an anxiety state and a significant experience of anxiety is characteristic of the disorder. Behavioral efforts to manage the anxiety also act to define the disorder which occurs in the context of a specific event that is traumatic enough to evoke agitation as a typical response.

Efforts to manage anxiety in post-traumatic stress disorder involve the experience of a repetition of the traumatic event that can occur in various forms. This repetition of the traumatic event reflects both an effort to master overwhelming trauma that the person experiences but at the same time reveals the persistent incompleteness of these attempts at mastery over the trauma. This repetition of those traumatic circumstances that have deeply affected the individual includes persistent memories of the trauma, dreams or flashback experiences about it, or the impending sense that the traumatic circumstances are being reconstituted by a precipitator that releases the traumatic memory.

The various precipitating traumas that can evoke the post-traumatic stress disorder include events such as catastrophes, accidents, assaults, and battle experiences. The person's experience as a result of such a trauma does not simply end in a typical reactive depression or dysthymic disorder. Rather, a more etched and scalding reaction resembling the original and severe trauma is seen. The presence of nightmares, repetitive dreams, flashbacks, and other such invasive recurrent thoughts reveals the presence of the newly reactivated psychological trauma.

The onslaught of such severe tension also will usually not produce phobic reactions or panic attacks. Rather, the overwhelming and pervasive experience of the traumatic memory generates a restriction of sensation and an overall psychological anesthesia. This sort of numbness or emotional anesthesia reflects the person's withdrawal from the interpersonal domain of involvements. Such an interpersonal retreat also corresponds to the person's emotionally washed-out texture of relating as well as an obviously depleted sense of interest in the world. In an overall sense, the appeal of the external world is significantly reduced as the focus on the traumatic circumstances or events becomes an increasingly central preoccupation.

As part of the post-traumatic stress neurosis some usual or typical anxiety symptoms may surface. These anxiety reactions include disturbed sleep, the well-known startle response in which the person seems to jump out of his skin in the presence of sudden stimuli when such stimuli are usually otherwise treated as innocuous. In addition, concentration can be impaired and memory negatively affected. As circumstances or even recollections that can be associated with the trauma further surface, then symptomatology will become exacerbated; in fact, an effort is often made to avoid participating in social engagements or even thinking about them, lest there is a chance that such interaction or thoughts can stimulate memories of the feared original event.

A special problem that has appeared with respect to this particular diagnosis of post-traumatic neurosis concerns what has become known as *survivor's guilt*. This pervasive experience of painful guilt can plague the individual who survives a tragedy when others have been killed, succumbed, or been victimized. A mild form of such a dynamic is often seen in families where more successful members try to minimize their achievements—especially when other family members are suffering acute hardships.

Sometimes an expost facto diagnosis of post-traumatic disorder can be confirmed when the person has a major catharsis through the reliving of the catastrophic event and seems later to be released from the psychological grip of the neurosis.

A final diagnosis of the anxiety disorders listed in table 7.1 is the atypical anxiety disorder—designated in *DSM-III-R* as anxiety disorder not otherwise specified—to be briefly noted here.

Atypical Anxiety Disorder

Relabeled *anxiety disorder not otherwise specified* in *DSM-III-R*, this category contains phenomena associated with anxiety neuroses that do not strictly adhere to the criteria of the diagnostic entities associated with the usually defined anxiety states. For example, there are individuals who may present with a rather broad spectrum of symptoms seemingly relevant to diagnoses within the range of neurotic anxiety disorders. These symptoms may include anxiety that is free-floating but not sufficiently persisting, or fleeting phobic feelings that are not entrenched phobias, and so forth. Such individuals do indeed experience palpable anxiety but a specific and identifiable syndrome is not particularly evident. This type of an array of partially defined syndromes would have been identified within the diagnosis previously known as mixed neurosis, but in the current *DSM-III* nomenclature the diagnosis is referred to as atypical anxiety disorder, and still further, in *DSM-III-R* as anxiety disorder not otherwise specified.

Throughout this chapter on anxiety disorders, what emerges is the attempt by classifiers to define diagnosis around a few central phenomena. Anxiety, or the palpable experience of anxiety constitutes one such central phenomenon. The *DSM-III* attempt in the case of the anxiety disorders, then, has been to combine general anxiety states with more specific phobic experiences and to separate these diagnostic states in terms of how symptoms of the anxiety are experienced and managed.

Looking ahead, there are other diagnostic categories within the neurotic range of functioning in which problems of anxiety are also central. The structure of these neuroses are designed in the personality specifically to avoid the experiences of anxiety and include bodily conversions, dissociations, and somatizations.

In the following chapter the neuroses that will be considered comprise two major groups: somatoform disorders, in which physical symptoms and hysterical conversions are major diagnostic indicators, and dissociative disorders, in which various types of psychological dissociation and depersonalization form the basis for the neuroses.

CAPSULE CLINICAL PROFILES OF PHOBIC DISORDERS

Phobias are indicated by an unusual or intense apprehension focused on a specific object or situation. The person experiences intense anxiety regarding this target and seeks to avoid it. Phobias are generally understood to be external displacements of internal fear, affects, and impulses.

Agoraphobia: An intense and compelling fear of open places where tangible boundaries are absent. The person craves the familiar and a clear route for return to the familiar which offer refuge and safety, insuring the viability of the ego. The core conflict may refer to dependency needs as well as fear of any possibility that urges and impulses may emerge. Fear of unleashing either aggressive or sexual impulses which becomes stimulated when terrain is unfamiliar may contribute to the need for a familiar safety situation where controls are assured. In addition to open spaces, fears include crowds, stadiums, elevators, vehicles, and tunnels—all of which relate to the absence of both egress and access to familiar, secure surroundings. During attacks, feelings of dread and terror prevail. Avoidance patterns to feared situations usually become intensely conditioned. Panic, anxiety, depression, and obsessional thinking can be generated in the overall process of agoraphobic concerns.

Social Phobia: An unrealistic fear about social embarrassment that leads to the avoidance of engaging in specific social outlets. An underlying sense of inadequacy is displaced onto circumstances in which the subject fears social scrutiny; social exposure and activities performed where others could view and evaluate the subject's performance engender distressing apprehension. The person's fear then justifies diminished risk-taking so that a need to remain dependently oriented is reinforced. Persons with social phobia have limited confidence and increased anxiety regarding control over reactions and impulses which may contribute to the need to establish avoidance of opportunities for social exposure and observation.

Simple Phobia: A specific irrational fear. Acrophobia (fear of heights) and claustrophobia (fear of closed spaces) are examples. These relatively narrow phobias are not as clinically debilitating as the social phobias because conscious strategies can be implemented to circumvent the problematic fearfulness. Anxiety related to impulse expression is thought to underly establishment of phobic targets as displacements of a feared impulse. Avoidance of the target then eliminates confrontation of the displacement of the troublesome wish and the fear of its expression.

CAPSULE CLINICAL PROFILES OF ANXIETY DISORDERS

In the neuroses, the general anxiety disorders and more specific phobias have been diagnostically separated with respect to how symptoms of anxiety are experienced and managed. In the anxiety disorders the experience of anxiety remains conscious and disturbing rather than neutralized through depression or absorbed into character patterns, as in the character or personality disorders. In the anxiety disorders, the symptomatology serves the purpose of either reducing, sustaining, binding, or mastering anxiety.

Panic Disorder: Periods of intense dread and apprehension appear in a frightening crescendo which are not easily or apparently linked to any specific occurrence or circumstance. Physical sensations may also appear ranging from dizziness or fainting to heart palpitations, sweating, nausea, or choking. Depersonalization feelings and fear of loss of control are also characteristic, along with fears of becoming crazy or dying. Reduced ego strength is seen and anticipation of panic becomes a debilitating feature. Issues of underlying anger often seem central, and dynamics of dependency and separation also appear to play a significant role in the underlying conflict.

Generalized Anxiety Disorder: Distressing anxiety defines this syndrome in the form of free-floating anxiety. Symptoms of anxiety include fearful anticipations—the central core—vigilance, motoric activity, and autonomic hyperactivity. Symptoms can include interrupted sleep, edginess, trembling, the startle response, facial strain, muscle aching, racing of the heart, and digestive and breathing problems. Ego strength is better developed than in panic states but needs for approval and acceptance make management of anger and overall impulse problematic. Repression is utilized as the main defense. Issues of dependency and separation constitute an important dynamic within the symptom picture since autonomous functioning evokes apprehension.

Obsessive Compulsive Disorder (or Neurosis): Symptoms involve repetitious intrusive thoughts or behaviors that are experienced as ego alien. Obsessions are intrusive ideas while compulsions involve repetitive physical behavior such that the person recognizes that something is wrong. The basic conflict involves control over impulses striving for expression. Focus on propriety and conscience dictates a strong emphasis on control. High standards of conscience underlie the inner tyrannical obsessive and compulsive imperatives as impulses repeatedly strive for expression. Control over anger and sexuality is an important preoccupation in this syndrome although the person is plagued with ambivalence regarding the contrast between yielding and stopping impulse expression. Anxiety is bound by symptoms that maintain equilibrium by partial expression and denial. The appearance of a multiplicity of symptoms can be overwhelming, leading to depression. Defenses include reaction formation, undoing, and isolation in a context of intellectually driven ideation patterns designed to insure control and to avoid surprise, especially with respect to the appearance of emotion.

Post-traumatic Stress Disorder: Involves acute and delayed types of terror reactions to traumatic, catastrophic, assaultive, accidential, or battle experiences. A specific exceptional, overwhelming event triggers the disorder; anxiety ensues with repetition of the event in memory, dreams, or flashbacks as attempts to master the tension still associated with the original trauma. Nightmares and recurrent thoughts invade the person's inner life, promoting withdrawal from interpersonal interaction and the possibility of a washed-out texture in emotional life. Experiences of disturbed sleep, startle response, and impaired concentration and memory occur.

Atypical Anxiety Disorder: A broad spectrum of symptoms are seen but not clustered to enable consistent definition. Free-floating anxiety of limited duration or fleeting phobias are examples of a range of anxiety related symptoms that do not qualify as an identifiable syndrome. Yet, sufficient symptoms of distressing anxiety do appear requiring diagnosis. This classification is labeled *Anxiety Disorder Not Otherwise Specified* in *DSM-III-R*.

CHAPTER 8

Conversion and Dissociative Reactions

In the evolution of *DSM* nosology the conventional and historical understanding of hysteria and the vicissitudes of hysterical reactions have been increasingly analyzed and separated into narrower categories. Thus, the various symptoms that comprise the neurotic disorder of the hysterias have been clustered in both *DSM-III* and *DSM-III-R* to form the array of diagnoses encompassing somatoform and dissociative disorders. These two major categories of somatization and dissociation largely parallel the nomenclature appearing in *DSM-II,* in which two forms of hysterical neurosis appeared: conversion type and dissociative type. In addition, *DSM-II* contained separate diagnostic categories for depersonalization and hypochondriacal neuroses. The refinement that has been attempted by *DSM-III/III-R* is to group the diagnostic references of hysteria into two major components. In the first of these components—somatoform disorders—bodily functioning is involved in the pathology, while in the second component—dissociative disorders—ego weakness appears in the form of dissociation of personality functioning.

In the broad history of psychopathology the various neurotic disturbances composing the hysterical disorders have played a major role in the shift from a speculative and organically oriented approach toward psychopathology to an essentially psychological appreciation of such hysterical processes. Fundamentally, the hysterical process is relatively straightforward, involving factors of suggestion that are involuntarily self-employed in an effort to eliminate anxiety. This apparent straightforward connection between suggestibility and intolerance of anxiety contributed to the use of hypnotic techniques in the understanding of hysteria as a psychological phenomenon. The nineteenth-century investigators of hysterical symptoms who utilized hypnosis and their precursors who relied on hypnotic suggestion for treatment are discussed in volume 1 of this primer, *History of Psychopathology*.

While apparently simple, the manifestations of hysteria can nevertheless appear in widely diverse syndromes. These clusters of hysterical symptoms can include features of multiple personality, the conversion of conflict and tension to bodily disorder, loss of memory, and preoccupation with bodily symptoms whether real or exaggerated. In an effort to be more descriptively refined and consistent with a modern scientific approach, the variety of manifestations of hysteria are detailed in *DSM* nosology in numerous circumscribed categories within each of the two major components, somatoform and dissociative disorders. The first grouping of hysterical syndromes considered in *DSM-III/III-R* are those primarily involving bodily disorders as an essential feature of the neurotic hysterical process. This major category is known as somatoform disorders, because somatic, physical symptoms play a central role in each of the diagnostic subcategories. While the physical aspects of the hysterical reactions considered as somatoform disorders may appear to have organic components, psychological conflicts are actually considered to be chiefly responsible for the neurotic process that culminates in such somatic symptomatology.

DYNAMIC FACTORS IN THE SOMATOFORM NEUROSES

The underlying psychological conflict involved in the somatoform disorders relates to feelings, desires, or impulses that if experienced and translated into behavior could evoke intense apprehension. Such direct expression of impulses would be sensed as dangerous and actually forbidden. Consequently, it is thought that intense anxiety is generated by these prohibited emotions and impulses even in anticipation of their surfacing. In all of the somatoform disorders, the conflict between direct assertion of hostile and sexual feelings on the one hand, and fear of their expression on the other, becomes converted to a preoccupation or symptom that involves some sort of bodily expression. Theoretically, the defense mechanism of repression is instituted to keep the conflict and its anxiety from awareness while the particular form of somatic expression of the emotion and associated tension symbolize the conflict and allow highly indirect emotional release. The nature of the feelings that are prohibited from overt expression are thereby managed in a psychologically safer way and thus they are not experienced or recognized. This repression accomplishes the major or primary gain of the disorder: emotions that appear to be dangerous and difficult to manage in adult functioning are avoided and do not have to be overtly faced and utilized in the service of mature functioning.

Secondary gain, important in all neurotic pathology, but especially significant in the hysterical neuroses, plays a particular role in the somatoform disorders. The concept of secondary gain refers to the observation that even though the debilitations of any pathological condition are painful, limiting, and unpleasant, certain gains that are secondary to the disorder accrue to the person who bears the disturbance. Among the secondary gains that correspond to the somatoform disorders, are the gaining of sympathy, encouragement, and attention consistent with a more immature state. Thus, the subject can avoid engagement of responsibility as well as suppress tension related to adult expectations. It is proposed that the fulfillment of dependency and attentional needs also satisfies derivatives of sexuality and that further, manipulation of others through symptomatology indirectly satisfies some of the sufferer's aggressive strivings.

Each of the hysterical disorders presented will consider the pattern of repression of affect associated with the particular disorder as well as the anxiety and conversion involved in each disorder. Such patterns of repression for each hysterical disorder will then reflect a focus of concern that centers on some kind of bodily experience. A resulting somatic symptom, then, symbolically reflects the conflict and allows for an unrecognized expression of emotion plus the increased possibility of secondary gain. Fear and tension can now be related to a symptom, as in all neurosis, while the greater anxiety regarding direct expression of emotion is eliminated or at least deflected from conscious attention.

The fear and tension now associated with bodily symptoms in hysterical neuroses reflect some of the anxiety that is present in every neurosis. In somatoform disorders, much of the neurotic anxiety surfaces in an unconscious form as guilt which then can be reduced by the painful, limiting, and self-punitive quality of the symptoms typical of the disorder. Thus, symptoms of conversions, bodily weaknesses, pain, and anticipation of major illnesses, in effect, assuage guilt as well as bind this form of anxiety. Even in the less agitated forms of somatization disorder where there appears a lack of manifest anxiety that nineteenth-century French researchers called *la belle indifference*, conversion symptoms dramatically eliminate the conscious experience of anxiety which now can be identified with the symptom's alleviation of guilt.

In *DSM-III*, the various somatoform disorders as well as the array of dissociative disorders are grouped as indicated in table 8.1. Considerable rearrangement, redefining, and renaming of categories has been realized in *DSM-III-R* which is presented in table 8.2.

One of the disturbances classified among the atypical somatoform disorders in *DSM-III* has been designated as a separate disturbance in *DSM-III-R*, the first of the somatoform disorders to be considered in the new arrangement. This new category is the body dysmorphic disorder, and its diagnostic criteria and psychological basis are described in the next section.

SOMATOFORM DISORDERS

Body Dysmorphic Disorder
(Dysmorphophobia)

This newly designated diagnosis considered in *DSM-III-R* is a condition in which an individual with a normal appearance overfocuses on what he considers to be some sort of physical blemish or fault. In some cases, there is no such demonstrable physical fault. In cases where a minor physical or appearance imperfection does exist, the degree of concern that the individual generates is quite exaggerated. However, from the point of view of differential diagnosis, the person with the body dysmorphic disorder is not delusional with respect to the physical flaw. There is, then, in persons with a body dysmorphic disorder, a capacity to recognize that an overemphasis is being placed on the degree of deficiency that preoccupies the individual. A further qualification in making the diagnosis of body dysmorphic disorder is that the overconcern or exaggeration of a presumed physical fault does not apply to the conditions of anorexia nervosa or transsexualism, diagnoses in which factors of physical appearance are also central to the disorder.

This diagnostic definition of body dysmorphic disorder in *DSM-III-R* broadens and formalizes the brief discussion that appeared in *DSM-III* under the category of atypical somatoform disorder. However, the body dysmorphic condition occurs relatively infrequently and its central symptom of an overfocus on a physical defect can be construed as reflecting the displacement of a sense of inadequacy onto an aspect of the body. Such a sense of inadequacy can further be presumed to relate to the individual's intense fear of effectively or safely expressing assertive or sexual feelings in a direct way appropriate to that person's age.

This displacement of feelings of inadequacy onto the body allows the person to avoid challenging circumstances by ascribing the defect in appearance to be one that is beyond personal control. The need to remain somewhat underdeveloped or immature to secure a feeling of safety can then be justified while the tension and distress of personal inadequacy feelings are displaced onto an anatomical reference. The underlying tension is then masked by the focus on the physical. The secondary gains involving sympathy and perhaps even indulgence from those who are unwittingly manipulated to feel sorry for the sufferer is apparent as an additional motive in the symptom formation of this type of hysterical syndrome.

TABLE 8.1. Somatoform and Dissociative Disorders of *DSM-III*

Somatoform Disorders

Somatization disorder
Conversion disorder (or hysterical neurosis, conversion type)
Psychogenic pain disorder
Hypochondriasis (or hypochondriacal neurosis)
Atypical somatoform disorder

Dissociative Disorders or Hysterical Neuroses (Dissociative Type):

Psychogenic amnesia
Psychogenic fugue
Multiple personality
Depersonalization disorder (or depersonalization neurosis)
Atypical dissociative disorder

In the next section, a form of hysterical neurosis that is much more common and dramatic will be presented, following *DSM-III-R* and table 8.2, a form referred to as conversion disorder. This disorder is also known both currently and in historical usage as hysterical neurosis, conversion type.

Conversion Disorder
(or Hysterical Neurosis, Conversion Type)

Individuals presenting a conversion disorder reveal a change in physical functioning that is often quite striking and suggestive of

TABLE 8.2. The Somatoform and Dissociative Disorders
of *DSM-III-R*

SOMATOFORM DISORDERS

Reference to DSM-III

New	Body dysmorphic disorder (or dysmorphophobia)
Was #2	Conversion disorder (or hysterical neurosis, conversion type), single episode or recurrent episode to be specified
Was #4	Hypochondriasis (or hypochondriacal neurosis)
Was #1	Somatization disorder
Was #3	Somatoform pain disorder
Was #5; renamed in *DSM-III-R*	Undifferentiated somatoform disorder
New	Somatoform disorder not otherwise specified

DISSOCIATIVE DISORDERS (OR HYSTERICAL NEUROSES, DISSOCIATIVE TYPE)

Reference to DSM-III

Was #3	Multiple personality disorder
Was #2	Psychogenic fugue
Was #1	Psychogenic amnesia
Same	Depersonalization disorder (or depersonalization neurosis)
Renamed in *DSM-III-R*	Dissociative disorder not otherwise specified

an impairment of a physical process. For example, visual perception may become constricted, thereby forming the symptom of tunnel vision, hands may lose sensation as in glove anesthesia, or limbs may become paralyzed. On closer scrutiny, the apparent physical basis for the disorder is untenable, since actual neurological pathways are not in any way physically implicated in the anesthesia or paralysis; that is, the anesthesia and paralysis are really hysterically determined. Further, psychological etiological factors become obvious either because of the conditions precipitating the onset of symptoms, symbolic expression suggested by symptoms, or because of secondary gains that are clearly evident. For example, the timing of symptom onset often reveals secondary gain factors such as the use of the symptom by the patient to avoid an undesirable challenge or responsibility, or the use of the symptom to gain help from people who would otherwise not be available.

Because of the psychological etiology and unconscious operation of conversion symptoms, it can be seen that the patient is unable to control or willfully alter the symptom. As a matter of fact, the attitude frequently displayed in relation to the symptomatic paralysis or anesthesia can be one of benign acceptance or indifference. When this type of indifference and emotional evenness appears, the psychological roots of the disturbance are betrayed by the individual's distance from appropriate emotions that would ordinarily accompany such symptoms. Not only is the symptomatic change in physical functioning in conversion disorder unaccountable on the basis of physical findings, but the symptoms also do not reflect culturally relevant functioning, such as in the case of accepted religious trance states, fainting, and so on. Further, conversion symptoms involve more than pain or impaired sexual functioning, as for example in the appearance of an occasional simple headache that helps avoid an unpleasant responsibility. In *DSM-III-R,* the specification of either a single episode of conversion disorder or recurrent episodes is included in the revision of diagnostic criteria for this disorder.

In terms of the dynamic factors promoting conversion hysteria specifically as well as somatoform disorders in general, the entrenchment and fortification of a repressive defense structure designed to limit accessibility to unmanageable or frightening emotions seems to be present. That the emotions usually protected include sexual and aggressive ones can be strongly considered since the conversion symptoms themselves make direct sexual and assertive expression very difficult to achieve. For example, a psychologically based symptom of muscle weakness or blurred vision effectively prohibits reliable, mature involvement in vocational, sexual, or family arenas. However, the passive elements involved in controlling others and in striving to be seductively dependent reveal an emotional presence that becomes only indirectly expressed. Thus, the conversion symptom itself seems to reinforce repressive defenses so that only harmless derivatives of the emotions appear in rather childlike or infantile form.

Along with the repressive stance, persons with conversion disorders tend to utilize denial defenses to screen out negative features of the environment. Further, the defense of reaction formation also is often present as a mechanism that enables a quality of tenderness to appear toward close family members instead of the hostility that may be actually relevant and present. The cumulative work of the defenses of repression, reaction formation, and denial helps promote the sense of martyrdom that can often be associated with individuals whose conversion symptoms are serenely but manipulatively used.

In addition, personality functioning in individuals exhibiting conversion symptoms is marked by a high degree of suggestibility. As a result of this proclivity toward suggestibility, an event felt by the individual to be unmanageable can, through a kind of self-suggestion, be reacted to in the form of a dramatic bodily change. The nature of this bodily alteration involves loss of function such as anesthesia or paralysis that itself symbolizes that person's weakness or inadequacy in coping with life's demands. Further, the effect of the symptom limits what the person can see, hear, be consciously aware of, or do. By means of such symptom formation, the environmental surroundings are successfully constricted and made more manageable, representing a subtle, but perhaps strategic gain for the person with the conversion disorder. In dynamic terms, the conversion symptom represented in the form of a bodily disability reflects in symbolic form the conflict between asserting oneself in relation to challenge and, because of anxiety connected to such risk, retreating to a posture of dependency.

Suggestibility also plays a part in the next disturbance among the somatoform disorders to be presented, the diagnosis known as hypochondriasis or hypochondriacal neurosis. In hypochondriasis, instead of producing conversions of conflict and tension to somatic phenomena, bodily reactions are suggestively misinterpreted to produce apprehensive preoccupations about especially threatening diseases.

Hypochondriasis
(or Hypochondriacal Neurosis)

Hypochondriacal neurosis differs sharply from conversion disorder in that the hypochondriac individual seems to interpret symptomatology unrealistically rather than displaying the comparative indifference often seen in connection with conversion symptoms. In hypochondriacal disorders, for instance, a headache is regarded as the probable indicator of a brain tumor, or a stomach ache becomes the signal for stomach cancer. In addition, floating phantom symptoms may appear so that the person becomes convinced of the veracity of a whole catalogue of symptoms. For example, the person may experience what seems like an arthritic symptom which, from moment to moment, appears and disappears and can become suddenly transformed into cardiovascular or any number of other disease possibilities.

The preoccupation with the direction in which the physical symptoms are leading becomes the essence of hypochondriacal neurosis. The symptoms on which the patient focuses are regarded as indicating a serious disease and the possibility of physical disorder becomes the central aspect of the person's life. Various somatic activities such as the heart beat or a cough can become especially focused upon as the patient's persistent bodily preoccupations shift targets. Medical consultations usually become part of the patient's way of life but the relationship to any particular consultant is sooner or later disrupted by the patient's disappointment when the physician cannot find a substantive medical disorder. Thus, as in all hysterical disorders involving physical complaints or pain, the individual's core psychological conflict in the hypochondriacal disorder also points in the direction of the inability of such persons to manage adult responsibilities. The patient's sense of personal inadequacy, which is covered over by intense focus on physical preoccupations, becomes justified through personal conviction that a serious disease is present. When confronted with the fact that such a disease cannot be established medically, the patient's unrecognized needs to control and make symptoms conform to a real medical ailment invariably frustrate those he consults. This frustration of the other person reflects the patient's displacement of hostility through passive-aggressive behavior, and reinforces the theoretical and clinical observations of the correlation between passive-aggressive traits and hypochondriasis.

An additional component of the hysterical disorders that involve physical complaints and bodily preoccupations is the need to be special that the patient attempts to derive by emphasis on pains and through the appearance of symptoms with unusual characteristics. Thus, the headache is not the usual tension headache, but is construed as far more special and unique, such as a symptom of a brain tumor. This type of device for supporting a posture of specialness is also consistent with the headaches presented by sufferers of somatoform pain disorder as it is known in *DSM-III-R,* or psychogenic pain disorder in *DSM-III,* where medication never seems to relieve the pain. Therefore, the pain is special as, by implication, is the bearer of the pain or subsequent symptom.

In spite of the multidetermined importance of symptoms in hypochondriasis and despite unrecognized needs to relate symptoms to dramatic medical conditions, the person's belief in the hidden presence of the preoccupying medical condition never actually becomes delusional in its extent. Therefore, the subject can admit to at least the possibility that the fear or belief about having the serious disease that is imagined is not necessarily based on fact. Yet, in the face of such an admission that rules out a delusional belief system, the underlying need for the belief and associated fear regarding the presumed serious illness pervades the person's functioning; pains and physical impairments continue to be misjudged as indicators of a serious medical condition. Although medical assessment does not uncover any physical process producing the symptoms about which the sufferer complains, the belief in or fear of the medical condition nevertheless continues. In order that the diagnosis of hypochondriasis conform to *DSM-III-R* criteria, the central belief and/or fear regarding a medical disease needs to last a minimum of six months; further, the symptoms utilized to form the basis for the presumption or fear about a disease cannot be associated with panic attacks.

Preoccupation with physical complaints also plays a central role in the next diagnostic subcategory of the somatoform disorders to be considered, following *DSM-III-R* and table 8.2, the somatization disorder. This disorder as described in *DSM-III-R* has been broadened somewhat from its *DSM-III* description. Nevertheless, its essence remains a variety of relatively long-term physical impairments in which a physical basis for the symptoms either is not present, or, if such a basis is found, then complaints far exceed the parameters that would be appropriate to the medical findings.

Somatization Disorder

In *DSM* nosology, a person diagnosed with somatization disorder presents a variety and range of actual physical symptoms that are persistent and long-standing sources of complaint. Theoretically, this focus on numerous physical symptoms that are worthy of complaint is regarded as a hysterical reaction because the adult responsibilities of life cannot efficiently be faced by the person with such a neurotically impaired ego. Thus, anxieties are managed by an overfocus on physical symptomatology which coincidentally secures for this neurotic type a host of secondary gains. Among these secondary gains are the avoidance of responsibilities and excessive reliance on stronger figures or authority types for counsel, guidance, decision making, and sympathy. Unlike the body dysmorphic disorder, in which the physical focus involves essentially imaginary or highly exaggerated body feature impairments, the physical symptoms central to the diagnosis of the somatization disorder indeed, actually occur. However, such physical symptoms either are psychologically rather than organically determined or, are psychologically exaggerated when organic contributions exist. In contrast with hypochondriasis in which bodily impairments or sensations are distorted to become signs of significant diseases, somatization disorder involves a range of physical complaints that are pervasively focused upon and for which medication or medical consultation is specifically sought.

Presumably, the primary gain obtained from this somatization disorder—which relates it to all the various forms of hysteria and provides the disorder with the neurotic imprimatur—involves the inadequate integration of emotions into independent, mature personality functioning. Thus, the sexual and directly assertive strivings necessary for adulthood are subverted to efforts to achieve sympathy, maintain dependency, and manipulate people through childlike weakness. While all of the hysterias share the avoidance of direct emotional expression and, more importantly, conscious awareness of the troublesome emotions involved, each form of hysterical neurosis manages the primary gain of avoiding integrating emotions into independent functioning differently.

Specifically, in the somatization disorder, the focus on a range of complaints crystallizes relatively early in development so that the chief symptoms will have persisted for some time before the age of 30. The presence of a long medical history is typical for this disorder. Symptoms usually can be understood from a psychological causative point of view since physical disturbances or injuries do not completely account for the complaints. The symptoms include some that are obviously psychological, involving conversion, and some that seem similar to neurological symptoms. The somatization problems include difficulty in swallowing, fainting, muscle weakness, double or blurred vision, and so forth. Other areas of complaint include gastrointestinal disturbances, such as nausea and diarrhea. Psychosexual symptoms include the inability to experience pleasure or the experience of pain during sexual intercourse. The remaining symptom categories are composed of various complaints of pain and other sensations involving cardiopulmonary functioning, as in palpitations, as well as symptoms of the reproductive organs in women such as some cases of painful menstruation.

In all, 35 different specific pain, conversion, physical, sexual and menstrual symptoms are listed in *DSM-III-R* with a minimum of 13 required to designate the diagnosis of somatization disorder. In addition, the symptoms that are identified are found not to stem from organic determinants, or, if they do, the degree of vocational and social interference is far greater than the organic involvement warrants. A further requirement for inclusion in the somatization diagnosis is that the particular symptom is one that necessitated prescribed medication, a consultation with a physician, or a change in the individual's way of life. For the symptom to be judged an indicator of somatization disorder in terms of *DSM-III-R*, its occurrence should not be in association with a panic attack.

Emphasis on pain components is prominent in the next diagnosis within the somatoform disorders to be considered, that of the somatoform pain disorder which was relabeled in *DSM-III-R*. In *DSM-III*, this diagnosis was known as psychogenic pain disorder. In this disturbance, physical discomfort itself becomes the basis of sympatomatology.

Somatoform Pain Disorder

This diagnostic category involves individuals who are concerned and focused on pain for a minimum of six months. The sensation of pain itself predominates over any physical impairments or physical symptoms. Assessment of this experience of pain in medical terms either reveals no injury or physical disorder related to the pain, or if medical findings are positive, the pain that is complained about and the resulting vocational and interpersonal deficits are far greater than the organic findings justify.

Differential Diagnosis

As a matter of differential diagnosis, many pain symptoms are included in the previously discussed subcategory of the somatoform disorders labeled somatization disorder. These symptoms include abdominal, chest, back, and joint pain, pain during urination, intercourse, and menstruation; however, as noted in the description of somatization disorder, at least 13 physical symptoms from a broad range of areas of disturbance are needed to determine the diagnosis. These 13 symptoms may or may not include pain. Further, headache pain is specifically excluded from the diagnostic criteria of somatization disorder. Thus, any focus on pain by an individual that is narrowly experienced without a relatively broad range of accompanying complaints regarding physical illness would, on a differential diagnostic basis, lead to consideration of somatoform pain disorder and not somatization disorder.

Dynamic Factors

In the somatoform pain disorder, psychological conflict becomes focused through symptoms of persistent and disturbing pain. The absence of a consistent, appropriate, or substantial organic basis for the extent of the pain is one of the factors enabling the classification of the pain disorder as a psychogenically based and psychological diagnosis. The factor that enables placement of the somatoform pain disorder among the somatoform disorders is the person's use of bodily pain reactions as a conversion phenomenon for underlying psychological conflict.

The observation that the development of this pain disorder derives from psychological conflict is further supported by the appearance of pain reactions that coincide with events in the individual's environment that might reasonably connect with a disabling reaction. For example, an individual who is socially unsure may develop severe headache pain when required to attend a social event. Rather than surfacing his fears, the headache represents one of possibly several physiological pain symptoms that reflect the conversion solution to the problem of attending the social event. The person's rationalization includes the fact that such headaches have been experienced in the past, that analgesics do not effectively reduce the pain, and that visits to physicians—even including new physicians accrued from doctor shopping—cannot really help relieve the pain. Therefore, participation in this important but actually feared social occasion needs to be canceled because of the pain symptomatology. Stomach aches, back aches, chest pains, and so forth are other pain syndromes that could appear in place of tension headaches in this clinical example.

Other Secondary Gains

As the preceding illustration reveals, psychological conflict largely related to dependency and inadequacy presumably becomes converted into hysterically based symptoms of pain. While both dependency and inadequacy are central needs in all of the hysterias, these important psychological dimensions often can also relate to the mechanisms of secondary gains. Apprehension that can arise from the potential surfacing of assertive and sexual feelings frequently amplifies the value of the dependency state. Pain symptomatology can then be formed that justifies dependency while demonstrating the person's inadequacy feelings. The secondary gains afforded by conversions into pain further reveal the psychological basis for the disorder. By means of secondary gain and in spite of an apparently disabling disturbance, some benefits paradoxically accrue to the patient.

For example, an event that the individual consciously or unconsciously feels inadequate to master can be avoided; sympathy and assistance are gained from people in the individual's social milieu, people who would not be available except for the presence of painful symptoms; and, a supportive figure or an authority becomes available for guidance and leadership even though the persistence of pain symptoms essentially nullifies the impact that the authority figure can make. The neutralization of the power of the authority figure implies that individuals with symptoms of hysteria gain strength by controlling through weakness. This effort to control through weakness also reflects the childlike strategy—albeit an unconscious one—as well as infantile conflicts that form the dynamics of the hysterical diagnosis.

Defense Patterns

As noted earlier, the defense mechanism that acts as the fulcrum of hysterical neuroses is the repression defense which also clearly plays a part in the somatoform pain disorder. Presumably, as tension over functioning as a sexual and assertive adult is repressed— symptomatology of enduring pain is actually promoted and developed to symbolize and confirm the person's feelings of inadequacy. What surfaces is the person's rationale that it is the various pains that are responsible for reducing the level of functioning and not any sense of inadequacy or fear of direct emotional expression. In addition to the overall repressive stance of this pattern is the development of passive aggressive tendencies. Passive aggressive tendencies within this pain context enable the displacement of hostility as, for example, in the enlisting of the aid of a physician to help control the pain symptoms and then unwittingly undermining the authority of the physician by a worsening of symptoms. Rendering the physican ineffective reveals a passive aggressive displacement in which hostility is used to minimize those who are enlisted for help. Correspondingly, the patient is able to retain power in the face of the helplessness presented by the pain syndrome. A further result of this passive aggressive displacement of hostility is the frustration that family members feel as they seek to help and comfort patients with this disorder. Of course, the continuing pain of the patient which is likely to worsen when the frustration of others surfaces then is likely to induce guilt in those who are close to the patient.

The passive aggressive character traits frequently observed in somatoform pain disorder as well as in other somatoform disorders can be presumed to reflect the underlying aggressive feelings that must find expression in safe, unthreatening behavior. The appearance of traits such as manipulativeness in such patients also reflects highly disguised hostile if not competitive strivings.

Two final subcategories that are used to classify somatoform disorders not meeting requirements of any of the main diagnostic entities complete this section of the nomenclature. A diagnostic category included in *DSM-III-R* as the undifferentiated somatoform disorder is discussed in the next section, to be followed by the diagnostic category labeled the somatoform disorder not otherwise specified.

Undifferentiated Somatoform Disorder

In *DSM-III-R* the undifferentiated somatoform disorder has nominally replaced *DSM-III*'s atypical somatoform disorder, but the *DSM-III-R* category remains utilized for the same type of disturbance as the *DSM-III* category. The diagnosis of undifferentiated somatoform disorder is applied when fewer physical symptoms are complained of than is required for a diagnosis of somatization disorder. In addition, the long-term preoccupation with the physical aspects of impairment characterizing somatization disorder diagnostically distinguishes it from the undifferentiated somatization disorder. In the undifferentiated somatoform disorder the individual's concern about physical illness does not necessarily appear before the age of 30, nor is it required to persist for many years, as in the somatization disorder. Thus, symptoms qualifying for inclusion in undifferentiated somatoform disorder are relatively limited in scope in terms of its differential diagnosis from the somatoform disorder. However, the various symptomatic complaints that are physically oriented endure for a minimum of six months and are not associated with any other somatoform disorder, sexual dysfunction, mood, anxiety, sleep, or psychotic disorder. As in the somatization disorder, medical assessment techniques reveal either no physical basis to warrant the complaints, or, when medical findings are present, the resulting complaints and social and vocational disruption is not at all in proportion to the physical findings established.

Somatoform Disorder Not Otherwise Specified

This classification is used simply for somatoform disturbances in which the criteria for the various diagnoses comprising the general category cannot be established. Such use may be necessitated when symptoms are not sufficient in number to permit a more precise somatoform diagnosis, for example, or when symptoms last less than the six-month criterion needed for some of the somatoform diagnoses.

In some instances of hysterical symptomatology the various pains, hypochondriacal preoccupations, somatized disorders, and conversion symptoms are amalgamated in an individual in such a way that no diagnostic entity among the somatoform disorders is sufficiently inclusive. In such a case, when an organic basis for the bodily problems cannot be established so that a psychological etiology is hypothesized, the residual categories supplied in the *DSM* nosology must be employed. In a disturbance involving a number of physical symptoms reflecting psychological etiology and lasting six months or longer, undifferentiated somatoform disorder is designated. For complaints involving hypochondriacal symptoms appearing for less than six months, somatoform disorder not otherwise specified can be utilized. Thus, either of these residual categories can serve for individuals involved with psychological conflict in which impulses cannot be managed adequately and primary and secondary gains are promoted by hysterical processes. Even in an unusual amalgamation of symptoms, the physical incapacities fostered by the complaints symbolically reveal the patient's underlying psychological inadequacy.

It should be noted that residual categories such as undifferentiated somatoform disorder and somatoform disorder not otherwise specified are necessary in descriptive empirically based nosologies such as that of *DSM-III* and *DSM-III-R* because a description of the disturbance will not always perfectly coincide with pure diagnostic entities. Such residual categories become less necessary in nosologies that are theoretically based because the principles of symptom formation can be categorized in terms of the qualities of a particular diagnostic domain even though specific manifestations of behavior are not always predictable. Thus, the *DSM* nosology contains more variants of the hysterical syndrome than are probably necessary. In the following section this profusion of hysterically based diagnostic entities is further elaborated in the dissociative disorders or hysterical neuroses, dissociative type, also listed in tables 8.1 and 8.2

DISSOCIATIVE DISORDERS OR HYSTERICAL NEUROSES, DISSOCIATIVE TYPE

In the previous section in which somatoform disorders were considered, it was apparent that a split between psychological functioning and bodily functioning was created by a characteristic psychological process employed to displace conflict and diminish anxiety associated with hysterical neuroses. The personality trait proclivities, defense mechanisms, and anxiety associated with psychological conflict in these diagnostic entities—and comprising the essence of underlying psychopathology—include various aspects of ego functioning in the personality. Bodily experience is also encompassed as an important ego function within an individual's overall psychological functioning. Therefore, the conversion of anxiety emanating from psychological conflict into bodily symptomatology, preoccupation, pain, and distortion in the conversion hysterias actually reflects the phenomenon of a division in the ego in which one important aspect is cut off from another. Ultimately, the condition of bodily distortions and physical pains that reflect and symbolize conflict—so that anxiety is diminished and bound in a bodily experience—occurs unconsciously, outside of the individual's awareness.

Consistent with the hysterical paradigm of a split in ego functioning, the second major grouping of the hysterical neuroses—those considered to be the various dissociative disorders—also revolves around the process of splitting of ego functions in the form of dissociative activity. These dissociative types of hysterical neuroses can often manifest symptomatology that is quite striking and even comparable in dramatic quality to the conversion types. Impairments of memory, inaccessibility of personal identity, and phenomena of multiple personalities as well as depersonalization experiences, form the symptomatology of the dissociative disorders. Overall, the various dissociative disorders all involve a symptomatic condition in which crucial aspects of the self are eliminated from consciousness through dissociation. Thus, in this group of disorders, important elements of the self, or important psychological functions, such as significant areas of memory or personal identity, are segregated and brought out of awareness by dissociation. One of the most dramatic forms of dissociative neurosis is the multiple personality disorder which will be presented first.

Multiple Personality Disorder

General familiarity with multiple personality disorder has developed through the popularization of writings such as Clecky's case study *The Three Faces of Eve* and Robert Louis Stevenson's fictional *Dr. Jekyll and Mr. Hyde.* In these works, dissociation of substantial, complicated, and relatively autonomous components of personality have given "split personality" some appeal as a term to summarize the striking division that is created between different and often opposing elements of personality. Since reality contact remains relatively intact in this disorder, even though the primary personality is unaware of any other personalities that periodically assume dominance, a psychotic state such as schizophrenia is ruled out. Thus, the schizophrenic condition in which the person's reality testing is tenuous or even fragmented so that the schizophrenic is split off from reality differs fundamentally from the hysterical neurosis of multiple personality disorder.

In multiple personality disorder dissociation enables the creation and simultaneous existence of more than one personality, each, no less, with considerable complexity as well as distinct identity. Among the multiple personalities existing in an individual with this disorder, a primary or basic personality predominates which provides a measure of day-to-day continuity for the person. This basic personality has no real awareness of any other existing personality units or subpersonalities. However, the other personality units that periodically surface may become dominant at different times. At these different times each personality subunit maintains its own distinctiveness and often possesses an awareness of all of the other personalities including the major or everyday one. The rather perverse purpose presumably served by the coexistence of multiple personalities dissociated and therefore distinct from each other is to maintain a semblance of completeness and integrity by retaining all aspects of functioning albeit in a highly protected, compartmentalized form. Such protective compartmentalization persists because pressure apparently exists in the development of the multiple personality to prevent the expression of various important aspects of personality. These different aspects of personality presumably are prevented from becoming integrated with each other because of the sense of danger their appearance evokes. It is assumed theoretically that a compromise is effected through the use of dissociation by which these central trends or aspects of personality can effectively be disavowed through dissociation for periods of time. Yet, since each personality strand continues to exist, retaining its complexity and distinctiveness, each of these aspects of personality can also retain the power to emerge into consciousness, express its individual inclination, and even consciously dominate the person during apparently safe but limited periods of time.

The repeated surfacing in awareness of parts of the personality that have been dissociated from consciousness and that thereby have not been integrated into overall personality functioning represents the partial failure of repression; that is, the ego has attempted, in effect, to exile certain personality components by expelling them from consciousness but their repetitious appearance also reflects the compromise represented in all neurotic symptomatology: unacceptable personality tendencies are partially eliminated from awareness, temporarily reducing or displacing the anxiety associated with them. Yet, these unacceptable tendencies continue to maintain an influence over functioning by their disguised but intrusive appearance in the person's behavior. In the multiple personality syndrome such disavowed aspects of the personality influence functioning by their periodic domination of the person. A process can be theoretically proposed for the existence and appearance of such multiple personalities by which mechanisms and patterns of defense structure are organized and function. In the following section these considerations of defensive utilization in the manifestation of the profusion of personalities in the multiple personality type will be considered.

Defensive Structure

In the genesis of the multiple personality type, a pattern of parental severity, authoritarianism, or rigidity which is assumed to have existed does not allow for the acceptance and integration of the various needs, attitudes, and impulses that emerge in the growing individual. As a result, repression as the major defensive maneuver becomes overextended and compromised. The repression is fortified by the additional defensive mobilization of compartmentalization. With the utilization of compartmentalization and its dissociative process, those needs, attitudes, emotions, and personality trait proclivities that could potentially create impasses and conflict that threaten the integrity of the ego are contained but not permanently blocked. Through the operation of dissociation, a more temporary but large scale blocking is thus accomplished.

Within the protective compartmentalization, the strength of the various unacceptable personality proclivities can become organized with remarkable depth and complexity and further acted out through the various subpersonalities that have developed. Because such unacceptable personality proclivities can be regarded as inimical to the well-being and security of the individual, dissociation is enforced to keep these aspects of personality segregated from one another and generally from consciousness as well. Thus, processes of repression, compartmentalization, and dissociation secure a sort of sanctuary for aspects of personality that could evoke a punitive parental reaction. The psychological cost of this gain in security is that the prohibited and threatening personality components do not participate in personality integration and there is a consequent loss of resourcefulness and maturational potential. Each dissociated proclivity and the personality features that embed it can never develop to become sufficient or complete enough to function fully autonomously or to influence personality functioning harmoniously. Each of the personalities that become dissociated remain compartmentalized to a degree, although the most thoroughgoing compartmentalization effects the primary personality which lacks awareness of any of the others.

Since it is apparent that there is a striving for expression by each of the important personality trends that are denied continuous influence in personality functioning, pressure is continually exerted against the dominant personality. This pressure by subsidiary personality components toward expression can also operate to redistribute and realign the dissociative force that maintains one personality as primary. Periodically, therefore, one of the dissociated personality components can overpower the dominant personality. At such a point, a necessary and relatively well-formed subpersonality emerges into consciousness. This subpersonality immediately becomes central in the functioning of the individual for a period of time that is limited but sufficient to enable securing of the idiosyncratic satisfactions centrally relevant to the needs encompassed by that particular personality unit. All of the personalities that emerge tend to have clearly identifiable qualities and frequently a classic triad of personalities can be delineated in the organization of any number of multiples when more than two exist.

The Classic Personality Triad

The major personality by which the person is generally known—and the one in which any conscious awareness of the presence of various subpersonalities is absent—typically manifests characteristics designed for more or less normal living. Since survival and security are major motivating factors of this dominant personality, its prominent trait cluster usually consists of an easy-goingness, a compliant style, dependent needs, and a largely cooperative nature. This profile of the primary personality is markedly different from the hidden personalities that necessarily emerge periodically to complete the individual, so to speak.

Interestingly enough, at face value, this personality in the dominant position could actually be considered as weak, nonassertive, or nonintrusive. Nevertheless, such a configuration can be the dominant part of the entire multiple personality matrix. It can be proposed that such a dominant part of the multiple personality generally forms around traits that have maximum survival value for that particular individual within the context of its environmental conditions.

Apparently, in the development of multiple personality, where the possibilities of punitive parental reactions are salient, a compliant, cooperative character would seem to contribute most to security and survival. In such cases however, both aggressive and sexual impulse components of personality are incompatible with the compliant, proper emphasis of the primary personality. Derivative characteristics of aggressive and sexual impulses are therefore intensively disavowed in the primary personality only to gain expression in other dissociated personality units. Hence, two other central tendencies emerge to form the classic multiple personality triad. One subpersonality embodies the critical, aggressive, and hostile predilections of the person and as a diagnostic syndrome can sometimes even reflect a paranoid pattern. The influence of dissociation and compartmentalization can keep this paranoid aspect of personality from becoming integrated with other personality traits, permitting narrow critical qualities to dominate its functioning. Just as the primary personality is rather skewed in a compliant dependent direction, the paranoid-like disposition in this subpersonality also reflects distortion as a result of the narrow range of its tendencies.

The third part of the typical multiple personality triad concerns impulses of sexuality. In this part, when it gains separate existence, a personality unit emerges that is seductive or even crassly sexual. In such a histrionic personality, characterology is formed that permits the person to be coy, gregarious, and socially intrusive. The overall coquettish quality can be quite intense and is as distant from the primary personality as is the paranoid-like component of this triad. Thus, it can be seen that a socially desirable but rather childlike dominant personality is designed with hostile and sexual impulses screened out and contained within a highly compartmentalized boundary. One of the unique features of the secondary, tertiary, and other personality components that form in the development of the multiple personality disorder is the continuing powerful and usually successful striving of the dissociated and unintegrated personalities to express themselves. Because of the nature of dissociation, which maintains separations, the various subpersonalities periodically do assume the dominant position and express themselves in terms of the individuality of the personality sector each embodies.

Empirical evidence indicates that the defense structure in the multiple personality disorder can create endless personality variants—each of which constitutes a consistent stamp of personality composed of traits, emotional styles, cognitive orientations, and other consistencies of the personality that are coherently integrated. For example, additional subpersonalities may cohere around traits reflecting artistic or creative talents with spontaneity and abstract expression as behaviorally dominant features. The integrations that occur within each personality unit are made possible by the compartmentalization of consistent qualities of functioning within each of the personality units that include, for example, traits, interests, and defenses. The operation of dissociation with respect to the divergent trends forming the core of the various subpersonalities—a separation that was presumably essential for emotional and psychological survival during various developmental stages—necessitates a fragmented overall character structure of the multiple personality type.

The adult with multiple personality is thus not completely discernible within this fragmentation and perhaps can only be more fully crystallized by an integration of the separated components that comprise this unusual personality type. These basic components that must be integrated include at least the need for social acceptance, the acknowledgement of sexuality, and the expression of anger and self-assertion.

The suppression of the central personality—a severe suppression of consciousness—along with efforts to develop a new identity is seen in the diagnosis of psychogenic fugue to be discussed in the following section.

Psychogenic Fugue

A general clinical consensus considers the basis for psychogenic fugue to be a dissociation that incorporates motoric activity with selective memory impairments. The motoric behavior physically carries the individual to a new location while the person's long-term stable identity is erased by a memory dissociation that occurs simultaneously with the travel. An experience of disorientation and confusion is likely to accompany these dramatic transformations that are connected with the operation of dissociation along with the creation of a new identity either in partial or complete terms. This last criterion of the presence of a new identity is a recent diagnostic criterion imposed by the *DSM-III/III-R* nomenclature.

One variant of psychogenic fugue involves the adoption of personality traits that are strikingly different from the premorbid stable and characteristic personality of the individual. Further complexities may be added to this new identity or personality, such as a new name, fictitious occupational history, and so forth. While psychogenic fugue always involves some construction of a new identity, the substitute identity is usually only partially composed. The general course of this disorder involves a purposeful quality demonstrated by the relocation and continuing functioning of the individual. It is this implicit purposefulness as well as the relocation phenomenon that differentiates psychogenic fugue from the more prominent confusion occurring in the otherwise similar disorder known as psychogenic amnesia.

Stressors that evoke substantial tension that the individual cannot regulate presumably stimulate the fugue episode. The function of the person's changed location or identity—an attempt to distance oneself from rejection, personal quarrels, or disaster—seems apparent. A goal of distancing oneself from any circumstance that may evoke anxiety is, of course, typical of the hysterias and is generally accomplished through alterations in body functioning or alterations of gross psychological functioning, such as memory loss.

Defense Structure

The dissociation manifested by memory loss, sudden appearance in a new location, and the adoption of a new identity, suggests the major role that the defense mechanism of repression plays in avoiding awareness of internal conflict. The fundamental psychological conflict together with the introduction of external stressors precipitate the fugue state. The accompanying anxiety generated by the intensification of internal conflict caused by a new stressor creates a circumstance in which the person's sense of adequacy and ability to cope is threatened. The underlying internal psychological conflict theoretically involves the fear of exhibiting assertive or sexual impulses as legitimate aspect of the person's autonomous identity. Because of the individual's feelings of vulnerability or inadequacy—which become more noticeable under the pressure of heightened emotions—it becomes necessary for the person to invoke additional protective mechanisms which in fugue amnesia result in the use of dissociative and regressive mechanisms. Through the institution of dissociation, a cluster of memories associated with the person's core identity are lost. Instead, motoric regressive trends are enlisted that reinforce the incapacity established by dissociation and its consequence, memory loss. In addition, the defense of denial is employed in the form of fabrication of a fictitious identity which is taken seriously by the subject for the time span of the fugue.

The mechanism leading to loss of memory concerning significant identifying data without the addition of a motoric component of travel characterizes the dissociative state constituting psychogenic amnesia. This disorder will be considered in the next section.

Psychogenic Amnesia

The diagnosis of psychogenic amnesia is characterized by an episode in which memory impairment occurs rather precipitously. The component of memory loss reflecting disorder usually involves personal identifying facts. The scope of such memory deficit is beyond any type of customary forgetfulness and organic or neurological dysfunction are not present. During the period of amnesia, confusion and loss of orientation are seen, and the amnesia usually passes as suddenly as it occured.

When the person's memory gaps are eventually filled in, the dissociative element of psychogenic amnesia can often be linked to a particular stress occurring in the individual's life. For example, the precipitating stressor may be a physical condition that threatens the person, thereby generating great tension. This tension becomes temporarily eliminated by the amnesia effected by dissociation. The stressor may also involve an activity that generates overwhelming anxiety because of the influence of conscience, as in sexual behavior that evokes intense, distressing feelings of guilt. In some cases experiencing an impulse itself—such as a sexual yearning that strongly registers—may be sufficiently unacceptable or threatening to precipitate psychogenic amnesia. As these examples suggest, if loss of recall were not instituted, considerable anxiety and/or guilt would be generated by circumstances and impulses in the individual's functioning. The individual suffering from psychogenic amnesia can neither tolerate this anxiety nor moderate it through less disruptive defensive maneuvers. In psychogenic amnesia, therefore, a memory block is erected that temporarily mitigates both the anxiety as well as the inability to manage the stressor. The insulation provided by this hysterical dissociative process allows the individual to gain time, which potentially affords some advantage in ultimately facing the conflict. A secondary gain is obviously accomplished by forgetting about the disturbing circumstance, which enables the individual to avoid facing the situation directly, and, at the same time, perhaps gain the attention, if not the sympathy, of others.

Variations of Memory Impairment

There are several kinds of memory impairment in psychogenic amnesia. These are described in the following listing.

1. *Localized or Circumscribed Amnesia:* This most common type of psychogenic amnesia involves memory loss regarding the circumstances involving a traumatic experience, such as loss of awareness of the facts of a serious accident until a few days pass, after which awareness returns.

2. *Selective Amnesia:* In this selective kind of amnesia, dissociation of memory affects only some of the details involved in traumatic circumstance, while other details are recalled.

3. *Generalized Amnesia:* In this rare type of psychogenic amnesia, there is a loss of memory for factors involved in an individual's life span.

4. *Continuous Amnesia:* This rare form of memory loss involves the span of time that follows a specific event or time and continues into the present.

Defenses

As can readily be seen from the central role of memory impairment in the diagnosis of psychogenic amnesia, the defense mechanism of repression is basic to the management of conflict in persons prone to this disorder, as it is in all hysterical disturbances. The mechanism of denial also serves to screen out information and attitudes that ordinarily offer clues to one's identity. The presence of confusion and disorientation perhaps also attests to the incompleteness of repression and the subsidiary work of denial that is necessary. The need for such repressive and denial defenses emanates from the person's anxiety whenever such anxiety is mobilized by potentially dangerous and threatening feelings. When circumstances arise that appear to require more independent and capable functioning than the individual typically is confident about, including the possibility of more mature management of assertive or sexual feelings, dissociation is then employed to create memory impairments. These memory losses are then utilized to promote distance from the provocative situation, securing a safer position through the manifestations of helplessness.

In the dissociation that triggers loss of memory, the affected individual experiences confusion and disorientation. An experience of disorientation associated with an alteration in the sense of self is also a salient feature in the depersonalization disorder considered next.

Depersonalization Disorder
(or Depersonalization Neurosis)

The state of depersonalization may occur as part of a variety of diagnostic disturbances. It is only when depersonalization exists as a central disturbance in its own right, interfering with interpersonal relating as well as vocational needs, that the hysterical type of disturbance known as depersonalization disorder is established.

Consistent with the general concepts applying to hysterical disorders that have been discussed throughout this chapter, a sense of inadequacy with regard to mature capabilities in managing impulses and emotions promotes a variety of dissociative and anesthetic experiences in the depersonalization disorder. At the experiential level the central phenomenon that characterizes this depersonalization disorder is either a person's intense sense of detachment from the self, as if viewing himself from outside, or feeling as if in a dream. The loss or diminished clarity about identity may be accompanied by a sense of alienation or a feeling that one is in a dream or trancelike state. Thus, the individual may feel unreal, mechanical, or unusually distant even from himself—standing apart from the self as it were. When these kinds of depersonalization experiences lead to substantial discomfort or distress because of their severity and continuation, a diagnostic state of depersonalization disorder can be considered, provided that the depersonalization is not a symptom of another disorder, such as schizophrenia. As in all neurotic phenomena, these feelings of unreality and a consciously experienced loss of self are ego alien, while reality testing, in the larger sense, remains intact.

At times, the transformation of experience caused by the depersonalization phenomenon also affects the way in which the environment is perceived. During the depersonalization episode, the individual's appreciation of his external surroundings suffers from a dislocation of the customary sense of reality. This unusual quality of perception is generally referred to in clinical terms as the sense of derealization.

Dynamics of Depersonalization

The variety and range of clinical phenomena constituting the depersonalization syndrome is a reflection of the difficulty the individual has in coping with mature, realistic requirements. As noted earlier, in the individual prone to hysterical reactions, a long-standing effort to maintain repression of threatening feelings and impulses makes it necessary to avoid and deny troublesome challenges that may require emotional involvement. In such individuals, when the demands of circumstances or of emotional expression become too great to be managed by the typical defense mechanisms of repression and denial, a characterological dissociative mechanism is mobilized insuring avoidance of the threatening situation and largely absorbing the person's energy. In this dissociative state, the various losses, feelings of unreality, occasional dizziness, and feelings of bodily change, all apparently unite effectively to remove the person from the circumstance of challenge. Since the transformation that changes the individual's sense of reality is not consciously dictated, a subjective sense of strangeness—often with intense anxiety including fears about becoming crazy—accompanies this depersonalized state. In the normal course of development, particularly in periods that are typically stressful, such as adolescent and preadolescent years, phenomena of depersonalization may first occur and then quickly fade in almost a natural way in response to circumstances that are temporarily overwhelming to the person. Such overwhelming circumstances are problematic in that they can be viewed as demanding more than the person is prepared confidently and adequately to manage. It is only in later years—when these periods during which overwhelming anxiety bypasses defenses of repression and denial to invoke the depersonalized condition—is it thought that the depersonalization neurosis becomes established.

Theoretically, periodic episodes of depersonalization occur in individuals who are unable to manage the emotions that are necessary in mature functioning. This deficiency of integrating emotion typically occurs during phases of increasing external pressure. This aspect of the depersonalization disturbance can impair the social and vocational roles that the individual is expected to fulfill. Consequently, the intensity and sustained quality of depersonalization becomes an interference in managing customary expectations. These impairments in the management of life's vicissitudes are a reflection of the depersonalization disorder, and any intense and sustained depersonalization that contributes to severe distress makes the diagnosis of depersonalization disorder a distinct possibility.

As in most of the hysterical neuroses, a person with the depersonalization disorder is likely to be someone who is unable to develop more than a dependent posture in his basic adjustment. The expectation for normal assertive functioning and sexual expression in an appropriate interpersonal context presumably evokes such substantial anxiety that the customary defenses of repression and denial are overwhelmed; a specific dissociative process then is set in motion to eliminate the anxiety and nullify the circumstances evoking the expectation of mature, independent behavior. The individual then becomes lost in the depersonalization that takes place and gains the advantage of escaping from the situation that is sensed as too threatening to be directly faced.

At times, when the extent of depersonalization is not thoroughgoing, but there are unusual experiences involving dissociations and derealization, a diagnosis of dissociative disorder not otherwise specified may be appropriate and is discussed in the following section.

Dissociative Disorder Not Otherwise Specified

As seen in tables 8.1 and 8.2, the final category for dissociative disorders of *DSM-III* is that of an atypical dissociative disorder which was renamed dissociative disorder not otherwise specified in *DSM-III-R*. This diagnostic consideration is employed for a variety of reactions based on dissociative processes which do not meet the full proportions of the various diagnoses in the specific dissociation based categories. Thus, this diagnostic classification is treated in the *DSM* nosology as a residual category.

This residual dissociative category includes clinical symptomatology of a dissociative nature such as states in which the experience of trance is central, and periods in which derealization is strongly felt while the depersonalization experience is relatively minimized or absent. In addition, states are included in this residual category in which dissociation occurs in reaction to pressures not normally encountered in life, such as in excessive persuasion or thought control.

In this chapter, the wide range of manifestations encompassed by hysterical processes has been considered. Bodily experiences and divisions in cognitive functioning represent the range of clinical phenomena of the hysterical neuroses. In the somatoform disorders—such as the conversion and pain disorders—bodily processes are enlisted to symbolize psychological conflict as a result of the inability to manage adequately the emotional demands of adult expression. All of the bodily processes that are utilized in somatoform disorders to displace, deny, and avoid, psychological conflict affect the body in ways inconsistent with the physiological basis for bodily functioning. It is this discrepancy from the known mechanisms of physiological functioning along with typical secondary gains that characterize the somatoform disturbances. The secondary gains involved in somatoform disorders consist of eliciting sympathy as well as finding authority figures to rely on for guidance. In addition, another important secondary gain of the somatoform disorders involves avoiding circumstances that are appropriately faced autonomously. These secondary gains reflect the essentially dependent nature of the individual and the substantive sense of inadequacy that make adult functioning intensely threatening. That the disorder allows avoidance of engaging aggressive and sexual functioning in a direct, mature, and appropriate manner exemplifies the primary gain that is accomplished. Passive aggressive tendencies such as inability to meet obligations, doctor shopping, and manipulating feelings of guilt in others frequently accompany these disorders.

The hysterical disorders encompassed by the dissociative diagnostic categories involve special emphasis on distortions in cognitive functioning such as memory, identity, and marked divisions in personality components. Individuals with dissociative reactions generally experience a sense of threat and vulnerability in connection with facing circumstances which must be handled independently. The overwhelming sense of threat ascribed to such circumstances elicits any number of dissociative processes, each of which can then become the basis of the particular diagnostic manifestation encompassed within the range of dissociative disorders. For example, memory failure regarding pertinent personal material constitutes psychogenic amnesia; physical travel away from one's usual location, with memory loss regarding past information and, possibly, the fabrication of new personal information constitutes psychogenic fugue; the inability to integrate sexual and aggressive components of personality successfully into overall personality functioning while dissociating separate identities that compete for control reflects multiple personality; finally, the experience of depersonalization and accompanying distress in response to the pressure of independent and adult functioning is the basis of depersonalization neurosis. Thus, it can be seen from this recapitulation of the commonalities involved in such psychological phenomena that a basic process of psychopathology characterizes this entire group of hysterical disturbances.

The presumed essential process in hysterical functioning is the sense of threat and danger engendered by circumstances that arouse the emotions of sexual and aggressive responses that must be incorporated into adult functioning. The individual's sense of threat regarding these emotions, and independent functioning in general, requires bodily conversion processes and cognitive dissociations to fortify the repression and denial that are no longer sufficient to enable the management of tension.

In the hysterical disorders the chief defense syndrome led by repression and denial needs to be reinforced in order to maintain the integrity of the individual and a working relationship with reality. When the essential relationship and interpretation of reality are not sustained because defenses and character structure are too fragmented, primary process material can become manifest and a psychotic disturbance will in all likelihood be indicated.

In *DSM-III* and *DSM-III-R*, the various psychotic disturbances are considered within several separate categories. In the following section, these psychotic diagnoses will be presented with respect to the schizophrenic and paranoid psychotic disorders as well as with reference to psychoses involving mood disturbances.

CAPSULE CLINICAL PROFILES OF SOMATOFORM DISORDERS

In the somatoform disorders, bodily processes are enlisted to symbolize psychological conflict. Either no physical bases for these disorders can be found, or, if physical findings are established, symptoms exceed the degree of disorder warranted by physical contributions. Secondary gains are particularly prominent in somatoform disorders, justifying a position of dependency and allowing subtle control and manipulation of people and circumstances. Primary gains involve the avoidance of sexual and aggressive expression according to appropriate and mature adult demands.

Body Dysmorphic Disorder (or Dysmorphophobia): A presumed physical imperfection is focused on by the person. A body delusion does not occur but the imperfection is nevertheless imagined or slight and greatly exaggerated. The sense of physical imperfection is considered a displacement of a sense of personal inadequacy. It is thought that perhaps the inadequacy feelings relate to the inability to feel confident or capable in expressing the sexual and assertive feelings appropriate for independent functioning.

Conversion Disorder (or Hysterical Neurosis, Conversion Type): A dramatic physical change appears that can include symptoms such as tunnel vision, glove anesthesia, or paralysis of limbs. No neurological disorder explains the appearance of these symptoms. The symptoms often seem precipitated by important events in the person's life and seem to generate secondary gain. The person may show indifference to the symptom, an indifference which can be a diagnostic indicator. The trait of suggestibility is seen. Repression of sexual and assertive urges, denial, and reaction formation assure the screening out of criticisms and permit friendliness and sociability to exist.

Hypochondriasis (or Hypochondriacal Neurosis): The person is overconcerned with bodily sensations and dramatizes or exaggerates the potential harm of these sensations, as in the appearance of a stomach ache that generates ruminations regarding stomach cancer. Phantom symptoms appear that can not be related to medical findings. The person's life tends to revolve around a catalogue of fears of physical disease. Passive aggressive traits and needs for control are dynamically intertwined with secondary gains. The person's somatic preoccupations become a function of the difficulty experienced with the demands of adult responsibilities. The person is never delusional, but special attention is sought in a childlike way, and its attainment is an important secondary gain.

Somatization Disorder: Actual physical impairments and disturbances occur but are psychologically based in spite of the usually long medical history that accrues. Examples of typical symptoms include swallowing problems, fainting, muscle weakness, inability to experience pleasure, and difficulties of cardiopulmonary functioning. Symptoms may be similar to neurological ones, but do not include panic attacks. A presumed goal appears to be the manipulation of others through weakness with a dependent need to rely on others for decision making and caretaking.

Somatoform Pain Disorder: Pain obtains for a minimum of six months and exceeds the intensity appropriate for any actual physical impairment that may be established. Specific pain experiences are generally emphasized rather than a wide range of complaints. No organic basis exists for the persistence and intensity of the pain. The etiology of the pain can relate to actual events that provide a rationale for the pain, such as lifting an object and then setting off a process of backache or pain. The pain symptomatology offers secondary gain by allowing control of others, especially authority figures. A key dynamic is the fear of direct emotional expression which is subverted to the passive aggressive stance taken by the subject. The manipulation process that the psychogenic pain can justify can reflect hostile and competitive motives.

Undifferentiated Somatoform Disorder: Fewer physical complaints are required for this diagnosis in comparison with other somatoform disorders. Complaints are not necessarily chronic nor do they need to begin before the age of thirty. Symptoms last at least six months and are not associated with psychosis or anxiety.

Somatoform Disorder Not Otherwise Specified: Symptoms last less than six months and the array of symptoms is too narrow for a more precise diagnosis. This diagnostic category also includes hypochondriacal symptoms appearing for less than six months.

CAPSULE CLINICAL PROFILES OF DISSOCIATIVE DISORDERS

The dissociative disorders involve a splitting of ego functions. Processes of compartmentalization and dissociative activity enable crucial aspects of the self to be segregated and disavowed as well as periodically expelled from consciousness.

Multiple Personality Disorder: This disorder is nonpsychotic since generally adequate reality contact is retained. Segregated subpersonalities develop that are aware of the major personality while the dominant one is unaware of the others. Each personality has a distinct identity and remains dissociated or separated from the rest. In this way, all aspects of functioning are maintained in a compartmentalized form—sexual in one personality, aggressive in another, creative in another, and so forth, while the dominant personality tends toward compliance and deference. While repression acts as the basic defense, so that the dominant personality is unaware of the others, compartmentalization and processes of dissociation separate the parts of the personality split off from the dominant one. It is thought that the subject's authoritarian and perhaps even abusive family history threatened important components of personality expression thereby prohibiting integration of various impulses of the personality. Dissociation secures safety at the cost of lost resources and maturational integration. The classic triad of the multiple personality is a dominant central personality based on dependency and compliance, a second aggressive, critical, and paranoid-like personality, and a third, sexual personality.

Psychogenic Fugue: In this disorder there is a suppression of the central personality which becomes dissociated and therefore inaccessible to the person. Motoric activity actually carries the person to a new location and the person's conscious identity is eradicated by the dissociation of memory. Disorientation and confusion are likely to be experienced. New identifying features are adopted, sometimes with relative completeness but more often in partial terms. The person's new identifying features are usually strikingly different than the usual characteristic personality. A new name and even fictional history may be created. Psychogenic fugue can be related to some tension in an important relationship. The person's usual reliance on the mechanism of repression becomes insufficient to manage the intensification of conflict and stress so that dissociative and additional defensive maneuvers are employed. Other defenses include regression that facilitates the motoric aspect of the disorder and denial that permits the acceptance of new identifying features with greater ease.

Psychogenic Amnesia: A loss of memory in the absence of any disturbance of motoric functioning characterizes this disorder. The dissociation that affects memory removes access to personal identifying facts. Confusion and loss of orientation can accompany this dissociative process. Onset is typically sudden as is the disappearance of the amnesia. Psychogenic amnesia is usually related to the appearance of an identifiable stressor. It is thought that sometimes the stressor is related to sexuality and a guilt-prone conscience. The memory block neutralizes both anxiety and the fear of the stressor. There are several different memory impairments, including *localized amnesia,* where the amnesia temporarily serves to avoid the pain of some recent trauma and the memory returns soon thereafter; *selective amnesia,* where some details are still remembered; *generalized amnesia,* where one's entire life is forgotten; and *continuous amnesia,* where amnesia occurs only from the time of the stressful event into the present. Repression and denial are intensively relied upon to manage conflict in persons prone to psychogenic amnesia.

Depersonalization Disorder (or Depersonalization Neurosis): Central to this disorder is a disorientation associated with an alteration in the sense of self as in the experience of detachment from self, or as if in a dreamlike state. The experience is ego alien and reality testing remains intact. The disorder is not, therefore, a schizophrenic one even though derealization experiences occur and self-identity is temporarily blurred. Dissociation shores up the defenses of repression and denial; by means of depersonalization, the dissociative process temporarily removes the person from the demands of life. Persons experiencing depersonalization neurosis frequently feel crazy and frightened regarding their own symptoms. Depersonalization symptoms can be experienced periodically during adolescence, but the diagnosis of depersonalization disorder is established by its disruptive presence in later years. Strong dependent features are present that can lead to difficulty in integrating all of the elements of mature emotional functioning.

Dissociation Disorder Not Otherwise Specified: This diagnosis is employed when dissociative reactions are of insufficient proportions to meet overall criteria for specific dissociation-based categories. Also included in this residual category are such dissociative disturbances as those in which trance experiences occur, or where feelings of derealization appear in the absence of an actual depersonalization event.

PART IV
Psychosis

CHAPTER 9
Psychotic Disorders

Reactions involving severe inconsistencies with reality as reflected by major impairments in such psychological functions as behavior, thinking, perception, affect or communicative expression signal the possibility of a psychotic disorder. Disorganization, confusion, and grossly impaired adaptation further support the likelihood of such a disorder, since psychoses consist of primitive, idiosyncratic, and egocentric functioning based on a fundamental break in contact with reality. Psychotic processes may involve disorders primarily of mood, as in the most severe affective disturbances, or disorders primarily of thinking, as in schizophrenia and the paranoid psychoses, or some combination in which both mood and thought reflect severe impairment. In chapter 6, psychotic disturbances that predominantly involved depression, elation, and the alternation or combination of these affective psychoses were discussed. This chapter presents the processes related to the various schizophrenic reactions, paranoid psychoses, and other psychoses that are classified in *DSM-III-R*. In addition, some traditional categories of schizophrenia useful to clinicians but omitted from current *DSM* nosology will be reviewed. The next section will consider psychotic phenomena broadly and schizophrenic features more specifically.

SCHIZOPHRENIA

In the active periods of psychoses, patients show distinct discontinuities in their ability to appreciate, interpret, and test reality. The unique characteristics of such a breakdown in reality testing have made the psychoses in general and the schizophrenic disorders in particular outstanding and unmistakable representations of psychopathology. This dramatic distinction that particularly characterizes schizophrenia, that of reflecting a break with reality, has given this disorder a unique position in the history of psychopathology. The added facts alone, that the active phase of many of the schizophrenic disorders can be markedly flamboyant along with the occasional but obvious presence of voices that are heard by the subject, focus on schizophrenia as the major manifestation of psychopathology to be identified and distinguished from nonpathological behavior. For these reasons the term "madness" has generally been synonymous with the psychopathology now identified as schizophrenia throughout the periods of history during which the diagnosis of psychopathology has been permitted. This point concerning the history of the diagnosis and interpretation of madness is made because certain trends such as those associated with religious influences have periodically preempted scientific methodology and confronted psychopathology on separate terms.

Approaches to Understanding Schizophrenia

In recent years, researchers, theoreticians and clinicians in a variety of fields have devoted considerable effort to understanding the nature of schizophrenia. These fields of investigation include biochemical research, genetics, psychopharmacology, neurology, as well as psychology. Yet, the basic mechanisms that underlie the schizophrenic disorders remain elusive. Nevertheless, the impressive contributions from the total range of research suggest the influence of a multiplicity of variables. The fact that schizophrenia tends to affect a fixed percentage of the population regardless of the cultural context implies an organic contribution. The preponderance of the disorder found in poorer economic strata and in family contexts reflecting disintegrating processes suggests psychological contributions to the etiology of schizophrenia, as well as the possibility of social factors in its distribution. Another approach to the etiology of schizophrenia suggests a pathologically prone constitution that environmental forces can play upon to induce manifestations of psychopathology.

A more subtle issue in diagnosing the various types of schizophrenic reactions concerns the question of whether a unitary phenomenon of schizophrenia is involved in all the types comprising the schizophrenic diagnosis or if a group of discrete disorders represents a more accurate description of the psychopathological processes that appear. Historically, a unitary conception of schizophrenia was implied when Emil Kraepelin introduced the notion of a major distinction in psychotic pathology between manic-depressive psychosis and dementia praecox, the earlier term for schizophrenia. By this division all thought disorders reaching psychotic proportions with poor prognosis and early onset were grouped together despite variations of subtype. Indeed, distinct subtypes were then added within the general schizophrenia classification, raising the question of whether all of the types reflected common pathology or could be better understood as separate syndromes. While little was known about schizophrenia outside of its symptom manifestations and course, it was convenient to maintain a unitary view of the disorder. However, more sophisticated research tended to emphasize the value of separating various forms of schizophrenia. As an example of the earlier unified point of view, Eugen Bleuler arrived at four major pathological manifestations designed to characterize all forms of schizophrenia. These four pathological indicators, or pathognomic signs, included disturbances in association, affect, autism, and ambivalence. In Bleuler's "four A's," a unitary conception is not only assumed but also given a diagnostic basis.

In more recent psychological research schizophrenic reactions have been divided in bifurcated diagnostic terms such as the process-reactive dimension and the poor-good premorbid theoretical distinction. Each of these theoretical dimensions reflects variations in severity of premorbid functioning, suddenness of symptom onset, and prognosis. Essentially, these theoretical conceptions place schizophrenia on a continuum. Clinicians and researchers then investigate variables associated with the extremes of the continuum. This method of investigation, involving an examination of extreme reactions, differentiates the more insidious schizophrenias characterized by withdrawal and gradualness of onset from the schizophrenias with more sudden, flagrant, and obvious symptomatology. The distinction between process and reactive, as well as between poor and good premorbid schizophrenia achieves a diagnostic separation corresponding to more severe, persistent forms of the disorder versus manifestations of schizophrenia that are more likely to develop periods of remission. The difference in onset characteristics, symptomatology, and prognosis have been correlated with a variety of perceptual, learning, social, and other variables, a difference which suggests the operation of distinctly different underlying pathologies.

Schizophrenia and the Current Nomenclature

In more traditional terms, reflected as recently as *DSM-II,* the schizophrenic disorders have consisted of subgroups designated simple, hebephrenic, catatonic, paranoid, chronic undifferentiated, and schizoaffective schizophrenia. This array of types demonstrates the difficulty in determining whether a unitary schizophrenic process underlies all the forms or whether more or less distinct psychopathological entities are involved, each with individual etiological processes as well as presumably distinct treatment requirements.

DSM-III initiated modification of the traditional categorization of schizophrenia by including under the classification of schizophrenic disorders the disorganized type, which overlaps pathology formerly represented by the hebephrenic type, the catatonic type, the paranoid type, and the undifferentiated type. A residual disorder is also included for those affected by symptoms after a severe episode of psychopathology subsides. These modifications in categorization were maintained in *DSM-III-R.* In addition, in both *DSM-III* and *DSM-III-R,* the schizoaffective type of schizophrenia is removed from the schizophrenia category and considered in a residual category of psychoses. In the same effort at reorganization, a schizophreniform disorder is proposed, also removed from the schizophrenia category, to encompass schizophrenic symptoms that lack the duration over time necessary in the revised nomenclature to achieve a diagnosis of schizophrenia.

Further, in *DSM-III,* a separate grouping of the relatively infrequently occuring paranoid disorders at the psychotic level is encompassed as a distinct category of psychoses. These diagnoses include paranoia, shared paranoid disorder, acute paranoid disorder, and atypical paranoid disorder. This group of disorders reflects the presence of a central delusional process without the appearance of schizophrenic findings. Continued modifications in the categorization of these paranoid disorders appear in *DSM-III-R.* In this *DSM* revision, the general category of paranoid disorder is given the primary label of delusional disorder with the reference to paranoid disorder as an alternate designation; the revised grouping encompasses the following types: erotomanic, grandiose, jealous, persecutory, somatic, and last, a residual type.

A final grouping of psychosis in *DSM-III* includes schizophreniform disorder, brief reactive psychosis, and schizoaffective disorder, as well as atypical psychosis. This final grouping is only slightly revised in *DSM-III-R*. In *DSM-III* and *DSM-III-R*, manic depressive psychosis and psychotic depression—two diagnostic categories with considerable historic tradition and both appearing in *DSM-II*—are classified among the affective disorders.

Table 9.1 presents the organization of the schizophrenic disorders appearing in *DSM-III* and *DSM-III-R* along with a parallel listing of the schizophrenic disorders considered within DSM-II. As table 9.1 indicates, *DSM-II* grouped several types of schizophrenia comprising different temporal durations such as acute schizophrenic episode, the chronic undifferentiated type, and the latent type in which extraordinary symptoms never surfaced. In

TABLE 9.1. Schizophrenic Disorders Classified in *DSM* Nosology

DSM-III	*DSM-III-R*
Disorganized type	Catatonic type
Catatonic type	Disorganized type
Paranoid type	Paranoid type
Undifferentiated type	Undifferentiated type
Residual type	Residual type

Course of Disorder
Subchronic
Chronic
Subchronic with acute exacerbation
Chronic with acute exacerbation
In remission

DSM-II
Simple type
Hebephrenic type
Catatonic type
Paranoid type
Acute schizophrenic episode
Latent (incipient type)
Residual type
Schizoaffective type
Childhood type
Chronic undifferentiated type
Other (unspecified) types

contrast, *DSM-III* introduces, and *DSM-III-R* continues, a means by which the temporal course of the schizophrenic process can itself be classified as part of the disorder. This five-part classification of *DSM-III/III-R* consists of subchronic, in which symptoms first begin to appear, with some continuing for more than six months and up to two years; chronic, when these symptoms last longer than two years; subchronic with acute exacerbation, essentially a resurgence of symptomatology in a person with the subchronic course of schizophrenia whose symptoms have become residual; chronic with acute exacerbation, a reappearance of symptomatology in a person with chronic schizophrenia whose symptoms have become residual; and remission. The classification of remission refers to a diagnostic state in which a person known to have had previous schizophrenic symptomatology currently shows no symptoms of the disorder. The classification by *DSM-III* and *DSM-III-R* of the time framework within which schizophrenic symptoms occur enables the various aspects of acute and chronic schizophrenic processes to be built into the diagnosis of each form of the schizophrenic manifestation.

Psychopathology of Schizophrenia

As a major psychopathological entity, schizophrenia in all its variants always involves disturbances among a number of dimensions. The choice of which dimensions to emphasize makes the difference in the diagnostic conceptualization of schizophrenia that is proposed by any theory of psychopathology and its related diagnostic system. Various considerations of schizophrenia have emphasized such qualities as the loss of abstract abilities, the resemblance to primitive, archaic, or childlike functioning, the sense of alienation from human experience and the interpersonal framework, and the loss of consistency in necessary reality testing. The presence of delusions, hallucinations, or withdrawal has also constituted major defining characteristics of schizophrenia in the conceptualizations of many researchers. Evaluation of disturbance in distinct areas of psychological functioning, such as Bluehler's diagnostic conception of schizophrenia, presents an understanding of schizophrenia in which hallucinations and delusions are of secondary diagnostic importance, while the significance of disordered thinking, emotions, and interpersonal contact is elevated to defining significance.

The approach represented by *DSM-III* and *DSM-III-R* to the diagnosis of schizophrenia emphasizes three specific factors or criteria. First, symptomatology includes delusions or hallucinations or impairments in affect, logical integrity, or behavioral reactions. The second major factor required by *DSM-III-R* for the diagnosis of schizophrenia is a time period of at least six months during which impairments reflecting schizophrenia are present. These impairments must include active psychotic symptoms consistent with schizophrenia—those indicated in the first of the three essential factors—for at least a week. The time period up to six months that is required for the *DSM-III-R* diagnosis of schizophrenia can be composed of the active symptoms—delusions, hallucinations, affect disturbance, distortions of logic, or aberrant behavioral reactions—which must persist for at least a week in addition to symptoms associated with the less severe prodromal and/or residual phases to reflect a minimum of six months in which schizophrenic symptoms have surfaced. The prodromal and residual symptoms will be described in the next section of this chapter along with the symptoms defining the active phase.

The third essential factor required to establish the diagnosis of schizophrenia is the presence of a process of deterioration. With respect to this criterion involving deterioration, a previously attained degree of functioning is compromised in the various spheres that involve personal functioning, such as vocational, social, and personal areas. Along with this deterioration, impairment in any number of psychological dimensions, such as thinking, emotion, perceptual ability, identity, relationship to reality, the use of volition, motoric, and even postural qualities can be present. The disturbances in these psychological arenas will be pointed out as they are relevant to the particular diagnostic types of schizophrenia that will be considered. Further, the diagnosis of the schizophrenic subtypes of simple schizophrenia, pseudoneurotic schizophrenia and latent schizophrenia, will also be considered, largely on the basis of their general usage by clinicians, although they do not specifically appear in the latest versions of *DSM* nosology.

The Schizophrenia Symptom Criteria as Defined by DSM-III

The outline of the particular symptom manifestations of the schizophrenic syndrome that will apply to the paranoid type, the catatonic type, the disorganized type, and the undifferentiated type is presented in table 9.2. These disturbances are represented by symptom elements of the *DSM-III* criteria for the diagnosis of schizophrenia. The concept of symptom element is referred to because *DSM-III*, and *DSM-III-R* as well, utilize three elements as criteria for the diagnosis of schizophrenia: symptoms, deterioration, and time duration of pathognomic features.

The psychological symptomatology listed in table 9.2 reflects the symptom framework for diagnosis appearing in *DSM-III* in which specific sorts of impairments are delineated and presented in some detail. The approach to this symptom element of the diagnosis of schizophrenia in *DSM-III-R* is somewhat modified in that this symptom element of diagnosis is condensed; consequently, most of the content details of symptomatology are eliminated. For example, although persecutory, grandiose, religious, and nihilistic content areas of delusions are considered among the symptom criteria for diagnosis of schizophrenia in *DSM-III*, such content details are minimized in the discussion of schizophrenia symptoms in *DSM-III-R*. While this treatment of the arrangement of diagnostic elements by *DSM-III-R* contributes to parsimony and perhaps efficiency, it substantially diminishes emphasis on qualitative characteristics of schizophrenic functioning. These qualitative features, such as religiosity, grandiosity, and persecution, are, however, important in the pathology of schizophrenia and, further, are invaluable in developing clinical and diagnostic refinement. Such diagnostic refinement allows greater appreciation of

TABLE 9.2. *DSM-III* Symptom Criteria for the Presence of
Schizophrenia

- Delusions characterized as bizarre or absurd
- Delusions with specific content, such as grandiosity, religiosity, nihilism, or bodily distortions; an absence of persecutory content
- Delusions with content of jealousy and persecutory themes along with any sort of hallucinations
- Hallucinations in auditory form with a superego texture noting the subject's behavior; occasional auditory hallucinations involving two-person dialogue
- Hallucinations of the auditory type intermittently experienced, but apparently not evoked by either depressive or expansive events
- Disturbed thought processes, including incoherence, associative and logical disturbances, and either flat or inappropriate affect, or any other floridly fragmented or confused behavior

the relevant pathological processes of schizophrenia. Therefore, the symptoms defined in *DSM-III* will also be included even though the specifics of these definitions have been dropped in the revised nomenclature. However, the modified symptom criteria of *DSM-III-R* will be referred to throughout the discussion and then presented comprehensively.

Inspection of table 9.2 shows that in *DSM-III*—and this continues in *DSM-III-R*—delusions and hallucinations constitute a central diagnostic indicator of schizophrenia. Delusions, one of the most obvious symptoms of psychosis, are fixed, false beliefs that are subscribed to with such perseverance that they become central preoccupations. The clear unrealistic nature of a delusion directly reflects the subject's loss of contact with reality. Hallucinations, on the other hand, are sensory experiences rather than thoughts. Hallucinations may involve visions, sensations on the skin, or voices that are heard, but in every case there is no external objective basis for the sensation. In schizophrenia, as in all of the psychoses, symptoms involving hallucinations are usually of the auditory type in which voices are heard without any external source, so that these auditory hallucinations are generated from within. As is true of delusions, auditory hallucinations are almost invariably obvious indicators of a break with reality.

Of the delusions found in schizophrenia and described in table 9.2, three specific categories can be abstracted. The first consists of delusions that may be considered incomprehensible, incoherent, or fragmented. These are referred to in *DSM-III* as bizarre or absurd, such as the subject's belief that special external forces are manipulating him or his thoughts. The second type of delusion would not be considered absurd insofar as the delusion is more coherent within the context of its basis in fantasy. Such delusions contain religious themes, grandiosity, ideas involving phenomena of death, or references to bodily distortions. However, the important point to note is the sharp distinction made between these first two categories and others, restricting these categories to delusions that do not contain persecutory themes. The issue of persecutory delusions or the collatoral theme of jealousy is assigned its own category, so that this third category of delusions would usually be correlated to the presence of hallucinations. In this third category of persecutory delusions with hallucinations, the hallucinations are not restricted to any given theme.

When the hallucinations take on a more specific and consistent character, the symptom would generally consist of an auditory hallucination, perhaps characterized by superego influence in which the voice heard tends to negatively evaluate or assess, or at least notice without benign implications, the subject's behavior. In less frequent instances, this type of superego based auditory hallucination could represent more than one voice so that the subject is actually listening to a conversation or at least an auditory exchange by at least two voices.

The remaining auditory hallucination category of *DSM-III* includes data from the subject reflecting intermittent hallucinations not resulting from any sudden event of depression, surprise, or expansive condition. Finally, a diagnostic profile qualifying as a schizophrenic syndrome includes verbal content that is generally incoherent, confused, illogical, showing associative disturbance or affect disturbance in the form of flat or inappropriate affect, or behavior that can be considered fragmented or bizarre.

DSM-III-R Symptom Criteria for the Diagnosis of Schizophrenia

The diagnostic framework comprising symptom manifestations utilized by *DSM-III-R* to arrive at a diagnosis of schizophrenia is somewhat different from *DSM-III*. Symptoms reflecting the active phase of schizophrenia are always necessary for the *DSM-III-R* diagnosis. In contrast, symptoms reflecting the prodromal phase (the phase preceeding the crystallization of the schizophrenic syndrome) and/or the residual phase (the phase that includes the reconstitution of the ego as the schizophrenic syndrome subsides) may be necessary to establish the diagnosis, depending on the length of time the active phase persists. The use of two groups of symptoms—those reflecting the active phase and symptoms associated with the prodromal and/or residual phase—is required for a diagnosis of schizophrenia, because active symptoms must be present for one week or more, but symptomatic signs of schizophrenia must be present for a period of time amounting to six months. Thus, to the extent that symptoms characteristic of the active phase of schizophrenia are not continuously sustained for six months, symptoms reflecting the prodromal and/or residual phases must appear over sufficient time to make up the difference. Through this combination of symptom groups, the six-month time criterion dur-

ing which symptoms must necessarily appear in order to establish
the *DSM-III-R* diagnosis can be met even with active symptoms
enduring only a week.

Symptoms of the Active Phase of Schizophrenia

The establishment of symptoms reflecting the active phase of
schizophrenia in *DSM-III-R* requires a finding of any one of three
categories of psychotic symptoms that appear for a week or more.
The first of these three categories of psychotic symptoms for diagnosing the schizophrenic condition involves the presence of bizarre delusions that are not consistent with the cultural patterns
of the subject. Such delusions reflect a fixed but false belief, and
reveal disordered thought, impaired capacity to rely on logic, and
confusion regarding reality. The possible range of contents of the
delusions is not presented in *DSM-III-R*—since the existence of
the delusion has taken precedence over its thematic content—but
would presumably remain consistent with the delusional content
outlined in table 9.2 derived from *DSM-III*. The delusional themes
that appear, then, are likely to center on preoccupations of persecution, grandiosity, religious themes, bodily inadequacies, or
nihilistic ideation, such as the subject's distorted conviction regarding his own or someone else's death or imminent demise.

The second of the three symptom possibilities that signal the
active phase of schizophrenia in terms of *DSM-III-R* criteria consists of distinct and more than brief auditory hallucinations. The
hallucinated voices may have the superego qualities of persecution
or foreboding, or they may simply be either a commentary, or an
interchange involving more than one voice. However, reference to
elation or depression is not to be involved in the hallucination, an
exemption that preserves the time-honored distinction between
psychoses involving thought and mood disturbances.

The third and last possibility of symptoms reflecting the active
phase of schizophrenia as defined by *DSM-III-R* consists of any
two of a number of symptoms that singly or in combination appear for at least one week. These symptoms include verbalizations
that reflect loose associations or incomprehensibility; behavior
consistent with a catatonic reaction, such as stupor, mutism, lack
of spontaneity, immobility, posturing, or excited but purposeless
motoric behavior; blunted affect or affect that is inappropriate to

the subject's context or the content of his verbalizations; delusions; and hallucinations. The occurrence of both delusions and hallucinations—in this third possibility of symptoms of active schizophrenia in which two are needed to establish the diagnosis—allows for their combined consideration either with each other or with another symptom in this last category. Thus, taken together, delusions and hallucinations may surface in some kind of combination with each other or with another symptom from this group for a week, thereby meeting the time requirement for active schizophrenia. When these delusions and hallucinations are considered separately however, as required in the first two symptom picture possibilities, the criterion of the appearance of symptoms for a minimum of one week for the diagnosis of schizophrenia may not be achieved. For example, each criterion—delusion or hallucination—may itself be sustained for less than a week. Table 9.3 summarizes the pathognomic symptom indicators of schizophrenia that define the active phase in *DSM-III-R*.

As can be seen from the distillation of the *DSM-III-R* psychotic symptom indicators for the active phase of schizophrenia in table 9.3, a complex array of impairments and distortions involving associations, affect, sensation (in the auditory sphere), and thinking, can reflect the existence of an active schizophrenic process. The guidelines offered by *DSM-III-R* provide definite rules for speci-

TABLE 9.3. Pathognomic Symptoms of the Active Phase of
Schizophrenia According to *DSM-III-R*

Either:
  Bizarre delusions present for at least one week—(first category in text)

Or:
  Distinct hallucinations present for at least one week—(second category in text)

Or:
  Any two of the following present for at least one week in combination—(third category in text):
    Loose or incomprehensible associations
    Flat or substantially inappropriate affect
    Catatonic reactions
    Delusions
    Hallucinations

fying the presence of the necessary indicator for this pathognomic symptom component—one of three necessary elements for the diagnosis of schizophrenia. The additional two elements relate to deterioration of functioning and the overall six month time period during which disordered functioning occurs.

Since signs of schizophrenia must be present for at least six months, either symptoms associated with the active phase may appear for the six month period or, if they are present for fewer than six months, symptoms associated with the prodromal and/or residual phases are needed to complete the six month requirement for the diagnosis of schizophrenia to be made.

Prodromal and Residual Phases of Schizophrenia

As indicated earlier, the prodromal phase of schizophrenia may precede, and the residual phase may follow, an active period of the disorder. The symptoms necessary for the diagnosis of the prodromal and residual phases reflect various specific manifestations of the person's confusion, disoriented functioning, disordered thought, and tenuous reality contact. The two phases are similar. They differ in that the prodromal phase is a precursor to the active phase and reflects a process of deteriorating ego-integrity, while the residual phase involves a process of reconstitution of ego-integrity and reality orientation. In this process of ego reconstitution, the restoration, or compensation of deteriorated functioning caused by the active schizophrenic process is partially accomplished. The symptoms necessary to establish the presence of either the prodromal or residual phase of schizophrenia as specified by *DSM-III-R* include any two of the following disturbances: schizoid-like behavoir; inability to manage one's appropriate social role; unusual behavior such as compulsive collecting or hoarding; poor self-care; affect disturbance involving flatness or inappropriateness; tangential associations, circumstantiality, or impoverishment of speech; magical thinking that includes a sense of what could be called universality, characterized by an affinity for clairvoyance and other kinds of being-in-touch; bizarre sensory experiences involving such sensations as forces or illusions; and loss of energy. These indicators of prodromal and residual schizophrenia presumably reflect less profound disorder in comparison with the symptoms reflecting the active phase of schizophrenia. However, the cumulative seriousness of such prodromal or residual symptoms impair functioning sufficiently to contribute to the diagnosis of an active phase of schizophrenia. This active phase is enabled by the presence of such prodromal and/or residual symptoms for a six-month length of time in combination with signs of the active phase, as shown in table 9.3, that endure one week or more.

Additional DSM-III-R Criteria for Schizophrenia

In addition to the symptoms that form the pathognomic diagnostic criterion of schizophrenia, considerations of the disorder in both *DSM-III* and *DSM-III-R* contain several other points of diagnostic importance regarding the pathology and course of the disorder. Other than the first diagnostic criterion, that of pathognomic symptom indicators, two other diagnostic considerations obtain. These include the second diagnostic criterion, which is the factor of deterioration in some important aspect of the person's typical level of functioning. The third diagnostic criterion is a time factor in the schizophrenic profile by which indications of schizophrenia are sustained for some period of at least six months with symptoms associated with the active phase present for at least one week. In addition to the diagnostic symptom criteria of tables 9.2 and 9.3 which correspond to *DSM-III* and *DSM-III-R* respectively, the deterioration of the patient's behavior within the parameter of a six-month duration of symptoms completes the *DSM* diagnostic criteria for the presence of the schizophrenic syndrome.

The various diagnostic criteria that are specified and required for the determination of schizophrenia according to *DSM-III-R* can now be formulated in summary fashion and are presented in table 9.4. As table 9.4 shows, the presence of one or two major symptoms characterizing the active phase of schizophrenia is required for a minimum of a week. These major symptoms are at the level of hallucinations, delusions, incomprehensibility, disorganized behavior, or impaired affect. If one or two of these major symptoms, and therefore the active phase of schizophrenia, are not sustained for six months, then lesser symptoms associated with a prodromal and/or residual phase must appear for a length of time that in combination with symptoms of the active phase reflect schizophrenic impairment for a minimum of six months. These lesser symptoms include such manifestations as unusual behavior, bizarre sensations, idiosyncratic beliefs, and so forth. No matter how long these lesser symptoms persist, the pathognomic symptoms of the active phase must be present for at least one week. In addition to the necessary symptomatic manifestations required for the diagnosis of schizophrenia in the six-month time period, deterioration in vocational, social, and personal spheres needs to reflect a compromise or demonstrate a distinct contrast with the premorbid level of functioning.

With the criteria for schizophrenia satisfied, the types of the disorder can be distinguished as described in the following discussion.

Paranoid Type

In the paranoid type of schizophrenia, delusions of a systematic nature or the presence of repeating auditory hallucinations focus-

TABLE 9.4. Diagnostic Criteria for Schizophrenia in *DSM-III-R*

Pathognomic Symptoms
   Presence for at least one week of:
      Bizarre delusions
            or
      Distinct hallucinations
            or
      Any two of the following:
         delusions
         hallucinations
         incomprehensibility or loose associations
         catatonic reaction
         disturbed affect

Impaired Functioning
   Deterioration in management of vocational, interpersonal, and
      personal-care spheres

Time Framework or Temporal Persistence
   Pathognomic symptoms sustained at least one week
   Pathognomic symptoms alone, or together with prodromal and/or
      residual symptoms sustained at least six months

Features Absent
   Significant affective disturbance, unless brief

ing on a consistent idea that is by definition false must be present. These hallucinatory and delusional experiences can frequently be characterized as thematically persecutory, grandiose, or jealous in nature. In addition, combinations of these themes or even themes involving religion, body distortions, or highly distorted delusional preoccupations with death may be present. In the consideration of thematic possibilities, *DSM-III-R* allows for greater generality of themes than did *DSM-III* since the latest revision, *DSM-III-R*, does not specify the requirement for any predominant theme. In contrast, *DSM-III* required the centrality of persecutory, grandiose, or jealous delusions.

In the first or persecutory type of delusions, the subject feels threatened and attributes either insidious or more direct, harmful motives to the imagined or projected source of the threat. In the second type of delusion, the grandiose variety, the person is involved in a paroxysm of self-congratulation or of a world salvation fervor. With this sensation, great personal power is experienced and the subject may engage in behavior designed to implement these expansive and grandiose goals. Religious delusions involve the subject with grandiose beliefs such as becoming or being a savior, or of being connected to important religious figures—perhaps hearing their commands or being selected by them as a special representative.

The third category of the paranoid type of delusion is characterized by a central core of jealousy which gains an obsessional grip on the subject's inner life. Further sorts of delusions that may occur outside of the preceding categories include delusions regarding bodily distortions which can incorporate beliefs that organs are missing or vitally damaged or that major flaws exist in anatomical functioning. Such distortions can also lead to feelings of fear or terror. Themes about death that can constitute delusional thinking often concern the subject's belief that death on a personal or even world scale either has occurred, is taking place, or is about to happen.

In addition to the delusions or hallucinations that become a singular focus in the paranoid type of schizophrenia, the diagnostic criteria of *DSM-III-R* require ruling out several characteristics often typical of schizophrenia. The characteristics that must be absent in order to establish the paranoid type of schizophrenia include confused speech, associations that are distinctly loose, tangential, or illogical, affect that is blunted or inconsistent with the individual's verbalizations or circumstances, catatonic reactions, and highly disorganized functioning. When these sorts of symptoms are absent, then the ideational and systematic delusional and hallucinatory symptoms are clearly central; such systematic delusional and hallucinatory experience characterizes paranoid thinking generally, and therefore are emphasized in the diagnosis of the paranoid type of schizophrenic disorder specifically. Thus, the delusional content in paranoid schizophrenia is not vague or incomplete but instead forms a seemingly coherent, often interrelated network of ideas that manifest an obvious and clear inconsistency with reality as a whole. This inconsistency rests on a flawed basis or unrealistic premise, or is based, simply, on an absurd core belief. Beyond the misconceptions involved in the delusional system of the paranoid type of schizophrenia, however, some logical threads may appear that reflect the systematic quality of the delusional system.

Defense Characteristics of
Paranoid Schizophrenia

The structure of paranoid delusional experiences are related to the presence of intellectual defenses and intellectualized, ideational character traits that are mobilized in an effort to maintain control over forceful and threatening feelings that are disturbing to the person. This reliance on intellectual defenses that become infused into the systematic delusional symptomatology in overt paranoid schizophrenia is largely responsible for the highly ideational cast of the paranoid schizophrenic's verbal behavior. Because of the involvement of intellectual defenses and the consequent ideational style to which these defenses contribute, the paranoid type of schizophrenia lacks the incoherence, disorganization, and affective disturbances often seen in other types of schizophrenia. In addition, the investment in intellectual defenses which promotes an ideational style that can control emotion explains the similarity in behavior and in needs to control emotion between paranoid schizophrenia and the obsessional character structure. In fact, this obsessive characterological formation can often be found to exist prior to the surfacing of the paranoid schizophrenic process. The obsessive characterology can actually serve as a long-standing facade that distinguishes the individual's personality and functioning. This obsessional character structure then serves to control emotion through a focus on thought processes both before the psychotic break—while the paranoid trend is latent—and after the break is reconstituted, when the paranoid schizophrenic process is in a state of remission.

In the paranoid type of schizophrenia, while the structure of the delusional system is ideational and systematic, the content represents both the projection of emotions that are unacceptable to the individual as well as the expression in compensatory terms of unacceptable feelings. In both cases, since the feelings are unacceptable, the projection and compensation defenses allow the expression of derivatives of these unacceptable emotions in unrecognized form. In the operation of the defense of projection, aggressive and destructive feelings are projected onto external figures and circumstances creating the mechanism by which the paranoid schizophrenic feels persecuted. Since the aggression has been externalized, the source of danger is then experienced as surrounding the individual, necessitating vigilance, scrutiny, and caution. This projection of aggression, therefore, evokes the sensation of threat from the outside which is the basis for the guarded, suspicious disposition that characterizes the paranoid stance.

The defense mechanism of compensation relates to underlying but profound feelings of inadequacy and inferiority that fundamentally and yet unconsciously motivate a person with paranoid ideation. Such intense feelings of self-doubt are mitigated through the compensation defense which then elevates the person's self-image and thereby facilitates feelings of grandiosity. Together with these defenses of projection and compensation, intellectual defenses help organize the ideational representations of the projected and transformed emotions—that is, inferiority into grandiosity and aggression into persecution—into a somewhat systematic network of ideas. These ideas reach delusional proportions in the paranoid schizophrenic state and become sufficiently systematic so that the feelings of aggression and doubt are eliminated and the transformations can be believed by the patient. Religious preoccupations and identification with the divine also support this compensatory transformation of feelings of inadequacy into the special feelings associated with divine identification. Further, instituting a connective bond with a higher power permits enlisting superior forces of divine proportions, as it were, as an aid to controlling the powerful impulses which the schizophrenic is struggling to manage.

In instances of persecutory delusions, the fear engendered in experiencing such morbid ideas reveals the degree of destructive aggression in the person that the projective defense mechanism is mobilized to manage. In projecting such frightening aggression, externalization of the aggression perhaps also allows the person to experience a detoxification of inner impulses which can tend to reduce the subject's underlying fears of destructiveness and explosiveness. When there is a failure to diminish the powerful destructive emotions that are troublesome for the paranoid schizophrenic subject, delusions related to the theme of nihilism may also appear in which a belief that the world will be precipitously destroyed represents a projection of aggression.

The frequently reported theme of jealousy in delusions of the paranoid schizophrenic also ultimately relates to the overwhelming sense of inadequacy that is basic to paranoid functioning. This grave feeling of inadequacy creates a paramount insecurity for the person that is translated by projection into the persistent belief that others are willing to abandon even basic commitments to the subject. In essence, the delusional theme of jealousy also reveals the person's sense of unworthiness of any other person's loyalty. A critical reaction by the paranoid schizophrenic subject toward the imagined infidelity and disloyalty of the object of the delusion then justifies the subject's expression of hostility. This hostility, along with profound inadequacy, represents the central emotions that the paranoid individual is striving to control. The presence in paranoid schizophrenia of grandiosity, fantasies of destruction, and expectations of hostile persecution all reflect the personality trait of criticality that is central in paranoid functioning. This trait of criticality is utilized by the paranoid subject continually to create a separation of self and object, thereby insuring the constant presence of an interpersonal condition that can be controlled.

Catatonic Type

In the catatonic type of schizophrenia, two distinct dimensions predominate that relate to bizarre postural and behavioral phenomena as well as unusual and bizarre affect expression. The first of these distinct dimensions involves a general restriction of behavior. In this restricted state of functioning, a low-level form of this disorder appears as a catatonic negativism in which the subject becomes either oppositional or neutral or generally resistive to the wishes of others. This negative stance persists in a pronounced manner. It appears strikingly unusual because of the disregard that the catatonic person maintains toward efforts at communication by others.

A more intense reaction within this dimension of restriction of behavior involves catatonic rigidity. Such catatonic rigidity involves actual postural resistance. The most intense type of restrictive behavior is represented by mutism and catatonic stupor. In spite of the apparent indifference to circumstances and communications in the surroundings of such a person, it should be noted that when the patient is in a catatonic stupor he may nevertheless be astute and fully aware of all circumstances and details around him. In spite of his stuporous and indifferent appearance, the patient in this so-called stuporous state may, in an emergency, be the only one who can calmly and directly proceed to the exit.

In contrast with the first dimension of restriction, the second broad category of the catatonic type involves an expansive orientation. A low-intensity form of such expansive behavior would include catatonic posturing in which inappropriate, rigid posturing takes place that then changes from time to time. This posturing is not the same as the resistive posturing of the first category of catatonic negativism. Posturing during catatonic negativism centers on the assumption of a bizarre posture from which the patient can be moved; the rigid posturing of the expansive form of the catatonic disturbance does not respond to external efforts toward change. The more familiar expansive manifestation of this catatonic type is reflected in catatonic excitement in which the subject can become explosive and even physically destroy his surroundings.

The criteria specified in *DSM-III-R* for the diagnosis of the catatonic type of schizophrenia involve the presence of functioning in which any one of the major catatonic symptoms predominates: stupor or mutism; negativism signified by unwillingness to cooperate with directions to move or efforts to be moved; assumption of a rigid, unmovable posture; excited behavior that is without purpose and unrelated to circumstances; or posturing.

The unusual symptomatology of the catatonic type generally focuses clinicians and researchers on symptoms. Yet, from a psychodynamic point of view, the posturing phenomena of the catatonic person may reflect an intense need to contain energy so that the fear of a highly destructive interaction with others is allayed. Thus, the posturing or rigid position represents, in effect, an extreme form of negativism or oppositionalism as a means of managing destructive potential. The explosive behavior within the expansive phase of catatonia can be viewed as reflecting an accumulation of energy that has not developed any kind of external discharge or attachment and, consequently, needs to be released. This energy is then exploded in what has become known as catatonic excitement. During the severe oppositional phases, such a person can be locked into an uncomfortable physical position for hours or days at a time. The posture can even be painful but the catatonic person will be unable to implement any volitional effort to become more comfortable. The catatonic symptom picture is, perhaps, a curious yet fertile ground for more than simply perfunctory descriptive diagnosis.

Disorganized Type

In *DSM-III-R* the disorganized type of schizophrenia is distinguished by three basic signs. The first, a symptom of disturbance in logical functioning, is referred to as frequent incoherence. This incoherence can be seen in impaired associations and communication. When the focus of this insufficient logic shifts from communication to behavior, then the pathological manifestation is signified by highly disorganized motoric behavior. The second symptom involves impairment of affect, in which expression of affect is characterized as blunted, or inconsistent with circumstances. Such inconsistency of affect may involve a kind of silly quality; or, the affective inconsistency may be reflected, for example, by laughter in the context of tragic news, or weeping in response to a humorous story. Thus, a bizarre quality is apparent in the symptomatology of incoherence or emotional inappropriateness that characterizes the disorganized type of schizophrenia.

The third criterion necessary for the diagnosis of the disorganized type of schizophrenia is an absence of catatonic behavior. It is apparent that in the tradition of *DSM* nosology, this disorganized type bears some resemblance to the previously designated hebephrenic schizophrenia in former *DSM* models. The absence of systematized delusions is no longer a diagnostic criterion for this disorganized type of schizophrenia in *DSM-III-R* as it was in *DSM-III*. However, any finding of systematized delusions in a suspected case of disorganized schizophrenia would be contradictory because, were these delusions present, they would actually act as organizational and cementing phenomena.

Undifferentiated Type

In the undifferentiated type of schizophrenia, the symptom picture is not a clear one, and, although there may be delusions, hallucinations, or associative disturbances, these impairments may also be combined in idiosyncratic ways so that the syndrome is a mixed one in which the criteria for other types of schizophrenia are not met.

Residual Type

The residual type of schizophrenia is diagnosed according to the standards of *DSM-III-R* when at least one previous episode of schizophrenia existed along with the continuation of some isolated symptoms such as those described previously as reflecting the prodromal and/or residual phase of schizophrenia as opposed to its active phase. Some of these symptoms may include manifestations of confusion, disordered thought, tenuous reality contact, poor self-care, and affect disturbance.

The above compendium of paranoid, catatonic, disorganized, undifferentiated, and residual types completes the consideration of the forms of schizophrenia comprising the current *DSM-III/III-R* nosology. Some types of schizophrenia that have been eliminated from the current diagnostic nomenclature nevertheless are familiar clinical syndromes that clinicians have traditionally observed. These traditional classifications known as the simple type of schizophrenia, pseudoneurotic schizophrenia, and latent schizophrenia are described in the following section. They are included to preserve continuity with the recent history of diagnosis and to provide clinical diagnostic description of syndromes that although no longer codified, nevertheless constitute useful clinical information.

Simple Schizophrenia

This traditional diagnostic entity of the simple type of schizophrenia was retained in the *DSM* nomenclature as recently as *DSM-II* but was subsequently dropped from the current versions. The category of simple schizophrenia does not correspond with the *DSM-III* and *DSM-III-R* conception of schizophrenia since obvious, overt symptomatology reflecting an active phase of psychosis as defined by active psychotic symptoms is not directly expressed. Instead, this diagnosis of simple schizophrenia is characterized by a slow, gradual, insidious process of deterioration most dramatically manifested by social withdrawal in which the person is clearly increasingly involved in autistic processes. Since such a process of deterioration includes manifestations in which interest in self-care diminishes, emotional expressiveness and affect is flattened, energy is greatly diminished, and interest and initiative in external phenomena are markedly reduced, it is apparent that the presence of a schizophrenic process is likely—that is, a loss of contact with reality and confusion in connection with relating to reality is evident. Further, since schizophrenia seems to apply as a diagnosis in such a clinical syndrome of autistic withdrawal, hallucinations and/or delusional functioning probably exist although they are not verbally expressed. Such hallucinatory and/or delusional activity is probably also sustained over time but the person's withdrawal, isolation, and social disinterest easily inhibit clinical detection of these decisive pathognomic phenomena.

The impoverishment of thought, behavior, and verbal communication that results as part of the insidious process of decline in simple schizophrenia is also consistent with the effects of a schizophrenic process. The presence of flat affect, withdrawal, and loss of energy and interest found in those suffering from simple schizophrenia can also suggest a pronounced sense of chronic depression which would seem to contraindicate the diagnosis of schizophrenia according to *DSM-III* and *DSM-III-R* standards. However, in clinical and theoretical terms, this affective disturbance of a depletion of mood perhaps reveals a continuum that obtains between depression and schizophrenia in the psychotic sector of psychopathology. Since losses centering on capacities for reality testing and involvement in the human world are significant factors in every schizophrenic disorder, it is likely that the emotion of depression will at some level and in some form be a necessary component or consequence of such losses. This component of depression would become more pronounced in those psychotic disorders such as simple schizophrenia in which both social losses are greatest and interpersonal interaction is most affected by deterioration.

The traditional disorder of simple schizophrenia corresponds with the process and poor premorbid dimension of schizophrenia referred to in psychological research on schizophrenic functioning. The slow, gradual development of symptoms associated with each of these perspectives on schizophrenia is also consistent with the poor prognosis encompassed by these research dimensions and usually encountered in simple schizophrenia. This poor prognosis contrasts with the schizophrenic reactions signaled by sudden, acute, obvious symptomatology in which a prognosis of remission can often be expected. The more sudden and overt schizophrenic reactions also correspond to higher level premorbid functioning.

The gradual decline characterizing simple schizophrenia typically begins early in life with symptomatic withdrawal and disinterest apparent during adolescence. This process of schizophrenic withdrawal remains extremely tenacious and difficult to reverse since social interest is increasingly substituted for by an autistic focus as the disorder relentlessly proceeds.

The diagnosis of pseudoneurotic schizophrenia is also omitted from the DSM-III-R nomenclature but has been a useful diagnostic conception utilized by clinicians. It will be presented in the following section. Like that of simple schizophrenia, the diagnosis of pseudoneurotic schizophrenia is vivid and provides the clinician with a diagnostic tool with which to understand a particular syndrome from the host of symptoms presented.

Pseudoneurotic Schizophrenia

The traditional diagnosis of pseudoneurotic schizophrenia which is absent from the current nosology is noteworthy as a syndrome because of the paradoxical blend of neurotic symptomatology imposed upon a more incipient schizophrenic underlay. Usually in the schizophrenic processes, symptomatology is generated so that primary process material becomes more visible, as, for example, in the appearance of hallucinations. In addition, even in the absence of hallucinations, active psychotic material is usually visible in the form of delusions or emotional expression with obvious impairment, as in the appearance of flat or inappropriate affect. Other examples of symptoms generated by a schizophrenic process can be the appearance of pronounced language or cognitive impairments as in word salads, and tangential and paralogical thinking. More subtle expressions of schizophrenic symptomatology are such phenomena as pronounced ambivalence in daily living. However, in the pseudoneurotic schizophrenic reaction a process that is considered schizophrenic because of decisive manifestations of confusion apparently contains sufficient restitutional qualities so that the schizophrenia—which is neither entirely latent nor visible— produces a host of neurotic-like behavior. This neurotic behavior comprises more or less the entire range of neurotic manifestations. Because of the presence of so many neurotic symptoms, the person is frequently in a state of disarray, disorientation, and disorganization. The net effect of this condition of confusion is defined and corresponds best to what has become known as pananxiety.

Pananxiety simply stated is the condition in which there is no conflict-free sphere in the personality. Every aspect of functioning—vocational, academic, interpersonal, marital, and so forth—is infiltrated with, and contaminated by, what the person experiences as anxiety, tension, or worry. Yet despite such a comprehensive concern about every aspect of life and each specific condition of functioning, the person remains fully ambulatory and maintains considerable ability to continue functioning. In addition, there is a relative absence of any substantial, active, significant psychotic symptomatology, and the person's fantasy is relatively usually free of primary process rumination. Instead of psychotic symptomatology, the range of neurotic symptoms includes the host of anxiety reactions discussed in this volume, even occasionally the experience of panic attacks, phobias, obsessive compulsive manifestations, hysterical conversions, and psychophysiological reactions.

Variations on the theme of pseudoneurotic schizophrenic symptoms occasionally include withdrawal features, emotional rigidity or overreaction, depression, unusual fantasies, and even sadomasochistic components. The combination of obsessional and depressed features on the one hand with hypochondriacal and hysterical features on the other, coexisting as they do in a single personality, apparently reflects the disorganizing influence of primary process material and impaired ego strength that produces the chaotic pananxiety syndrome manifested. In certain idiosyncratic cases, micropsychotic episodes have been noted featuring a symptomatic triad: feelings of depersonalization or derealization, ideas of reference as in paranoid ideation, and hypochondriacal preoccupations.

As noted, this particular diagnostic entity of pseudoneurotic schizophrenia, although not included in the *DSM* nomenclature, has been useful to clinicians for some time. It is especially valuable, for instance, in the differential diagnostic endeavor of evaluating syndromes suggestive of schizoaffective psychosis or severe hysterical disorder; in determining whether to treat for schizophrenia or neurosis; and in encapsulating diagnostically the particular type of chaos manifested in a presenting disorder. The key component of this clinical condition is the emotional and psychological chaos or confusion, in the absence of obvious psychotic symptomatology, which encompasses the special symptom of pananxiety. When this pananxiety is definitively identified, the diagnosis of pseudoneurotic schizophrenia then clarifies that schozoaffective psychosis as well as severe hysterical personality both need to be ruled out. The diagnosis of pseudoneurotic schizophrenia also indicates that the clinical issue at hand is to monitor carefully the underlying incipient schizophrenic process by strengthening ego functioning. This ego strengthening is usually achieved by offering reassurance and structure that addresses the level of neurosis in order to more effectively harness, better focus, and tranquilize the subject's pananxiety.

A third type of schizophrenia not included in current *DSM* nomenclature is the latent schizophrenic syndrome, which will be considered next.

Latent Schizophrenia

The diagnosis of latent schizophrenia has been helpful in encapsulating the functioning of patients who have never had an overt psychotic break with reality but who nevertheless show signs suggesting the presence of a schizophrenic process. Such patients present a well-organized character structure which serves to contain an underlying schizophrenic process. An extensive investment in a character structure which is well integrated provides a relatively strong facade that tends to mask the psychotic potential that is present. The presence of a latent schizophrenic process—that is, one that has never directly revealed itself—can be indicated by functional deficiencies determined by careful clinical scrutiny. For example, the individual may be unusually slow or underachieving in relation to intellectual capabilities, without concrete findings of learning disability or overtly interfering anxiety consistent with a neurotic level of pathology. Similarly, vocational functioning may be unusually below the levels suggested by the individual's apparent capacities.

In clincial terms, careful interviewing of a person with latent schizophrenia may yield subtle but identifiable suggestions of tangential associations, unusual affect responses, and particularly, interpersonal relating that is distant and essentially uninvolving, if not actually inappropriate.

Since the diagnosis of latent schizophrenia essentially involves a personality disorder with only hints of more profoundly disturbed psychopathology beneath the surface, psychological testing is often required to confirm the diagnosis. Typically, a passive aggressive, dependent, or obsessional characterological personality style can be clearly determined, especially since such kinds of characterological control of emotion or investment in reinforcing a dependent position can be instrumental in assuring containment of underlying schizophrenia. Psychological testing would then reveal more concrete signs of schizophrenia than the clues alone that appear in interview and review of history. Such signs may include transparencies in projective graphic material, poor judgment in placement of otherwise well-organized figures and drawings, and noticeably poor form quality in responses to Rorschach ink blots. Stories constructed to Thematic Apperception Test stimuli may well be coherent and logical while reflecting both lack of interpersonal depth of relating and devisiveness.

The essence of the pathology involved in the diagnosis of latent schizophrenia is the need to manage exceedingly turbulent emotions that cannot be comfortably channeled. Therefore, to a considerable extent, character traits are utilized to keep inner agitation and primary process material at bay. This singular and long-term investment in emotional control prevents the full potential development of ego strength from being realized, and institutes a deficiency in functioning that is reflective of the underlying schizophrenia with which the individual is actually struggling.

The diagnosis and corresponding behavioral manifestations of latent schizophrenia are different from that of pseudoneurotic schizophrenia in two ways. First, in latent schizophrenia, under-achievement in vocational and other areas is typical, whereas in pseudoneurotic schizophrenia a standard of excellence can indeed be sustained in several areas. Second, in latent schizophrenia, the personality is not infected with pervasive anxiety, which, as pan-anxiety, is the pathognomic sign of pseudoneurotic schizophrenia. The minimal appearance of anxiety in latent schizophrenia is due to the extensive elaboration of a containing character structure in contrast to the underlying character in pseudoneurotic schizo-phrenia in which a complex and mixed character picture exists. Paradoxically, it is this pananxiety of the pseudoneurotic schizo-phrenic that insures uniformly high standards of functioning by continually fueling the person's motivation. In contrast, in latent schizophrenia a continual source that energizes achievement mo-tivation is absent, thereby creating conditions leading to variable functioning or even poor functioning as in underachievement.

The latent component in the diagnosis of latent schizophrenia refers to the absense of overtly obvious psychotic signs. However, under conditions of significant pressure, the integrity of the indi-vidual's character structure could be expected to fragment and the schizophrenic process would then become clearly manifest in a psychotic break.

This consideration of traditionally useful clinical diagnoses completes the discussion of schizophrenia, the most commonly oc-curing psychosis and its various types or groups of psychotic re-actions. The most frequently occurring form of schizophrenia is the paranoid type and the presence of paranoid thinking appears as well in a variety of diagnostic categories in addition to schiz-ophrenia, as for example in the paranoid personality disorder it-self. In the next section, another diagnostic representation of par-anoid symptomatology will be presented—the relatively rare psychosis known as the delusional or paranoid disorder.

DELUSIONAL (PARANOID) DISORDER

In the historical development of modern diagnostic nomenclatures culminating in *DSM-II*, paranoid schizophrenia was distinguished from several other disorders that contained components of paranoid ideation. These other disorders involving paranoid elements included the character disorder known as paranoid personality, the involutional paranoid state, and the psychotic condition simply labeled paranoia. The diagnosis of paranoia in *DSM-II* was based on a personality profile characterized by a complex paranoid system of thinking that was considered psychotic since delusional ideation was the central pathological feature. Although this psychotic condition of paranoia was chronic, its paranoid thought pathology did not interfere in any appreciable way with the remainder of the patient's disposition, functioning, and personality, except by constricting the conflict-free sphere of ego functioning. In DSM-II, these various psychotic paranoid conditions (involutional paranoid state and paranoia) were suggestively related to schizophrenia or paranoid personality—an example of diagnostic uncertainty.

In *DSM-III* and *DSM-III-R*, in spite of the deletion of the clinical diagnosis of involutional paranoid state, the observation that paranoid pathology could appear in a variety of diagnostic forms is clearly asserted. Not only is the paranoid personality disorder retained, but in the psychotic context, a firm separation is made between paranoid thinking in the context of schizophrenia and the paranoia that is connected to the narrow delusional or paranoid disorder. This diagnosis of psychotic delusional or paranoid disorder is one of four groupings of psychosis in the current *DSM* nomenclature. These four groupings of psychosis in *DSM-III* and *DSM-III-R* include those within the classification of the affective disorders, the schizophrenic disorder, the delusional or paranoid disorder, and finally, those few psychotic disorders not currently considered classifiable in any of the first three categories. In the following section, the psychotic disorder known in *DSM-III-R* as the delusional or paranoid disorder and its variant forms will be considered.

DIAGNOSTIC ORGANIZATION OF DELUSIONAL (PARANOID) DISORDER

In *DSM-III* and continuing in its revision, *DSM-III-R*, diagnostic history seems to have inexorably created a need to understand and analyze the psychopathology manifested in paranoia in greater detail. In addition to the previously described paranoid schizophrenia, as well as the diagnosis of paranoia offered in *DSM-II*, *DSM-III* and *DSM-III-R* offer several further differentiations within the psychotic paranoid diagnostic configuration. In *DSM-III* these further distinctions within the psychosis of paranoia include paranoid disorder as a major category utilizing the term paranoia itself, and several subcategories labeled shared paranoid disorder, acute paranoid disorder, and a residual category called atypical paranoid disorder. Table 9.5 lists these paranoid disorders as they appear in *DSM-III*.

This section of *DSM-III* nosology comprising delusional or paranoid disorders is an attempt to include psychotic diagnostic aspects of paranoid psychopathology not subsumed as an aspect of schizophrenia. The question of whether such a classification scheme is valuable, given the rarity of the diagnostic entities involved, however, is answered in the negative by the revision of this category in *DSM-III-R* in which one paranoid or delusional disorder has been defined with variant types differing only by the nature of the delusional theme that can be specified.

The revision of this section of the nomenclature as it appears in *DSM-III-R* reorganizes the psychosis of paranoid disorder quite substantially, including a change in the name of the general classification to delusional disorder. Perhaps these revisions reflect the continuing difficulty in adequately classifying the various manifestations of paranoid ideation that appear in various forms of psychopathology. The subtypes of the delusional or paranoid disorder specified by *DSM-III-R*, based on the content of the central delusion, are *erotomanic, grandiose, jealous, persecutory, somatic,* as well as a residual category designated *unspecified,* if no single

TABLE 9.5. Paranoid Psychosis in *DSM-III*

Paranoid Disorder

Delusions involving persecution or jealousy that last a week or more without distinct hallucinations, unusual behavior, or affective disturbance

- Paranoia: Symptoms as above lasting six months or more
- Shared paranoid disorder: Symptoms as above but based on identification with another person's paranoid delusion
- Acute paranoid disorder: Symptoms as above but lasting less than six months
- Atypical paranoid disorder: Residual category for the amalgam of traits and paranoid delusions that cannot be classified elsewhere

delusional idea is central. Table 9.6 indicates the specific variants comprising the delusional disorder in *DSM-III-R*. It is informative to note the major difference in the category types delineated in *DSM-III-R* in comparison with *DSM-III*. This difference reflects not only a significant reconceptualization of the psychotic paranoid pathology that is under consideration, but also suggests the traditional difficulty in characterizing this unusual and rare diagnostic sector.

The fact that several diagnostic entities comprising psychotic paranoid disorders in *DSM-III* were dropped from *DSM-III-R* and the displacement of another diagnostic entity—shared paranoid disorder into a different category entirely in *DSM-III-R* (psychotic disorders not elsewhere classified)—supports the long-standing uncertainty about the composition of these diagnoses. While the *DSM-III* categories have been considerably revised and reorganized, several new components of delusional or paranoid disorder have been demarcated in *DSM-III-R*. These new components will be considered next.

Diagnostic Criteria of Delusional Disorder

In *DSM-III-R*, the delusional or paranoid disorder is characterized by the presence of a delusional system containing ideas involving

TABLE 9.6. Delusional Psychosis in *DSM-III-R*

Delusional (Paranoid) Disorder

- Delusions that reflect fixed false beliefs are present but not bizarre
- Hallucinations usually are not present but, if present, are not distinctive
- Functioning outside the sphere of delusional ideation is not unusual in quality
- Affective, schizophrenic, and organic symptoms are not significant

Subtypes

- Erotomanic: delusion of a special person's love
- Grandiose: delusion of special power, knowledge, value, identity
- Jealous: delusion of infidelity of partner
- Persecutory: delusion of harmful treatment or plotting
- Somatic: delusion of physical impairment or illness
- Unspecified: multiple delusions or themes different from above

persecution, specialness, bodily disturbance, or jealousy. Yet, as might also be the case in a disorder of a characterological type, associations are generally intact, the person remains coherent rather than confused, and clinical symptomatology, such as delusions, do not contain the bizarre content, affect, or overall style of bizarre schizophrenic delusions. Consistent with the absence of such unusual symptomatology, hallucinations are either absent or only minimally acknowledged. Finally, this delusional disorder is not accompanied by any inappropriate emotion corresponding to delusions that are present.

Several different types of delusional disorder can be specified by characterizing the essential theme of the paranoid delusion comprising this psychotic disturbance.

There are five delusional types as well as a sixth category that acts as a repository for delusional content not corresponding to the basic five.

Erotomanic Type: This type of delusional content involves ideation in which another person, generally of a special status, is regarded as having amorous feelings for the subject.

Grandiose Type: In this type, false ideas are maintained regarding expanded powers, value, knowledge, or identity, any of which may become focused on a presumptive relationship with someone famous or even on a divine figure.

Jealous Type: A delusional fixation on the imagined infidelity of the subject's partner comprises the content of this type of delusion.

Persecutory Type: In this type, delusional importance is placed on the misconception that the subject—or someone close—is being unfairly and perniciously treated. Such a delusional system can lead to utilization of police and courts for redress of grievances, only to result in dismissals that are utilized to further the persecutory delusional system.

Somatic Type: In this type, a belief reaches delusional proportions that a physical impairment, disorder, or medical condition exists.

Unspecified Type: This category is reserved for delusions that are not encompassed by the types enumerated or for delusional disorders in which multiple themes appear with none assuming primacy.

In the next section, the remaining psychotic disorders included in *DSM-III* and *DSM-III-R* are discussed.

PSYCHOTIC DISORDERS NOT ELSEWHERE CLASSIFIED

This entire category represents a residual grouping containing five psychotic reactions that are presented in *DSM-III-R* as unrelated to one another. Thus, except for the presence of a variety of disparate psychotic symptoms, no common theoretical dimension unites the diagnostic entities included. Since manifestations of these psychotic syndromes are seen clinically, these diagnoses require inclusion in the nomenclature and are therefore inserted on an essentially clerical or residual basis. This residual basis is reflected in the label given the diagnostic grouping of these disparate psychoses: psychotic disorders not elsewhere classified. The same atheoretical grouping obtains in *DSM-III* with a difference mainly in the ordering sequence. However, this parallel residual category in *DSM-III-R* is expanded by the addition of one entry from a separate category in *DSM-III*—that of shared paranoid disorder. This diagnosis of shared paranoid disorder is included among the paranoid psychoses in *DSM-III* although in *DSM-III-R* the disorder appears as a disconnected residual classification relabeled induced psychotic disorder. The loss of clinical or theoretical coherence uniting the psychotic reactions included in this residual category brings focus to the use instead of the symptoms of psychoses as the unifying thread. These psychotic symptoms that alone are used to impose unity include delusions, hallucinations, catatonic behaviors, loosened associations, disorganization, or the sustained infiltration of affective impairment in a thought disorder. Symptoms in the disorders included in this residual category are never sufficient to establish a diagnosis of schizophrenia.

Table 9.7 presents a composite of the residual disorders as classified in *DSM-III* and *DSM-III-R*. The particular disorders will be discussed in the order in which they appear in *DSM-III-R*.

Brief Reactive Psychosis

In brief reactive psychosis, the disorder appears with a sudden on-set and recedes with a sudden return to typical nonpsychotic func-tioning. The duration of this acute but brief reactive psychosis ranges from a few hours to no more than a month. The pathological pro-cess involved in this disorder resembles that of reactive depression considered in previous traditional diagnostic formulations, such as that in *DSM-II*, especially in terms of precipitating causes. Just as in reactive depression, where a psychosocial stressor can directly engender an acute depressive reaction, so too, in the brief reactive psychosis, a psychosocial stressor can release psychotic symptom-atology. Therefore, the development of psychotic symptoms in di-rect relation to a stressful stimulus event is an important distin-guishing criterion for the diagnosis of brief reactive psychosis. The clinical profile of such reactive psychotic behavior involves dis-turbance of association, expressions of delusions or hallucinations, or catatonic or disorganized behavior along with emotional agi-tation, turbulence, or the presence of confusion. It should be noted that increased pathology preceding the psychotic episode is not consistent with this diagnosis. Instead, in order to diagnose brief reactive psychosis, no unusual or new psychopathology becomes apparent preceding the occurence of the psychological stress. Thus,

TABLE 9.7. Psychotic Disorders Not Elsewhere Classified

DSM-III

Schizophreniform disorder
Brief reactive psychosis
Schizoaffective disorder
Atypical psychosis

DSM-III-R

Brief reactive psychosis
Schizophreniform disorder
Schizoaffective disorder
Induced psychotic disorder
　(shared paranoid disorder)
Psychotic disorder not otherwise specified
　(atypical psychosis)

schizophrenic symptoms associated with the prodromal expression of schizophrenia do not appear in the clinical profile prior to the turbulence of brief reactive psychosis.

Simply because the disorder is brief, it should not be confused with inconsequential pathology. For example, cognitive processes may be quite disrupted, disorientation can be present, and there can be intense stirrings and out-of-control shifts of feelings. Age of onset is often during adolescence, and the disorder is expected to last in most cases for only a few days. A differential diagnosis must be made between this brief reactive psychosis and schizophreniform disorder which is considered next.

Schizophreniform Disorder

In the schizophreniform disorder, the subject exhibits much of the necessary behavior to be diagnosed as schizophrenic, including that of bizarre delusions, persecutory or grandiose feelings, hallucinations (primarily auditory), associative confusion, catatonic reactions, disordered affect, social isolation, and so forth. Table 9.3 presents the necessary pathognomic symptoms of schizophrenia comprehensively. The deterioration in functioning that is a criterion for schizophrenia is not a necessary part of the clinical profile of the schizophreniform disorder, although such impairment may occur. However, the issue of duration of this disturbance is a major criterion that gives the disorder its special character. In order to diagnose the schizophreniform disorder, the person should exhibit the schizophrenic profile based on the pathognomic symptoms in table 9.3, as well as the prodromal and residual symptoms indicated in table 9.4, for less than six months. In addition, *DSM-III-R* allows for specification of prognostic considerations in this schizophreniform disorder. Therefore, the diagnostic designation includes the specification of either "without good prognostic features" or "with good prognostic features." The latter designation is made and a good prognosis expected if two or more of the following positive prognostic indicators appear: major psychotic symptoms occur within four weeks of the first departure from premorbid functioning; confusion or disorientation develops during the psychotic period; affect does not become flattened or attenuated; and social and vocational adjustment have been adequate prior to psychosis. These indicators of good prognosis are consistent with research and clinical findings that a sudden symptomatically florid manifestation correlates with a greater likelihood of remission, while a slower, more gradual onset with insidious deterioration correlates more poorly with remission.

Schizoaffective Disorder

In this disorder, mixtures in the symptom picture of schizophrenic and affective psychotic disturbances are seen. For example, psychotic features consistent with schizophrenia characterize the subject's cognitive behavior, such as delusions, hallucinations, or loosened associations, together with a major depressive or manic reaction in the affective sphere.

Traditionally, the schizoaffective disorder essentially contains affective disorder qualities and schizophrenic qualities in almost equivalent proportions and was classified in *DSM-II* as one of the types of schizophrenia. It should be noted that in the schizoaffective disorder, the various symptoms of schizophrenia as well as affective disturbances create an idiosyncratic diagnostic entity that bridges affective psychotic disturbances in which cognitive fragmentation is relatively limited, with the schizophrenic disorders in which cognitive impairment is preeminent. It is the sustaining presence of major affective disturbance along with a typically pronounced delusional system that is the paradigmatic manifestation of the schizoaffective disorder. Generally, the delusional system that develops is not congruent with the mood disturbance; that is, the delusions are usually not related to manic or depressive affect. Instead, the disordered thought symptomatic of this diagnosis is more consistent with persecutory themes and other qualities reflecting paranoid ideation.

In *DSM-III-R* the balance between cognitive and affect disturbances in the schizoaffective disorder is weighted somewhat in favor of cognitive impairment: delusions or hallucinations must occur for a minimum of two weeks in the course of the disorder together with the profile comprising either major manic or depressive symptoms; the mood symptoms are not brief but they must recede for at least a two-week period, insuring the primacy of disordered thought; yet the presence of disordered thought is insufficient by itself to establish schizophrenia. If the mood disturbance previously or currently includes a period of elation, the bipolar type of schizoaffective disorder is specified; if, on the other hand, only depressive features have occurred, the depressive type is specified.

Induced Psychotic Disorder
(Shared Paranoid Disorder)

This diagnosis, classified in *DSM-III* as one of the paranoid psychotic disorders but reclassified in *DSM-III-R* among the theoretically unrelated residual disorders does indeed reflect paranoid ideation and pathology. In this disorder, the subject exhibits the general profile of the delusional or paranoid disorder; that is, persecutory delusions can be present, along with emotion that corresponds appropriately to the delusional content, with an absence of any bizarre quality, an absence of confusion, and probably little evidence of associative disturbances. This syndrome further involves an absence of major hallucinatory experiences or significant affective disturbance. Yet the specific feature of the induced psychotic disorder that distinguishes it from other psychotic reactions is what has become known clinically as shared paranoia, that is, a folie à deux-like experience. The delusional system begins to emerge as a result of identification and internalization processes with another person who exhibits an entrenched, clear-cut, crystallized paranoid delusional system. The person with whom the identification is made is usually someone with whom the subject has consistent personal contact, such as a companion or family member. Thus, a delusion emerges in someone close to an individual in whom a delusion is already present. The induced delusion shares the thematic quality of the original one. Diagnostic closure is achieved by ruling out any findings of the presence of psychosis or schizophrenia in prodromal form before onset of the shared delusion in the identifying individual.

Psychotic Disorder Not Otherwise Specified
(Atypical Psychosis)

This residual category briefly known as atypical psychosis completes the larger residual category of psychotic disorders not elsewhere classified. In *DSM-III-R* this diagnostic classification is reserved for disturbances in which any psychotic symptoms are manifested but not in sufficient scope to qualify for a fuller, more meaningful diagnosis. Such symptoms may include delusional or hallucinatory cognitive experience, loosened thought processes, confusion, disorganized functioning, or catatonic reactions, but these symptoms never fulfill criteria of better-established psychotic diagnoses. As symptoms develop further, or more information is secured that would warrent further diagnostic refinement, the diagnosis can be revised accordingly. However, in psychotic reactions with unusual, idiosyncratic, or erratic symptoms, the diagnosis of atypical psychosis can be maintained.

As can be seen in this chapter, the tradition most recently encapsulated by *DSM-III/III-R* of descriptive, empirical categorization increasingly elaborates finer discriminations of the actual behavior of individuals but has not yet included the dimension of a metapsychological basis to explain diagnostic issues. Nevertheless, recognition of diagnostic shift does surface in the *DSM-III* and *DSM-III-R* nomenclature. This issue of diagnostic shift of course implies that changes, restitutions, deteriorations, and overall variations of the pathological process is assumed to be occurring in the person. The concept of the diagnostic shift also can be a bridge to further incorporation of metapsychological considerations in the nomenclature in the way suggested throughout this volume by the discussion of a metapsychological view of paranoid psychopathology as well as the character disorders. The connections between behavioral and theoretical considerations of paranoid pathology would include issues of ideational control over emotions of hostility and criticality, and compensatory grandiosity in relation to feelings of inadequacy; the expression of these pathological processes at the level of either characterological or psychotic functioning; imbeddedness within or outside schizophrenic processes or affective disturbances; and developmental issues that provide historical underpinnings to the pathology.

The focus on symptomatology in diagnostic criteria without corresponding incorporation of metapsychological foundations to advance theoretical coherence creates certain disadvantages. This focus on symptoms prevents the derivation of diagnostic findings from the broad fabric of personality and therefore prevents diagnosis from ultimately constituting a shorthand and derivative form of psychopathology. Perhaps in future nosological efforts the dimension of metapsychology and the development of a theoretical network will permit a broader and more powerful diagnostic synthesis. Such a synthesis would include the psychopathology, personality functioning, and diagnostic issues engendered by theoretically accounted for connections integrating personality and psychopathology.

In the following chapter, several diagnoses of special interest and importance to clinicians will be presented in order to provide an additional diagnostic map of those conditions clinicians frequently encounter in practice. These are usually considered symptom disorders.

CAPSULE CLINICAL PROFILES OF TYPES OF SCHIZOPHRENIA

A variety of symptoms reflect the presence of the general state of schizophrenia. This catalogue of symptoms includes discontinuities in appreciating reality, loss of abstract abilities, resemblance to primitive archaic functioning, regression, confused associations, disturbances in affect expression, bizarre ambivalence, the presence of autistic reactions, a sense of alienation, the experience of delusions and hallucinations, and withdrawal. Generally, these symptoms reflect a disturbance primarily in thinking and secondarily in affect expression as well. The *DSM-III-R* requirement for the diagnosis of schizophrenia includes: (1) the presence of active symptoms: intense delusions or hallucinations or a combination of less intense delusional or hallucinatory experience, affect disturbance, logical disturbance, or behavior disturbance; (2) active symptoms entrenched for at least a week and with or without lesser symptoms for six months; and (3) deterioration in various spheres of life, such as occupational, interpersonal, and personal care. Thus, three elements are required as criteria in the diagnosis of schizophrenia: (1) symptoms, (2) deterioration, and (3) duration of pathognomic features. The combination of symptoms appearing during the active phase as well as in prodormal (incipient) and residual (recovery) phases establishes the diagnosis. The less severe prodromal and residual symptoms include confusion and disorder in thinking, emotion, perception, reality testing, motoric, and volitional functioning.

Paranoid Type: Systematic delusions or repeating auditory hallucinations that focus on a consistent but false idea must be present. These delusions may incorporate persecutory, grandiose, or jealous ideation. Also present may be body distortions, religious ideation, or overall preoccupation with death. Other psychotic symptomatology such as peculiar verbalizations or incomprehensibility do not qualify the syndrome as paranoid. Ideational and intellectual defenses resemble obsessional character traits. Projection and compensation are major defenses that transform aggressive and inadequacy feelings into the experience of persecutory delusions and grandiosity. Defenses of displacement (of aggression), repression (of terror), projection (of criticality), intellectualization (of feelings), and compensation (of inferiority feelings), erase the profound self-doubt thought to be the core underlying pathology of the paranoid. This self-doubt also relates to the emergence of feelings of jealousy while divine evocations act as a compensatory balance to pervasive critical feelings toward the self.

Catatonic Type: Two major dimensions seen in the catatonic patient are: (1) restriction of behavior as in oppositionalism, or actual postural resistance—stupor or mutism; and (2) expansive excitement and explosiveness. Even in the postural state or the state of seeming paralysis, the patient is lucid although immobile and perhaps temporarily mute.

Disorganized Type: The three conditions for the diagnosis of the disorganized type of schizophrenia are: (1) disturbances of association as seen in incoherence and/or in disorganized motoric behavior; (2) affect disturbance as in blunted or inconsistent expression; and (3) lack of posturing as in catatonia.

Undifferentiated Type: In this type, delusions, hallucinations, and associational disturbances are combined in unusual ways. A mixed picture unfolds that does not satisfy standard criteria of any other type.

Residual Type: A diagnosis of residual type is made when one previous episode of schizophrenia existed and most active symptoms have diminished while isolated symptoms from prodromal or residual phases persist.

Simple Schizophrenia: Although not included in *DSM-III* or *DSM-III-R* nosology, the simple type of schizophrenia is nevertheless encountered clinically, especially in hospitalized populations. A gradual loss or process of deterioration can be seen in this disorder, including social withdrawal and autistic behavior. Personal care habits deteriorate markedly, affect becomes flat, and overall interest in the world becomes severely reduced. Hallucinations and delusions are implied in the syndrome although withdrawal negates their expression. Impoverishment of thought, behavior, and verbal communication is typical. Chronic depression also appears. The decline inherent in the process of deterioration begins early in life and is especially apparent during adolescence. Prognosis tends to be poor.

Pseudoneurotic Schizophrenia: This type of schizophrenia is not included in *DSM-III* or *DSM-III-R* nosology. Nevertheless, because of its unique clinical picture it retains clinical value. Essentially, in the pseudoneurotic type, neurotic symptoms are imposed on the surface upon an incipient schizophrenic underlay. Cognitive impairments can include paralogical thinking and word salads. Yet, sufficient restitutional processes exist so that rather than florid psychotic behavior, what is seen is a host of neurotic-like behaviors. A disarray is frequently observed in such persons and the presence of pananxiety is the paramount symptom of this diagnosis. Usually, active psychotic signs are absent. Present are anxiety attacks, phobias, obsessive compulsive behavior, hysterical symptoms, conversions, and psychophysiological reactions. Depression can also appear. In more serious manifestations of pathology, a triad of symptoms appear: depersonalization feelings, ideas of reference, and bodily symptoms.

Latent Schizophrenia: This disorder is not included in the nomenclature of *DSM-III/III-R* although it is a diagnostic entity frequently noted in clinical work. A well-organized character structure contains an underlying schizophrenic process so that the person has not experienced a break with reality. Thus, psychotic potential is masked. Yet deficiencies can be seen, including a poor achievement record in comparison with ability reflected by intellectual functioning and the absence of any learning disability. Vocational functioning is also below capacity. The person's associations may be tangential, and affect and interpersonal responses can be somewhat distant. Characterology can include passive aggressive, obsessional, and/or dependent features utilized to manage underlying turbulent emotions.

CAPSULE CLINICAL PROFILE OF
PSYCHOTIC DELUSIONAL DISORDER

This diagnostic category encompasses psychopathology based on a systematic delusion of paranoid and psychotic proportions. The systematization is thorough but restricted to the delusional area so that for the most part unusual or bizarre behavior does not surface.

Delusional (Paranoid) Disorder: In this disorder delusional ideation occurs but the effect of the delusion on functioning is limited. Therefore, overall behavior does not appear unusual in spite of the existence of a markedly delusional idea. Delusional themes may center on ideas of persecution, specialness, bodily disturbance, or jealousy. Outside of the delusional area, the person with a delusional disorder remains intact and coherent. Bizarre content or ideation is usually absent from the delusional system as well; hallucinations are rare, and emotion is also usually appropriate rather than disordered or flat. The following types of delusional ideation are found:

Erotomanic Type: Delusion of being loved by a special person.

Grandiose Type: Delusion of power or association with powerful figures.

Jealous Type: Delusional ideation that focuses on the infidelity of a partner or loved one.

Persecutory Type: Delusional themes in which the subject receives unfair treatment.

Somatic Type: Delusional belief that subject is either physically defective or diseased.

Unspecified Type: A category reserved for delusions not corresponding in idea to the other central categories in which specific themes are prominent.

CAPSULE CLINICAL PROFILES OF
DSM-III-R PSYCHOTIC DISORDERS
NOT ELSEWHERE CLASSIFIED

These diagnostic entities comprise a residual grouping of psychotic reactions that are not related to one another. Each of the diagnostic entities contains a distinct psychopathological cast.

Brief Reactive Psychosis: In this episodic disorder, symptoms include delusions or hallucinations, associational disturbance, catatonia, as well as a variety of other psychotic symptoms. Symptoms appear suddenly and just as suddenly disappear. This temporary episode may endure not longer than a few hours to no more than a month. In most cases the episode lasts only a few days. Symptoms are usually tied to some specific stressor and no symptoms preexisted the presence of such a stressor. In addition no new pathology should be seen before the appearance of the stressor. Onset of the disorder is usually identified in adolescence.

Schizophreniform Disorder: This diagnosis involves symptoms of a schizophrenic disorder, including delusions, hallucinations, or the remaining pathognomonic schizophrenic signs, but the duration of symptoms is not as long as in schizophrenia. Therefore, in the schizophreniform disorder, the important diagnostic distinction is that the schizophrenic symptoms are visible for less than six months and features of deterioration are absent.

Schizoaffective Disorder: In this disorder there is a mixture of schizophrenic and affective psychotic symptoms, including disturbed cognition—such as delusions, hallucinations, or impaired associations—as well as disturbed affect. Delusions that are experienced are usually not congruent with specific manic or depressive moods, but rather tend to reflect persecutory themes.

Induced Psychotic Disorder: In a folie à deux sharing, an individual without signs of schizophrenia acquires, through identification, delusional thinking that is similar in theme to that of a person with whom the identifier is close, such as a companion, or spouse. In this particular disorder specific paranoid ideation is seen.

Atypical Psychosis: This residual category includes individuals who exhibit either a variety of sparsely evidenced psychotic symptoms or fragments of symptoms.

PART V
Selected Clinical Conditions

CHAPTER 10
A Sampling of Additional Clinical Conditions

A proliferation of diagnostic classifications has taken place in the evolution of *DSM* nosology. That is, there is an ever-increasing expansion of diagnoses as *DSM* development is traced from the first edition to the current revision, *DSM-III-R* leading to *DSM-IV*. These diagnostic classifications have clinical value insofar as a wide array of maladaptive and pathological behaviors can be organized into syndromes and thereby more easily conceptualized in diagnostic language. Presumably, this diagnostic language can represent broader underlying pathological and personality dimensions. In this sense of parsimony, development in *DSM* structure can help the clinician to see a broad range of psychopathology. Yet, in the *DSM* nosology, this multiplicity of psychopathological phenomena is organized with reference to symptoms and psychological demographics such as duration of symptoms and so forth. The problem that is created is that such behavior is not classified with respect to explanatory reference or with attempts at underlying theoretical consistency. The inexorable direction that such diagnostic scrutiny is taking begins to resemble what might be described as a dictionary of syndromes or even as a dictionary of symptoms.

The zeal of classifiers to try to reach basic common denominators on a manifest atheoretical and empirical level and pure diagnostic categories which are characterized by clear syndromes is actually resulting in what could be considered narrower listings of individual symptom clusters and even of single symptoms alone. Such development in the evolution of diagnosis would seem ultimately likely to yield a fragmentary effect in overall diagnostic organization.

An example of this tendency to focus on descriptive symptoms can be seen in the case of sexual dysfunction where issues such as premature ejaculation and impotency problems are viewed as discrete diagnoses rather than representative of any underlying hysterical or conversion condition or as part of a dormant but debilitating accumulation of depression or anger, which would then give the presence of the symptom increased meaning. Such a trend toward focusing on discrete symptoms undoubtedly reflects the growth of behavioral treatments centered upon symptomatology alone. What seems to be omitted both in the behavioral approaches and in the ensuing conceptualizations of diagnosis is the importance of a personality network that theoretically encompasses any symptomatic manifestation. This tendency toward specific focus on symptom disturbances can tend to shift the organization of the nomenclature toward a cookbook of recipes in which limited entities are considered according to the fashions of treatment.

In spite of what appears to be a tendency toward simplification in diagnosis and the organization of the nomenclature, this chapter will review several significant clinical syndromes that are frequently encountered in clinical work. These clinical entities will be described in terms of symptomatology and theoretical links will be proposed to provide an etiological and clinical basis for each syndrome. The clinical conditions discussed include sadistic, masochistic, or self-defeating personality disorders; exhibitionism and voyeurism; the sleep disorders of insomnia and narcolepsy; the eating disorders of anorexia and bulimia; and the diagnosis of attention deficit disorder. This sampling of special clinical problems also suggests that *DSM* nosology will most likely continue to develop more numerous discrete diagnostic entities as the system evolves.

AGGRESSIVE IDEATION:
SADISTIC AND MASOCHISTIC DISORDERS

These disorders of sadistic and self-defeating functioning involve aggressive ideation and behavior in a context in which cruelty or humiliation is inflicted or experienced in a manner related to domination or self-sacrifice. The proclivities encompassed by sadistic and masochistic functioning may join pairs of individuals in which complementing roles are fulfilled. Yet a dispositional tendency in terms of character structure generally underlies the sadistic or masochistic orientation in a given individual. Therefore, even complementing aspects of sadomasochism between people is based on individual characterology and appears in each person at the level of a personality disorder.

Sadistic Personality Disorder

On a descriptive level, sadistic personality features considered in *DSM-III-R* nosology include the manifestation of cruel behavior, the expression of physical pain in the object that is caused by such cruelty, and the implementation of discipline towards others that ranges from low-level violence to extremes of torture, all resulting in some sense of pleasure for such sadistic persons. The sadistic cruelty inflicted on others reflects covert sexual connotations and can play a perverse part in the sexual bonding and needs of individuals or couples. However, sadistic behavior is broader than these sexual implications because such behavior apparently rests on the dimension of domination versus submission in human relationships, and therefore concerns the contamination of needs for power, yielding, aggression, as well as sexuality.

It can be proposed that the sadistic character structure is designed to manage rather punitive superego strivings by acting out in aggressively controlling ways sadistic behavior which insures that the anxiety associated with such cruel impulses does not register. In this sense, a defensive insulation usually becomes prominent and neutralizes any empathy for the suffering person.

Along with the superego imperative to act out the sadistic impulse, there seems to exist in the sadist an internalized permission to act out as in identification with the aggressor. This implies that the sadistic person dichotomizes the world into victims and victimizers and is able to identify with the victimizer. Such identifying with the aggressor together with the subject's distancing mechanism, permits the sadist to sever any empathic connection with the victim. All imperfections and impurities are then attributed to the victim so that the sadist is able to experience power, and aggressive dominance, and perhaps unacknowledged sexual satisfaction, as this domination triad begins to govern the entire personality. When sexual excitement and fantasies are overtly and significantly associated with the creation of physical domination, control, suffering and humiliation of a victim, the diagnosis of sexual sadism can be considered.

Additional theoretical connections with respect to psychoanalytic understanding suggest that sadistic personality functioning may derive from early developmental experiences in which the subject experienced personal sacrifice and injustice.

Differential Diagnosis

In the context of character structure, especially as codified in *DSM-III-R* and leading to *DSM-IV*, the sadistic personality can be discriminated from that of the paranoid, psychopathic, and passive aggressive personalities with respect to several dimensions. The individual in whom a paranoid character dominates is engaged in hostile and critical projections toward the world in order to avoid profound self-criticism associated with the experience of inadequacy, inferiority, and intense self-doubt. Such a characterological configuration differs from the characterological strivings in the sadistic personality in which a primary satisfaction in the expression of hostility itself becomes central.

In the psychopathic personality, hostility, aggression, and destructive behavior are generally a function of the strong motoric need and action-orientation of this character type in order to avoid a profound state of inertia or even psychic paralysis. In the occurrence of any state of inertia, such psychopathic types report the experience of an inner deadness that in turn generates frightening or terrifying feelings. Here again, hostility and aggression are not primary satisfiers but secondary side effects of the psychopath's particular form of managing inner tension. Thus, any aggressive acting out is related in the psychopathic character structure to the inability to stop behavior and engage in thoughtful contemplation. Further, the poorly controlled expression of the aggressive impulse in psychopathic types generally relates to a goal of obtaining a desired stature or possession through immediate action, because planning and considerations of conscience cannot be reflectively engaged. Pleasure in domination and aggressive behavior is therefore secondary in psychopathic functioning, not primary as in sadistic functioning.

In the case of passive aggressive character structure, a major aim of the passive aggressive pattern is to avoid a sense of disempowerment. The passive aggressive behavior is thus a self-empowerment through the process of disempowering others. Because of the sense of an impending feeling of becoming overpowered, the passive aggressive behavior is actually an attempt to balance forces between self and object. In comparison with the sadistic person, the passive aggressive personality can be considered relatively benign in the net effect of his hostile behavior since the goal is to express hostility safely and always indirectly by surreptitiously frustrating others, rather than humiliating or victimizing them overtly. Therefore, the passive aggressive person's experience of pleasure concerns covertly defeating authority figures or neutralizing their power rather than experiencing such behavior as the direct achievement of profound pleasure.

It may be seen that the sadistic person is not merely interested in being critical, as in the paranoid act. He is not interested in merely expressing aggression because of inability to manage control, as in the psychopathic act. He is not at all interested in covertly neutralizing the power of authorities through frustration as in the passive aggressive act. Rather, the sadistic process seeks pleasure in the extreme, requiring extreme but planned, overt measures. The effect of these measures is to achieve dominance over a victim, and to humiliate in order to gain primary or direct gratification in the infliction of aggression and pain. Simultaneously, a sense of power is assured by the immunization from empathy in the dehumanization of the object.

Masochistic Personality Disorder
(Self-Defeating Personality)

In the masochistic personality, only some opposite features to the sadistic person exist. For the most part, the masochistic person is engaged in a range of functioning that results in self-defeating circumstances for the person. Thus, the element of masochism is considered only one aspect of the self-defeating behavior, so that the *DSM-III-R* nosology defines the entire syndrome as a self-defeating personality disorder. Although the *DSM* nosology considers this sort of self-defeating behavior as emerging in early adulthood, it is nevertheless clear that clinicians begin to see the self-defeating patterns in childhood and adolescence as well. In addition, although the *DSM-III-R* characterization of this disorder indicates that self-defeating persons are attracted to situations which can be easily undermined, it may be more useful to examine such self-defeating behavior with respect to particular character patterns.

It can be hypothesized that persons with a self-defeating character pattern have had early experiences with parental figures who were either, on the one hand, overambitious for the child, thus setting the conditions for protest behavior, or on the other, not supervisory enough, thereby setting conditions for anger. In either case, the net effect may be that such persons can perhaps develop passive aggressive patterns of the passive type, leading to procrastination, delay, and fragmentary attempts to complete work. In the self-defeating character structure, such passive aggressive attempts presumably are not designed as much to serve passive aggressive character needs as they are to insure the goal of non-achievement. Thus, the subject is spared a full confrontation as a result of disappointing the overambitious parent with claims that the work takes too long and is too demanding, and, in this way of rationalization, can transform a failure into a gain. In such circumstances, the person begins to enter the realm of continual low-level suffering and hardships both in personal relationships and occupational experiences. For example, such persons may effectively prevent others from helping them by making poor choices in their associates or by rejecting truly helpful efforts of others. In addition, such persons may make poor choices in developing goals and can frequently experience depression when goals are compromised. In the extreme form, self-defeating persons engaging in consistently implemented masochistic activities begin to accumulate multitudes of frustrations and can then even become physically ill. Such persons also tend to offer others assistance, and when for one reason or another they are not appreciated, they become angry and can experience rejection and humiliation.

Psychoanalytic Implications

In terms of the experience of pleasure, such persons also inundate themselves with work tasks which are in a continual unfinished state, so that opportunities for pleasure are severely curtailed. Finally, in the exaggerated form of giving assistance to others, the self-sacrifice that may even be unsolicited is frequently ignored by others, leading to further experiencing of hurt feelings in the subject.

The masochistic or self-defeating personality frequently reaches the point at which psychological pain and even sexual and affectional rejection is experienced as abuse. Yet, in terms of psychoanalytic understanding of this kind of personality, the entire syndrome of self-defeating behavior, masochistic features, and the experience of abuse seems to render a subliminal familiarity and even pleasure and gratification that make the intimidation, humiliation, and submission self-perpetuating. It is the organization of these self-defeating behaviors in the context of secret and usually unacknowledged gratification that forms these persistent personality patterns into a specific character structure.

Further, from the psychoanalytic perspective, it is thought that the operation of a punitive superego is played out in the masochistic victim's encouragement of a submissive, self-limiting or perhaps even abused posture. Since a presumed sadistic parental introject allegedly requires satisfaction, obedience, and humiliation in the service of punitive drives, the masochistic yielding to this punitive parental introject can engender a well-disguised satisfaction, that is, the gratification of this parental introject. The connection as well to a need for self-defeat based on guilt that requires assuaging through repeated self-diminishment is also a theoretical consideration in the operation of masochism from the psychoanalytic point of view.

PARAPHILIAS: EXHIBITIONISTIC AND VOYEURISTIC BEHAVIOR

In *DSM-III-R*, both exhibitionism and voyeurism are considered separate sexual disorders under the general category of paraphilias, referring to sex related disorders. In its Greek roots, the word "paraphilia" refers to a feeling of love, as expressed in the term *philia*, and the prefix *para-*, indicating beyond, aside from, or amiss. Thus, both in exhibitionism and voyeurism, sexual gratification is not sought through direct sexual experience such as fondling, kissing, or intercourse. Rather, the excitation can occur through limited sexual display and observation focused on strangers, essentially, who are unaware of their participation as a sexual object. The main aim, then, in the paraphilias is to create the feeling of gratification albeit without direct interpersonal or sexual connection.

Exhibitionism

The exhibitionist engages in a series of acting out behaviors in which the genitals become exposed to an unsuspecting person. Sexual excitement is increased if the unsuspecting person does not flee, thus creating the sense of some compliance. The impulse to engage in such exhibitionistic encounters is based theoretically, in psychoanalytic understanding, on an attempt to gain personal reassurance and power through a noticeable effect on the unsuspecting person. The welcomed effect on the unsuspecting person is verified by a strong reaction such as in a reaction of shock. In this way the sexual quality of exhibitionism seems to be fused with needs for reassurance.

The reassurance of the person's integrity, intactness, and power or potency by the reaction of surprise to exposure, theoretically relates to the psychoanalytic concept of castration anxiety derived from the phallic period of psychosexual development. The recognition conveyed to the exhibitionist by the reaction of the observer serves to reduce anxiety pertaining to value, potency, and adequacy, the derivative concerns stemming from castration anxiety. That the sense of power may be essentially more important than the implication of sexual appeal and sexual gratification seems to support the prevailing hypothesis that the exhibitionism need not lead to sexual completion as in sexual contact with the object.

Voyeurism

In the voyeuristic tendency, the issues of power and recognition are again considered major goals in sustaining the voyeuristic act in a compensatory attempt to repair feelings of helplessness and inadequacy. While no real motive of sexual contact with the observed person is sought, a fantasied contact is generated that temporarily contributes to an aura of strength, connection, and control. Since engagement in actual and more personal contact is anticipated as threatening, then the voyeuristic urge seems to act to provide reassurance of potency in the absence of actual contact. Voyeurs are frequently more attuned to such disembodied connections with people and often display defensive insulation in any primary relationship. The voyeur may also engage in a variety of sexually related activities such as compulsive masturbatory activity while watching the sexual behavior of others, seeking unsuspecting persons in the state of disrobing, or utilizing pornographic materials to look at. In all cases, the activity is solitary, usually requires planning, and tends to detract from and impede the deepening of any personal relationship. However, the voyeuristic person secures the gains of a feeling of safety, control, and reassurance about personal intactness and power that are necessary, given the presumed underlying fearfulness of entering sexual and social relationships fully and directly. The voyeuristic person's emphasis on looking as a source and contributor to sexual gratification and a temporary sense of adequacy is often traceable to developmentally early experiences in which sexuality or sexually implicit behavior was witnessed. Such early, premature views of adult sexual encounters or seductive behavior may have been overwhelming to the subject so that continued voyeurism represents repetitious behavior and attempts toward mastery of the early and incomplete experience. Further, the early and probably overwhelming voyeuristic experience, often also accidental, establishes a template through which later experiences of sexuality are expressed in ways strongly influenced by the original experience.

Clinically, it is sometimes seen that both exhibitionistic and voyeuristic impulses can be expressed by a single person while in other cases persons may be exclusively one or the other. Psychoanalytically, the voyeur is considered to be governed by passive defenses regarding fears of phallic assertion. Such passive defenses generate a receiving and even dependent orientation to protect against the threat associated with more active efforts at mastery and satisfaction, particularly in the sexual area. The voyeur's emphasis on looking involves a taking in and thus establishes new empowerment. In fact, both voyeurs and exhibitionists have reported feeling nurtured as well as empowered by their respective acts and frequently experience depression, emptiness, or personal weakness when deprived of the repeating behaviors involved in

these disorders. Correspondingly, such personalities are pervaded
with feelings of reassurance and worthiness when the acts are successful. These positive feelings compensate for the experience of
emptiness and depression the individual feels when forced to forgo
the acting out.

When discovered in the acting out event, both exhibitionistic
and voyeuristic persons can become extremely frightened and dis-
traught, and will desist from further acting out for some time.
However, as time elapses, the feeling of loneliness and the urgency
for self-reassurance are inexorably reasserted, triggering renewed
acting out in spite of any residual apprehension. The terror and
distress of actually being caught in the act does not seem to result
in a resolution of the conflict. Rather, being caught in the act con-
firms the person's worst fears—that of inadequacy, ineptness, personal weakness, and in psychoanalytic terms, overall castration fears,
including the experience of humiliation and guilt. Thus, it seems
that this cycle of the exhibitionistic and voyeuristic acting out can
only be resolved with the working through of concerns regarding
intactness, needs for power, recognition, nurturance, and alleviation of underlying depression, as well as creating the possibility of
deepening any primary relationship.

SLEEP DISORDERS:
INSOMNIA AND NARCOLEPSY

In *DSM-III-R* leading to *DSM-IV* classifiers have turned their attention to various forms of sleep disorders such as dream interruption states, as well as insomnia. For the purposes of a clinical
discussion of sleep disorders in this section, the analysis of insomnia and narcolepsy will primarily be concerned with clinical findings useful to clinicians regarding the overall manifestations of insomnia and narcolepsy.

Insomnia

DSM-III-R characterizes primary insomnia essentially as a difficulty in initiating or maintaining sleep, a difficulty compounded

by the experience of daytime fatigue. The criterion used to establish the presence of insomnia concerns sleep difficulty occurring periodically during the week and lasting for at least one month.

To describe insomnia in more precise terms, this disturbance concerns not merely a difficulty in initiating or maintaining sleep but has implications for the sleep cycle itself. The sleep disturbance occurs largely in three ways, each of which can become a characteristic and identifying problem for the insomniac. First, is the insomnia in which a person finds it extremely difficult to get to sleep initially. Individuals with this kind of insomnia become conditioned to expecting the experience of tension as bedtime approaches because they anticipate difficulty in gaining sleep. Yet the conditioned response of tension is a secondary response and, even were that tension regarding the expection of sleep disturbance to be neutralized, the condition of insomnia could still obtain.

The second major kind of insomnia is referred to as mid-night awakenings. This type of insomnia may be preceded by two specific conditions. The first is the condition in which initiating sleep was very difficult and, after the person was eventually able to sleep, several hours later a mid-night awakening nevertheless occurred. Second, if the insomnia condition consists of mid-night awakenings, then the awakening occurs even with those individuals who have not had the problem of getting to sleep.

The third phenomenon of insomnia concerns early morning awakenings or dawn insomnia. In this type of insomnia, persons, whether or not they had difficulty in initiating sleep or experienced mid-night awakenings, nevertheless awaken considerably before sunrise, certainly before 5 a.m., and more likely than not, closer to 4 a.m. In such cases a return to sleep is rare.

The clinician will be able to conceptualize the insomnia condition based upon this paradigm of the three kinds of insomnia: initiating sleep, mid-night awakenings, and dawn insomnia. In all three kinds of insomnia, persons experience daytime fatigue, irritability, and agitation. It would seem that the presence of such symptoms are reasonable based on the simple experience of sleep deprivation. Yet this simple explanation of sleep deprivation actually is not sufficient to explain the myriad of symptoms that occur as a result of the insomnia.

More specifically, what actually occurs that is so deleterious to the person and creates a sleep pattern lacking the necessary restorative properties of sleep is that the person experiencing insomnia of the various types described does not actually sleep with the correct sequence of sleep stages. The restorative property of sleep occurs when the sleep stages begin with stage 1, light sleep, followed by stage 2, somewhat deeper sleep, followed by stage 3, which begins the prelude to the deep sleep of stage 4, and then is followed by the dream state. The sequence should repeat itself this way roughly every 90 minutes throughout the night in order to accumulate a pattern of normal sleep and the overall satisfying experience of sleep restoration. Of course, during various types of insomnia this sequence of sleep stages is interrupted, and the interference produces a disturbance in the circadian rhythms or circadian sleep-wake pattern. It is this interruption in the necessary circadian pattern that promotes the symptoms of fatigue, irritability, and agitation that insomniacs experience during the daytime.

Psychodynamics

From a theoretical point of view, insomnia is likely to become active during periods when individuals experience some breach in an important relationship. Such a breach can be defined in terms of marital separations, threats of separation, or at least difficulty with the primary partner that reaches a threatening point. This connection between the symptom of insomnia and the disturbance in relationships implies that at least in functional insomnia, in the absence of organic etiology, the symptom of insomnia itself does not appear as a random phenomenon. It could be helpful to clinicians to realize that the insomnia condition just as quickly disappears after the repair of a breach in a relationship as it appears during a separation. Of course, the issue of dependency as a personality need becomes an important feature of the psychodynamic context of the insomnia symptom; that is, the greater the presence of dependency, the greater the probability that a severe insomnia symptom will derive from events of separation. For example, dependent youngsters who leave home to attend college frequently arrive at the college student health office complaining of the inability to sleep as well as of a host of other symptoms. Thus, there may be variations on the theme of separation and, as dependency increases, the likelihood for insomnia to appear also increases.

Clinically, it becomes evident that the psychodynamic context of insomnia forms a triad of components. This insomnia triad of personality components consists of issues of separation, features of dependency, and, finally, the experience of depression as well as, in many cases, a subsumed condition of disatisfaction, anger, and even rage. The pivotal event that can release the symptom of insomnia seems to be the separation experience. A consequence of such a sequence resulting in the symptom of insomnia can be the experience or expression of anger or rage or depression.

Other separation issues which the clinician needs to recognize can include loss of a job, death of a loved one, or geographic relocation which involves separation from familiar structures. Presumably, the extent of dependency within the personality will affect how pronounced the insomnia may become. The clinician should also consider that some of these variations of separation examples can be repaired quite quickly by skilled intervention or even minimal intervention, while other kinds of separations become quite devastating and require involved and enduring clinical effort. As the psychodynamic context indicates, insomnia is considerably more than a sleep disorder represented by symptoms alone.

Narcolepsy

Although the *DSM* model considers excessive sleepiness under the heading of hypersomnia disorders, nevertheless, excessive sleepiness usually seen by clinicians relates to the condition of narcolepsy. In recent years, this condition of narcolepsy has gained considerable attention. While it was previously considered a rare condition, it is currently being treated with greater urgency and the condition itself is now regarded to be widespread. Before it was understood, sufferers were hospitalized and treated for a variety of different disorders, including even schizophrenia. Recent research has conclusively shown that narcolepsy is organically based and contains genetic markers.

Fundamentally, narcolepsy is a sleep disorder organized as a tetrad of symptoms. The first symptom is the narcoleptic attack itself in which the sufferer feels an inexorable pull into sleep. From the psychological point of view, this is perhaps adaptive because research also shows that this disorder generates a disruption in the sequence of sleep stages so that during the first symptom of the actual narcoleptic sleep attack the person is dragged into sleep and is instantly dreaming. Were the person not to be sleeping, the dream would presumably carry out its dramatic imperative to be portrayed, and the person would then behave as if he were hallucinating. The sleep attack can last from a few minutes to more than a half hour, and can occur several times throughout the day.

The second symptom of the narcoleptic tetrad is cataplexy. In the manifestation of this symptom, the subject reacts to a particular stimulus which causes a paralysis of voluntary musculature and physical collapse; for example, the individual may drop in a heap. The stimulus that triggers this cataplectic symptom is usually one containing the element of surprise, such as an unexpected loud noise or the punch line to a joke. The attack can last several minutes, but the person lying in this cataplectic state is conscious and aware of his surroundings. The person can gradually come out of the attack either as its effects subside or through the mere touch of another person. The cataplectic attack is entirely different from a seizure generated by the condition of epilepsy.

The third symptom of the narcoleptic tetrad is known as sleep paralysis, in which the person is entirely in a state of helplessness or paralysis. This state occurs either during the moments of falling to sleep or in the moments awakening from sleep. A fourth symptom, associated with the sleep paralysis, is the final major symptom of the tetrad, known as the hypnagogic hallucination. This hallucination generally occurs during the sleep paralysis and constitutes a dreamlike state in which the dream or hypnagogic images are so vivid that even after awakening the subject feels certain that the hypnagogic events actually did occur. When shown how such events would not be possible, the subject will usually intellectually concur that it was a dream and yet, is reluctant to relinquish acceptance of the experience of the hallucinatory images because they were so extraordinarily vivid.

Psychodynamics

Narcoleptic persons frequently show dependency features of personality and a psychological overlay to the basic organic syndrome of compelling sleepiness. With respect to the characteristic of dependency, the narcoleptic disorder frequently becomes initiated by some separation period during adolescence or early adulthood;

again, attending college away from home for the first time or moving into one's own first apartment can stimulate the manifestation of the syndrome.

Further, it should be noted that in a clinical sense narcolepsy may be diagnosed either when the entire tetrad exists or when any part of it exists, even in the absence of the primary narcoleptic sleep attack. The dependency feature of personality can be considered an effect of the special assistance such persons begin to need from others over a long period of time. In extreme, but not rare cases, such persons, because of the unusual nature of the syndrome and its effects, become effectively unemployable. Thus, the end result in many cases is a dependency or reliance on one's family or special agencies for support and supervision.

EATING DISORDERS: ANOREXIA AND BULIMIA

The diagnoses of anorexia and bulimia as eating disorders have gained widespread attention, especially in the past decade, and statistics regarding these syndromes have indicated that their prevalence is greater than previously realized. In general, anorexia and bulimia have in common as symptoms disturbed and self-destructive patterns in the intake of food, in the perception of body image, including weight and size, in conceptions regarding nutrition and health, and in rituals surrounding weighing and scrutiny of the body. Eating in binges along with the ejecting of food after it has been eaten is a symptom found only in bulimia. Both disorders center on obsessions regarding food or eating, as well as body size.

Several characterological qualities appear in the functioning of anorectics and bulimics. These include dishonesty because of the deception that is compulsively maintained about food, eating, and appetite. Further characterological issues typically encompass involvement in power struggles, narcissistic preoccupations, compulsive rituals, and an unconscious but obvious striving to avoid engaging directly in concerns associated with adult functioning unless narcissistic components are predominant. Thus, an adult level of intimacy in relationships, engagement of a range of areas, and sensitive care for other people are rarely revealed by persons with eating disorders since their characterology centers instead on rather regressive, self-centered, and compulsive preoccupations. A core of insecurity with impaired self-esteem and self-identity leads to a compensatory overfocus on personal appearance, size, weight, and eating patterns. This over-focus provides compensatory sources of accomplishment, self-identity, and control. Attention is gained and the basic threats involved in being unable to cope with challenges of maturation and management of adult responsiblities are avoided. Although in many cases both anorexia and bulimia coexist, in most instances they are found separately and it is possible to view them as separate syndromes.

Anorexia Nervosa

The central feature of anorexia is the compulsive effort to lose as much weight as possible and to become as thin as possible. The Greek roots of the term mean loss of appetite, but appetite is never actually lost at all. This eating disorder is motivated by an excessive fear—almost a phobia—of weight gain. As such, when the anorectic, typically a young woman, views her physical image in the mirror, she emphatically misperceives the size and weight reflected by the image that she is scrutinizing with utmost dedication. The misperception is characterized by a persistent overestimation in size so that no matter how thin the person becomes, she is never thin enough; she always perceives herself as too fat. The danger to many anorectics is that they become emaciated to the point of malnourishment leading all too often to physical disease, complications, and even to death.

Statistically, anorexia occurs much more frequently in young women, although children and adolescent boys can also express this disorder. The disorder typically begins to appear during high school years and develops further during young adulthood. Although many theories have been proposed regarding the etiology of anorexia, no single therapeutic intervention has been consistently effective in the majority of cases. What is known is that the disorder seems to be a result of a psychological conflict which is managed in a symptomatic way: intake of food ceases or is profoundly reduced, even though at the beginning, or even the end stages of the illness, appetite may still be intact. Thus, anorexia, a term referring to the loss of appetite, is more of a catchword for this disorder than an accurate description of it, since many appetites persist—for food, attention, and control.

Physiologically, according to the *DSM* model, anorexia can be diagnosed when there is, in women, an absence of at least three consecutive menstrual cycles—amenorrhea—as a result of the drastic weight loss and its physiological effects; an intense fear of gaining weight even during periods when the person is emaciated, and a loss of fifteen percent of body weight. Thus, for the anorectic, the continual loss of body weight by a variety of means and in spite of dramatic physiological changes and interpersonal reactions is the central overt striving.

As the anorectic's compulsive dieting and weight loss continue, a number of ensuing consequences may appear that are partly derived from physiological changes. The anorectic who becomes emaciated may appear disoriented and reveal disordered thinking; depression with suicidal impulses may surface; a manipulative, petulant, covertly tyrannical stance may be detected; acute sensitivity to noises and odors can develop; social isolation often becomes emphasized, with only mechanical participation in life's necessities; finally, alcoholism and shoplifting may emerge as problems reflecting the strain anorectics encounter in logically directing their behavior patterns.

Taken together, the mental set of an anorectic usually reflects a person who is goal directed toward a narrow weight-loss perspective, and who is highly motivated with single-minded determination to lose weight. This sort of fanaticism is psychologically understood as guided and fueled by compulsive needs related to desperate attempts by anorectic persons to seek to gain control of their life.

The Issue of Control

Such needs for control appear to emanate from the anorectic's covert sense of the unmanagability of life's pressures, requirements, and responsibilities. These difficult pressures for the anorectic include the expectations of significant people in the anorectic's circle. Most profoundly, the challenge of embracing the responsibilities required by maturation with an integrated sense of personal identity is the area in which threat and lack of control is most pronounced.

Thus, a specific psychodynamic issue reflected in the interpersonal sphere for anorectics can concern the significant individuals in their life whom the anorectic ultimately needs either to feel safe from or to control. In fact, in many of the theories regarding anorexia, researchers refer to the presence of a controlling mother figure or dominant caretaker. Such a parental figure can exercise control through direct monitoring and supervision of the child that sets the stage for the child's rebellion against the inordinately suffocating parental control. In such cases, the rebellion can grow out of a sense of resentment because the child senses the absence of concern from the parent regarding the nurturance of the child's individuality. In place of this nurturance, the child can experience that the parents' own needs have taken over and can only be gratified by absorption into the parental need system. As a means of developing some sense of independence and separate self-identity, the adolescent's typical rebellion is intensified by the food and bodily centered focus played out by the anorectic.

A second type of rebellion also may appear in the anorectic sufferer. In this second kind of rebellion, the child may experience the parent as unable to be pliable and as exceedingly narcissistic, so that rather than a fear of suffocation through oversupervision, in this case rage is the foundation of the rebellion. This rage is presumably directed to the same parent who has, in effect, abandoned the child to the parent's own narcissistic need system. In the first kind of rebellion, it could be hypothesized that to resist taking in food feels like a lifesaving technique—an avoidance of suffocation. This rather unusual solution of refusing food, then, has an equally idiosyncratic conclusion; that is, if not taking in food prevents suffocation, then the proof of survival is in the persistence toward seeking to look thinner.

In the second kind of rebellion, however, based on rage toward the parent who is experienced as narcissistic, it may be the case that by precluding the entire issue of feeding, eating and nourishment, the anorectic prevents the narcissistic, abandoning parent from exercising the controlling power of the parent in the first place. The compulsive nature of the anorectic's behavior, therefore, can be an effort to gain a controlling grip on the environment in a general sense, and, more specifically, to gain a sense of control with respect to the overcontrolling or narcissistic parent—to render such a parent ineffective.

In order for the anorectic to maintain compulsive behavior, denial mechanisms are utilized to facilitate the continuing loss of weight as a means of forestalling any trace of accumulation of weight. In contrast, a weight gain could, in symbolic terms, constitute yielding to the dominating parent and relinquishing control as well as symbolically acknowledging the experience of being abandoned by the narcissistic parent.

In terms of identification with the same sex parent, it can be proposed that anorectic young women either become identified with the overcontrolling mother or the narcissistic one. In either case, a component of regressive immaturity is generated through such identifications since the evolution of a specific, comfortable self-identity, separate from that of the parent, has not been achieved. This failure to progress in adaptively resolving the identity crisis in the transition from childhood to adulthood occasions the more immature focus. An effort to form an identity founded on control of food intake and body size, which also negates parental expectations, takes the place of the transformation involved in engaging adult responsibility.

The father figure in the anorectic's family structure is perhaps likely to be a somewhat aloof character type whose need for control or concern with his own boundary conditions may be emphatic. Such a father figure would not be likely to be outspoken. Therefore, with the presence of a controlling mother the child is not usually able to depend upon the father for protection or solace or for providing the necessary balance in the family, especially with respect to the mother's interest in power or her immaturity. As a result, the anorectic patient is frequently one who feels psychologically ill-equipped to face the challenges of life. This sense of intense inadequacy develops especially during adolescent and early-adult years. The anorectic's grave fear of assuming increasingly mature roles that would be necessitated by continued normal development can contribute to self-defeating motivation to remain undeveloped and to misperceive the excesses of physical shrinkage. By the use of compulsive food avoidance and denial of weight loss, development itself is both diminished and denied. Life challenges are then avoided by the anorectic who feels frightened and inadequate except in the narrow area of weight control. Therefore this area of weight concern is presumably singled out for mastery as a rebellion against figures sensed as either overly controlling or as narcissistically absorbing.

Since sexuality is also understood to be an adult related com-

ponent of intimacy and the deepening of relationships, the anorectic's condition, with its compulsive preoccupation with food and
body size, contributes to disinterest in sexual activity. Therefore,
both in the sexual sphere of functioning as well as in non-sexual
areas, the anorectic can, through this condition of compulsive body
preoccupation, presumably assert either control or individuality or
both, although this assertion is at great physiological and psychological cost.

Bulimia

This rather contemporary diagnosis of bulimia—the term, from
its Greek roots, means insatiable hunger—concerns the phenomenon of binge eating and the vicissitudes surrounding this sort of
impulse problem. The impulse involved with binge eating stems
from the sufferer's obsessive concern with body weight, food, and
eating. The binge eater's inability to sustain denial and compensatory mechanisms enables recognition of the acting out patterns.
This realization regarding such uncontrolled compulsive behavior
often yields depression as the individual pursues a host of behaviors, rituals, and fantasies surrounding food, appetite, eating, and
purging.

The symptom of purging essentially constitutes an undoing
mechanism and represents a clear reflection in behavioral terms of
the intense psychological conflict experienced by such a person.
Purging is an attempt on the part of bulimics to cancel or undo
what they consider the self-damaging effects of the feeding frenzy.
Purging itself includes an entire strategy involving various tactics
for expelling food that has already been ingested. Vomiting is
characteristic and comprises the main undoing technique of the
binge eater. Laxatives as well as diuretics are also utilized in order
to negate the food that has been compulsively consumed. The institution of exercise regimes, precipitous diets, and periods of vir-
tual starvation are also employed to undo the effects of compulsive
eating. In addition, these practices manifest the bulimic's obsessive
focus on eating habits and body concerns.

In the diagnostic criteria of *DSM-III-R* the process of binge eating consists of at least two periods of excessive consumption per
week with regular behavioral engagement of undoing attempts over

a three-month period. This particular criterion is the major descriptive information needed to diagnose bulimia although additional criteria include a great deal of food consumption in a small amount of time—typically, high caloric food items—secretiveness and even deception in revealing eating habits, and, finally, great weight fluctuations.

It is apparent that the bulimic person, like the anorectic, is extremely concerned with body shape, and feels tortured because, despite such concern with body size, binges, secret eating, and purges are both planned and repeatedly practiced. Thus, the bulimic sufferer experiences an approach-avoidance conflict in which a realization takes place that the contradictory behaviors compulsively enacted have a disordered, humiliating quality. Since issues of appearance are quite important to bulimics, the embarrassment they suffer and the depression they experience can be quite demoralizing and despairing. It should be noted that bulimics are often normal in weight, so that the entire syndrome of binging and purging is frequently inconsistent with the person's physiological needs regarding weight and body size. However, this inconsistency reflects the misperception of body image as a central symptomatic phenomenon in the bulimic disorder.

The Issue of Control

The compulsive binge eating of the bulimic reflects an obvious loss of control and, correspondingly, the purge which terminates the binge reestablishes and reconstitutes the person's sense of control. Thus, the repetitive cycle of binging and purging reflects the continued, unresolved, central issue of control with which the bulimic is struggling. Usually, the binge-purge syndrome is, temporarily for any particular episode, extinguished by associated clinical phenomena such as insomnia or the development or preoccupation with a range of physical illnesses, usually emanating from the repetitious cycle of binging and purging.

The similarity between the anorectic and the bulimic in terms of unclear self-identity, control needs, and misperception of body size is focused on the fear of gaining weight and efforts to control amounts of food ingested or retained. The main difference between the two disorders concerns the use of denial and undoing and the resulting way in which anxiety is experienced. The anorectic sustains strong denial mechanisms and will protest when it is suggested that something is wrong. In contrast, the bulimic is quite concerned about the idiosyncratic eating pattern, does not deny the problem, and is in a never-ending conflict with manifest anxiety about trying to end the compulsive agony of the doing and undoing ritual. Yet, the bulimic person seems also to be controlled by covert psychological forces that interfere with accurate assessment of weight and size, such as the sense of pressure that creates a compulsive striving for reduced size. This striving for reduced size with the implication of a more admirable appearance is regarded as highly desirable insofar as it can be a means of inflating deficient self-esteem. A quest for an ultimate sense of adequacy, coherence and stable positive self-regard can be considered to underlie the bulimics' misjudgment of body size and compulsive attempt to reshape themselves, doing and undoing, in order to attempt also to secure a sense of personal control and an esteemed body image.

In the development of the bulimic syndrome it can be considered that the chief characteristic of the family's major parent-figure concerns the issue of ambition for and criticism of the child. In the case of the relationship between girls and their mothers, the mother of the bulimic may either be a controlling and/or narcissistic type who is generally dissatisfied with the child's achievements. Such mothers may tend to be perfectionistic toward their children. This perfectionism toward the child can be part of an acting out equation on the mother's part. That is, such mothers can be anxious or intrusive and are able to reduce the effects of their own anxiety by focusing and expressing perfectionistic needs toward the child. The child, in turn, would usually feel inadequate and unaccomplished and may feel depressed and anxious. In the bulimic episodes, it appears that the child is always trying to reach some ideal or perfection concerning size and body shape. Of course, this ideal can never be satisfied. Such a bulimic person is usually both impulsive and compulsive and correspondingly given to sudden bursts of trying to perfect herself. Yet, the internalization of identification issues between mother and daughter presumably make it impossible for the child to become satisfied with herself. Instead, she is engaged in an endlessly unsuccessful attempt at control in the form of a repetition compulsion. Just as the mother is always dissatisfied with the child vis-à-vis the mother's perfectionistic projection on the child, so too the bulimic child will always feel dissatisfied and can never achieve the state of perfection that is compulsively and pervasively sought. In this sort of hypothetical and perhaps prototypical family, the father figure is seen as weak and is similarly minimized by the ambitious, driving, and seemingly compulsive and anxious, perfectionistic mother.

On a prognostic level, most clinicians would agree that bulimia has a better predictive outcome than does anorexia. The probable reason for a better prognosis in bulimia relates to the factor of denial. The anorectic sustains denial with a virtually impenetrable rigidity, while some bulimics can recognize being embedded in a problem of their own creation about which they feel anxiety, humiliation, and despair. Thus, anorexia seems to resemble a consolidated characterological condition in which the experience of anxiety is minimized. Anxiety about personal imperfection is avoided by the acting out comprising the anorectic syndrome. In contrast, the bulimic struggles with repetitive doing and undoing, which involves considerable anxiety. Consequently the bulimic disorder has more of a neurotic cast, which suggests greater accessibility to clinical working through. It would seem that the anorectic, in implementing denial mechanisms, may not be able to struggle as readily with underlying conflicts until such denial mechanisms abate.

ATTENTION DEFICIT DISORDER

For many years hyperactivity in children and poor concentration in adults were not recognized as possible parts of an overall syndrome. Hyperactivity appearing in children was frequently subsumed as an autistic phenomenon, while the lack of concentration in adults was treated as a manifestation of anxiety, or as an effect of depression. In addition, there was a general sense in the clinical field that such symptoms were vaguely organic in nature.

In recent years, as recognized in *DSM* nomenclature, phenomena of hyperactivity and reduced concentration have been recognized as possible aspects of a single syndrome that may occur in childhood and become etched as a personality configuration that can be sustained throughout life.

The attention deficit disorder exemplifies such a problematic diagnostic entity. Considerable new material is currently being synthesized so that clinicians can identify this syndrome during various stages of life. It seems appropriate to cite attention deficit disorder as a conclusion to this volume, based on the importance of understanding diagnostic parsimony and the relevance of diagnosis itself.

Attention deficit disorder has been misdiagnosed in the past, and persons suffering with this syndrome have at various times been considered organically damaged, autistically impaired, psychopathic, hyperactive, and so forth. The attempt by *DSM* classifiers to finally crystallize the various symptoms of attention deficit disorder into one major syndrome is an example of how attempts at diagnostic identification can ultimately be helpful to persons experiencing the life problems associated with a particular syndrome.

Since the various diagnoses covered in this volume have included for the most part those syndromes associated with adults, so too the attention deficit disorder appearing in childhood before the age of nine is included here because of its enduring nature ultimately creating havoc in adult life.

In childhood, the attention deficit disorder comes to be noticed in a general way by parents and teachers so that the child is considered different from the other children on the basis of higher activity level. More specifically, this type of hyperactivity encompasses behavior of fidgeting, restlessness, deficient self-discipline, significant distractibility, noticable impatience, obvious impulsivity, difficulty in completing tasks, as well as numerous other similarly impaired capacities.

From the cognitive point of view, attention span is affected negatively and interests are short-lived and rapidly changed. Rather than being loquacious, the child is considered to be inappropriately talkative. Instead of being considered curious and engaging, the child is assessed as intrusive and interrupting. Accidents and forgetfulness are often seen, and the child is frequently accused of being deliberately oppositional; however, because of various attention-span problems, such a child frequently has not actually heard instructions. These children have also been diagnosed in the psychopathic range as conduct disorders because they often find themselves in dangerous situations in which they exhibit impulsiveness and excitability. It should be noted that such individuals are definitely not psychopathic, and that their behavior during potentially dangerous conditions is not determined by issues of manipulation or any of the so-called psychopathic motives, such as expedience, exploitation, and so forth.

In adulthood, all these qualities in the attention deficit disorder become expressed in derivative form in terms of excessive job changing, reduced ability to complete work, the appearance of euphoria in starting something new and corresponding depressive feelings when tasks remain incomplete. The adult sufferer of the attention deficit disorder is aware of such problems and is sometimes quite dispirited at the paradoxical state in which the problem is visible but he does not seem to have the power to do anything about it. Relationships become unstable because such persons are frequently inclined to have temper tantrums as well as sudden shifts of interest. These persons are not necessarily affected intellectually, but, because of their short attention span, may score somewhat lower on standardized intelligence tests.

This disorder is currently considered to stem from a neurobiological basis. The major symptom of hyperactivity as well as many of the other symptoms of this disorder can now be treated with medication. The importance of diagnosing this disorder cannot be overstated because persons suffering from it find themselves inexorably pursuing directions that lead to high unemployment, encounters with police, as well as untoward experiences involving divorce and emotional traumas consisting of lifelong intermittent depression, low self-esteem, and an overall pessimistic view of their position in life.

Understanding and identifying such a syndrome also helps differentiate the functional psychodynamic aspects of disorders from those aspects that are organic and neurologically based. When syndromes are accurately identified, diagnosis then relates to specific psychopathology which in turn contains referents to the matrix of personality and to issues of etiology, prognosis, and treatment. Such connections between the identification of syndromes, the formulation of etiology and diagnosis, and the understanding of psychopathology and personality, ultimately contribute to the enhanced understanding of the person, and exemplify the purpose of this volume.

CAPSULE CLINICAL PROFILES OF ADDITIONAL DISORDERS

Sadistic Personality Disorder: In this disorder, the presence of cruel behavior results in perverse pleasure. Sadism is often related to underlying sexuality and aggression and strivings for power and dominance. A punitive superego structure leads to acting out of cruelty while identification with the aggressor becomes significant in the character structure. In the identification with the victimizer's power and domination, empathy for others is lost. A domination triad of needs exists, consisting of power, aggression, and sexuality. The sadistic personality differs from paranoid, psychopathic, and passive aggressive personalities because of the centrality of the need to gratify urges of hostility directly.

Masochistic Personality Disorder: In this disorder, also referred to as self-defeating personality, the person behaves in self-sabotaging ways that produce humiliation, defeat, and suffering. Development of passive patterns lead to procrastination and delay, insuring the accumulation of failures and the appearance of consistent low-level functioning. Pleasure opportunities are rejected overtly, sabotaged, or are restricted by the taking on of responsibilities that remain unfinished. Self-sacrificing attitudes appear that are frequently unsolicited and even unappreciated by others. Perverse pleasure reinforces the entire pattern.

Exhibitionism: In *DSM-III-R* exhibitionism is considered a sexual disorder or paraphilia in which sexual gratification is achieved indirectly by sexual display behavior. In this kind of behavior, genitals are exposed to unsuspecting strangers leading presumably to a sense of empowerment. Generally, in this disorder, sexuality is fused with a need for reassurance. The most basic concerns regarding reassurance involve the person's integrity, intactness, and power.

Voyeurism: The issue of empowerment is central in this disorder. It is presumed that the voyeuristic act neutralizes any sense of inadequacy on the part of the voyeur. Thus, the voyeuristic act gives the voyeur, who is generally fearful of interpersonal closeness and assertiveness, a sense of power and a feeling of safety and intactness. It would be expected, therefore, that primary relationships are insulated, and, further, that the acting out aids in the defense against the further deepening of any primary relationship. It is thought that the voyeur has had early experiences of witnessing some sexual or seductive behavior. A feeling of depression can accrue when the acting out is checked.

Insomnia: Insomnia is a sleep difficulty diagnosed after one month of the experience of sleeplessness. *DSM-III-R* defines insomnia as difficulty in initiating and maintaining sleep with the experience of daytime fatigue. Clinicians are most concerned with three kinds of insomnia: (1) initiating sleep; (2) mid-night awakenings; (3) dawn insomnia. Daytime fatigue is due to interference with circadian sleep-wake pattern or stages of sleep. Psychodynamically, insomnia can be due to separation anxiety or a breach in or threat to the fabric of a primary relationship. Insomnia, especially in dependent personalities, may begin because of concerns about separation. Insomnia is associated with a triad of symptoms: (1) separation, (2) dependency, and (3) depression and anger.

Narcolepsy: A disorder of excessive sleepiness with an organic basis. A tetrad of symptoms comprise the disorder: (1) narcoleptic sleep attack in which the subject feels dragged into sleep; (2) cataplexy in which there is a loss of voluntary muscle control and physical collapse, usually to stimuli that surprise the subject—although he remains aware of the environment; (3) sleep paralysis or the state of paralysis either at moments of falling asleep or at moments of coming out of sleep; (4) hypnagogic hallucinations associated with sleep paralysis where the person strongly beleives the events of the dream took place. Such hypnagogic hallucinations are images that are hypervivid. Psychodynamic possibilities associated with narcolepsy include dependency features of the personality, and separation events are highly implicated in the onset of this disorder.

Anorexia Nervosa: In this disorder, there is a compulsive attempt to lose as much weight as possible based manifestly on an exaggerated misperception of one's size as well as excessive fear of weight gain. The downward spiraling weight loss can lead to symptomatic physiological effects such as amenorrhea, and in some instances, death. This eating disorder occurs mostly in young women during high school or early adult years. Compulsive preoccupations with food, body size, and weight are central issues. It is thought that the anorectic is rebelling against strong parental control by asserting control over food intake, weight, and physical appearance. The anorectic's mother is often considered the dominant parent figure, regarded as being controlling, perfectionistic, and perhaps narcissistic, while the father is typically thought to be aloof, weak, or ineffective. The anorectic presumably feels inadequate and ill-equipped to meet the psychological challenges of maturation and the syndrome enables avoidance of academic, vocational, and social expectations. Because clear self-identity and a sense of personal control are limited, the focus on weight, body size, and food intake provide compensatory experiences of control and definition of personal goals.

Bulimia: Bulimia is a disorder of impulsive binge eating associated with purging as an attempt to undo the feeding frenzy. Depression can result from the impulsive eating and purging. Vomiting is the main purge mechanism, while laxatives and diuretics are also used, as are diets, exercise, and even periods of starvation. The bulimic person experiences great weight fluctuations. Secret eating is typical. Bulimia is thought to represent an effort to cope with concerns about lack of self-control, the preempting of personal control by others, as well as inadequate self-image. The focus on an ideal body size and weight temporarily compensates for poor self-esteem while the pattern of ingestion and purging evokes a paradoxical sense of self-regulation beyond the control of others. Within the binge-purge cycle, compulsive binging and purging reflect the central issue of control and its regulation and locus. Denial mechanisms are not as strong as they are in anorexia, allowing bulimics to be more aware and anxious about their symptoms, suggesting somewhat more favorable prognosis.

Attention Deficit Disorder: This disorder is considered biologically based and can be treated with medication. The syndrome appears in childhood and includes hyperactivity and reduced concentration. The child is talkative, involved in accidents, forgetful, and restless. In adulthood the syndrome includes fidgeting, restlessness, poor self-discipline, distractability, impatience, impulsivity, inability to complete tasks, poor attention span, rapidly changing interests, and excessive job changes. Euphoric feelings with respect to new ideas are experienced while a depressed mood prevails when interest declines. Relationships are usually threatened by temper outbursts as well as unsustained vocational engagement. Thus, psychosocial implications form a disturbing overlay to biological difficulties.

Conclusion

In this volume, an overview of the diagnostic nomenclature as applied to adults was presented. This overview encompassed both *DSM* classifications as well as diagnoses considered important to clinicians but not derived from the *DSM* codification. Seventy diagnostic entities were examined with respect to behavioral manifestations of specific psychopathology, including symptom clusters or syndromes, as well as other aspects of personality, such as defense mechanisms, emotion, and developmental considerations. This approach to understanding the deeper aspects of diagnosis in its relation to psychopathology allowed, wherever possible, a three-dimensional exploration of each diagnostic entity. The premise of this exploration into diagnosis rested on the conception of diagnosis as a reflection and shorthand language for the vicissitudes of psychopathology, which in turn was viewed as an expression of the distortions involved in the basic fabric of personality.

The implication of this holographic view of diagnosis, derivative psychopathology, and basic personality fabric was to enable a comprehensive and in-depth depiction of the individual rather than providing a surface focus limited to behavioral phenomena. Thus, this diagnostic primer was meant to integrate, wherever possible, the atheoretically and behaviorally based approach to diagnosis of the current *DSM* model with dynamically oriented theoretical and metapsychological conceptions of psychopathology and personality.

In the *DSM* nomenclature, especially in *DSM-III* and *DSM-III-R,* recognition is given to multidetermined causes for psychopathological manifestations, since there is the opportunity to diagnose both a clinical syndrome on Axis I and a pathological character structure known as personality disorder on Axis II. For the first time within *DSM* nosology, a diagnosis can formally be composed of several diagnostic subentities or levels of psychopathology. Arising from this conception of levels of diagnosis is an implication that personality imprints have a depth, the importance of which is underscored by the derivative of character which becomes identifiable throughout the entire range of psychopathological manifestations.

However, the diagnostic effort represented by *DSM-III* and *DSM-III-R* utilizes a philosophy by which surface phenomena—because they are readily observable largely as behavioral manifestations— are the key components used to build the diagnostic nomenclature. The essential inner functioning of the disturbed individual, the complex pathological network of traits, defenses, fantasy and emotion is avoided for the sake of behavioral clarity and behavioral research. Yet, the avoidance of psychodynamics, theory, and metapsychology diminishes the capacity to realize the essence of any individual's disturbance, the etiological imperatives that ultimately form the diagnosis, and the compelling divisive conflicts which identify the all-important sources of anxiety. A drawback of the *DSM* nomenclature, therefore, seems to be its promulgation of disembodied diagnoses such as, for example, impotence, exhibitionism, or agoraphobia, that are not related to pathological processes that would provide a context for disturbed functioning. In this sense, without direction toward underlying pathological factors, the foundation for this nomenclature is weakened and reduced. These proposed limitations of the *DSM* nosological approach do not encourage efforts at building a broad, meaningful psychology. Such a meaningful psychology would relate the various pathologies to understandable processes, broadening the heuristic strength of the relationship among the domains of diagnosis, psychopathology, and personality.

In this volume, aspects of this potentially meaningful psychology based on interconnections between personality, psychopathology, and diagnosis have been integrated with the various diagnostic entities wherever possible, both those included in *DSM* nomenclature and those conventionally utilized by clinicians but excluded from the *DSM* system. Some of the components of this integration have included, on an etiological level, such issues as developmental concerns, identification with parental figures, and the process of trait development; on a metapsychological level, references to psychic structure, psychosexuality, anxiety, and defenses; and, with respect to conscious experience, references to emotion, fantasy, and, only finally, behavior.

The value of such an integration between the *DSM* approach with its focus on behavior and the attempt in this book to locate the behavioral level in the fabric and structure of personality is perhaps that an integrative approach provides a perspective on symptoms and diagnosis that is more complete, meaningful, and ultimately more precise and useful. This integrative perspective can promote the development of a picture that diagrams the three levels that abstract the psychology of the individual—the basic personality structure or characterology, its psychopathological manifestations, and, finally, the language of diagnosis, which is no more than simply an encapsulated language for this psychopathology. Thus, this diagnostic representation of psychopathology can indeed reflect the organizational code for the entire domain of personality.

The diagnostic point of view represented in this book with its multidimensional considerations of factors relevant to precision in diagnosis may not only expand the relevance of psychopathological phenomena and personality functioning, but may also perhaps claim special relevance for understanding the individual being assessed. This understanding is enriched by regarding individual diagnosis as an organization of a complex network of character structure, particular relevant emotions, trait clusters, and defensive syndromes that are all amalgamated in keeping with the etiology of the particular dysfunction in question. These distinctions of systems and subsystems within the individual again imply that it is worth unifying nosological approaches by theory, thereby demonstrating some reasonable measure of internal consistency, validity, and systematic coherence.

With respect to organizing a diagnostic nomenclature so that a basic theoretical parsimony is achieved, a variety of approaches can be taken. In this volume, a particular and new approach to the organization of diagnosis, especially characterology, was presented. In this approach, the basic character styles of the *DSM* system were categorized according to those variables considered relevant to the very basic question concerning the formation of character structure in the first place. This question concerning the formation of character structure asks why character structure is necessary at all and secondarily, if it is assumed that character is indeed necessary almost as an axiom of human nature, then the question remains on what basis character forms.

The particular approach in this book has sustained a basic psychodynamic position in the understanding of character: that is, that character structure in a psychoanalytic frame evolves as a survival response to the management of the general state of tension and more specifically with respect to the palpable experience of anxiety. With regard to the management of tension and anxiety, most psychodynamic theorists would agree that such tension and anxiety is generated from the vicissitudes of the emotions. Thus, the relative degree of acceptability in expressing particular emotions in the interpersonal context of development presumably creates a gradient of tension and anxiety. This anxiety can intensify, subside, or perhaps be determined generally in response to the ways in which defense mechanisms manage emotion, and most trenchantly by the more permanent particular characterological dispositions that are encouraged.

In this volume, part 1, which deals with character structure, can therefore be viewed as setting the stage for basic underlying dispositions to be associated with the entire range of diagnoses on all psychopathological levels. This means that every diagnosis more or less contains a character structure, and each character structure develops from the presence of emotion and from defenses and enduring traits that are designed to manage these emotions. These emotions also include the important experiences of anxiety and tension that constitute the signals of interpersonal threat, apparently requiring the creation of a characteristic protective apparatus—the character structure.

The organization of such character structures in this book has therefore been grouped according to basic ways in which emotion appears to be governed. Thus, four categories of the regulation of emotion constitute a model through which to understand the organization of character—the foundation of all diagnosis. This presentation of character and diagnosis has suggested that diagnostic parsimony is gained when the character structure is based on control of emotions or its dyscontrol, or avoidance of interpersonal situations by distancing emotion, or by the use of emotion to safeguard the interpersonal condition, especially by insuring the successful gratification of dependency needs.

Even though the understanding of character structure as the basis of each of the diagnoses covered in this volume cannot be precisely or consistently applied to each diagnostic entity, wherever possible references to the complex linkages of character and various components of personality have been included in the analysis of many of the diagnostic syndromes.

The attempt in this book to utilize the entire personality configuration in order to comprehend the individual better may contribute to continued studies of diagnosis in which it may be further appreciated that the diagnosis itself is merely an abstracted language for the vicissitudes of psychopathology, which in turn is embedded in an understandable system of personality. This volume, *The Diagnostic Primer,* and its companion first volume, *History of Psychopathology,* perhaps represent another step in this direction: to show through the history of psychopathology how psychopathological phenomena generated diagnostic referents in an inexorable progression through centuries to the point that such referents became more consistently connected to their psychopathological sources and finally to basic personality derivatives. Through this attempt to integrate these various domains in the psychology of the person, a more comprehensive understanding of the person rather than a fragmentary approach may be developed, also leading to the eminently important aim, that of approaching a more coherent conceptualization of human nature.

RECOMMENDED READINGS

DSM Classification and Psychopathology

Diagnostic and Statistical Manual of Mental Disorders. 1980. 3d ed. Washington, D.C.: American Psychiatric Association.
Diagnostic and Statistical Manual of Mental Disorders. 1987. Rev. 3d ed. Washington, D.C.: American Psychiatric Association.
Frazier, S. H. and A. C. Carr. 1983. *Introduction to Psychopathology*. New York: Aronson.
Spitzer, R. L., A. E. Skodol, M. Gibbon, and J. B. W. Williams. 1981. *DSM-III Casebook*. Washington, D.C.: American Psychiatric Association.
Webb, L. J., C. C. DiClemente, E. E. Johnstone, J. L. Sanders, and R. A. Perley. 1981. *DSM-III Training Guide*. New York: Brunner/Mazel.

Personality and Character Structure

Coen, S. J. 1988. Sadomasochistic Excitement. In R. A. Glick and D. I. Meyers. eds., *Masochism*. New York: Analytic Press.
Deutsh, H. 1965. *Neuroses and Character Types: Clinical Psychoanalytic Studies*. New York: International Universities Press.
Freud, S. 1959 (1908). Character and Anal Eroticism. In J. Strachey, *The Complete Psychological Works of Sigmund Freud*. Standard Edition, vol. 9. London: Hogarth Press.
Freud, S. 1961 (1931). Libidinal Types. In J. Strachey, ed., *The Complete Psychological Works of Sigmund Freud*. Standard Edition, vol. 21. London: Hogarth Press.
Freud, S. 1958 (1911). Repression. In J. Strachey, ed., *The Complete Psychological Works of Sigmund Freud*. Standard Edition, vol. 12. London: Hogarth Press.
Freud, S. 1961 (1905). Three Essays on the Theory of Sexuality: Sexual Aberrations. In J. Strachey, ed., *The Complete Psychological Works of Sigmund Freud*. Standard Edition, vol. 19. London: Hogarth Press.
Freud, S. 1957 (1915). The Unconsious: III. In J. Strachey, ed., *The Complete Psychological Works of Sigmund Freud*. Standard Edition, vol. 14. London: Hogarth Press.
Giovacchini, P. L. 1984. *Character Disorders and Adaptive Mechanisms*. 2d. ed. New York: Aronson.

Grotstein, J. S., M. F. Solomon, and J. A. Lang, eds. *The Borderline Patient*. New Jersey: Hillsdale, N.J.: Erlebaum.

Gunderson, J. G. 1984. *Borderline Personality Disorder*. Washington, D.C.: American Psychiatric Press.

Jenike, M. A. 1986. *Obsessive Compulsive Disorders: Theory and Management*. Littleton, Mass.: PSG Publishing.

Kellerman, H. and A. Burry. 1981. *Handbook of Psychodiagnostic Testing: Personality Analysis and Report Writing*. New York: Grune & Stratton.

Kernberg, O. F. 1975. *Borderline Conditions and Pathological Narcissism*. New York: Aronson.

Kernberg, O. F. 1984. *Severe Personality Disorders: Psychotherapeutic Strategies*. New Haven, Conn.: Yale University Press.

Leites, C. 1979. *Depression and Masochism*. New York: Norton.

Lion, J. R. 1981. *Personality Disorders: Diagnosis and Management*. Baltimore, Md.: Williams & Wilkins.

Masterson, J. F. 1981. *The Narcissistic and Borderline Disorders: An Integrated Developmental Approach*. New York: Brunner/Mazel.

Meissner, W. W. 1978. *The Paranoid Process*. New York: Aronson.

Millon, T. 1981. *Disorders of Personality: DSM-III, Axis II*. New York: Wiley.

Reich, W. 1958. *Character Analysis*. London: Vision Press.

Reik, T. 1941. *Masochism in Modern Man*. New York: Farrar, Straus.

Salzman, L. 1985. *Treatment of the Obsessive Personality*. New York: Aronson.

Schad-Somers, S. 1981. *Sadomasochism: Etiology and Treatment*. New York: Human Sciences Press.

Shapiro, D. 1981. *Autonomy and Rigid Character*. New York: Basic Books.

Shapiro, D. 1965. *Neurotic Styles*. New York: Basic Books.

Wolberg, A. R. 1973. *The Borderline Patient*. New York: Intercontinental Medical Book Corp.

Zales, M. R., ed. 1984. *Character Pathology*. New York: Brunner/Mazel.

Affect Disorders

Davis, J. M. and M. W. Maas. 1983. *The Affective Disorders*. Washington, D.C.: American Psychiatric Press.

Jacobson, E. 1972. *Depression: Comparative Studies of Normal, Neurotic and Psychotic Conditions*. New York: International Universities Press.

Mendelson, M. 1974. *Psychoanalytic Concepts of Depression*. 2d. ed. New York: Spectrum.

Paykel, E. S. 1982. *Handbook of Affective Disorders*. New York: Guilford.

Schuyler, D. 1974. *The Depressive Spectrum*. New York: Aronson.

Shneidman, E. 1985. *Definition of Suicide*. New York: Wiley.

Wetzel, J. W. 1984. *Clinical Handbook of Depression*. New York: Gardner Press.

Neurotic Disorders

Abse, D. W. 1959. Hysteria. In S. Arieti, ed., *American Handbook of Psychiatry.* Vol. 1. New York: Basic Books.

Alexander, F. 1965. *Psychosomatic Medicine.* New York: Norton.

Bliss, E. L. 1985. *Multiple Personality, Allied Disorders and Hypnosis.* New York: Oxford University Press.

Brownell, K. D. and J. P. Foreyt. 1987. *Handbook of Eating Disorders.* New York: Basic Books.

Bruch, H. 1973. *Eating Disorders: Obesity, Anorexia Nervosa and the Person Within.* New York: Basic Books.

Cooper, A. M., A. J. Francis, and M. H. Sacks, eds. 1985. *The Personality Disorders and Neuroses,* vol. 1. New York: Basic Books.

Dupont, R. L., ed. 1982. *Phobia: A Comprehensive Summary of Modern Treatments.* New York: Brunner/Mazel.

Fenichel, O. 1945. *The Psychoanalytic Theory of Neurosis.* New York: Norton.

Freud, S. 1955 (1895). Studies on Hysteria. In J. Strachey, ed., *The Complete Psychological Works of Sigmund Freud.* Standard Edition, vol. 2. London: Hogarth Press.

Garner, D. M. and P. E. Garfinkel, eds. 1985. *Handbook of Psychotherapy for Anorexia and Bulimia.* New York: Guilford Press.

Gray, M. 1978. *Neuroses: A Comprehensive and Critical View.* New York: Van Nostrand Reinhold.

Grinker, R. R. 1974. *Psychosomatic Concepts.* New York: Aronson.

Horowitz, M. J., ed. 1977. *Hysterical Personality.* New York: Aronson.

Johnson, C. and M. E. Connors. 1987. *The Etiology and Treatment of Bulimia Nervosa: A Biopsychosocial Pespective.* New York: Basic Books.

Kales, A. K. and J. D. K. Kales. 1984. *Evaluation and Treatment of Insomnia.* New York: Oxford University Press.

Kellerman, H. 1981. *Sleep Disorders: Insomnia and Narcolepsy.* New York: Brunner/Mazel.

Kelly, W. E., ed. 1985. *Posttraumatic Stress Disorder and the War Veteran Patient.* New York: Brunner/Mazel.

Krohn, A. 1978. *Hysteria, the Elusive Neurosis.* New York: International Universities Press.

Lewis, H. B. 1971. *Shame and Guilt in Neurosis.* New York: International Universities Press.

May, R. 1977. *The Meaning of Anxiety.* New York: Norton.

Milman, D. and G. D. Goldman. 1973. *The Neurosis of Our Time: Acting-Out.* Springfield, Ill.: C. C. Thomas.

Minuchin, S. 1978. *Psychosomatic Families: Anorexia Nervosa in Context.* Cambridge, Mass.: Harvard University Press.

Neuman, P. A. and P. A. Halvorson. 1983. *Anorexia Nervosa and Bulimia: A Handbook for Counselors and Therapists.* New York: Van Nostrand Reinhold.

Pasnau, R. O. 1986. *Diagnosis and Treatment of Anxiety Disorders.* Washington, D.C.: American Psychiatric Press.

Roth, S. 1980. *Narcolepsy and Hypersomnia*. Basel: S. Karger.

Scrignar, C. B. 1984. *Post-traumatic Stress Disorder: Diagnosis, Treatment, and Legal Issues*. New York: Praeger.

Turner, H. A. and J. D. Maser. 1985. *Anxiety and the Anxiety Disorders*. Hillsdale, N.J.: Lawrence Erlebaum Associates.

Psychosis

Arieti, S. 1978. *Interpretation of Schizophrenia*. New York: Brunner/Mazel.

Bellak, L., ed. 1958. *Schizophrenia: A Review of the Syndrome*. New York: Grune & Stratton.

Costello, C. G. 1970. *Symptoms of Psychopathology: A Handbook*. New York: John Wiley & Sons.

Gottesman, I. and J. Shields. 1982. *Schizophrenia: The Epigenetic Puzzle*. New York: Cambridge University Press.

Helzer, J. E. and S. B. Guze, eds. 1987. *Psychoses, Affective Disorders, and Dementia*, vol. 2. New York: Basic Books.

Jackson, D., ed. 1960. *The Etiology of Schizophrenia*. New York: Basic Books.

Shapiro, S. A. 1981. *Contemporary Theories of Schizophrenia: Review and Synthesis*. New York: McGraw-Hill.

Index

Ideation (*Continued*)
23, 24, 28, 31, 33-34, 37, 40, 42,
43; schizoid, 33-34, 37; in
schizotypal personality, 107, 116;
see also Paranoid ideation
Ideational defenses: in paranoid
schizophrenia, 239-40, 262
Identification, 259; in anorexia, 287;
in bulimia, 290; with feared
aggressive process, 166; in passive
aggressive personality, 84-85;
incomplete, in psychopathic
personality, 60, 66; with parental
figure, 25-27, 29, 31-32, 36, 101,
298; in sadistic personality
disorder, 271, 294
Identity: inaccessibility of, in
dissociative disorders, 200, 201,
207, 208, 210, 213-14, 217;
fragile, in narcissistic personality,
54, 55, 56, 57, 58, 71; loss of, in
depersonalization disorder, 210,
218; loss of, in psychogenic
amnesia, 208, 218; loss of, in
psychogenic fugue, 206, 207, 217
Identity confusion: in borderline
personality, 95, 96, 97, 98, 99,
100-1, 115
Impotence, 76, 270, 298
Impulses, 65, 140, 145; in
agoraphobia, 157, 159, 179;
avoidance of anxiety through
expression of, 145; defenses
against, in phobias, 163; and
depression, 139; in generalized
anxiety disorder, 168, 169; in
obsessive compulsive disorder,
171, 174-75; in psychogenic
amnesia, 208; in psychopathic
personality, 67; in social phobia,
160, 161, 180; in somatoform
disorder, 184, 199
Impulsivity: in attention deficit
disorder, 292, 296; in borderline
personality, 97, 98, 116; in
psychopathic personality, 61, 62,
67, 69, 71
Inadequacy, sense of: in anorexia,
287, 296; in depersonalization

disorder, 210, 218; and
depression, 131; displaced onto
body, in somatoform disorders,
187, 191, 215; in hysterical
personality, 71; in major
depressive episode, 127, 146; in
paranoid personality, 28, 29, 41,
272; in paranoid schizophrenia,
241, 262; in psychogenic fugue,
207; in somatoform disorders,
196, 197, 213; in voyeurism,
276-77, 278, 294
Inadequate personality (character
type), xiv, 13, 70, 72, 73, 77, 87,
88-93, 94, 114; clinical case
illustration, 91-93; clinical profile,
94; developmental issues in, 90-91
Induced psychotic disorder (shared
paranoid disorder), 226, 253, 255,
259; capsule clinical profile,
265-66
Inferiority feelings, 54, 131; in
hysterical personality, 50, 51; in
paranoid personality, 28-29, 41
Inner life, deadened: in psychopathic
personality, 62, 64, 65, 69, 71
Insomnia, xvi, 76, 270, 278-81; 289;
capsule clinical profile, 295;
psychodynamics of, 280-81; types
of, 279, 295
Insularity: of compulsive personality,
20; in emotion controlled
character type, 15, 16, 40, 43; in
emotion dyscontrolled character
type, 43, 71; of paranoid
personality, 25, 28
Intellectualization: in emotion
controlled character type, 15, 16,
20, 21, 22, 25, 28, 34, 40, 42; in
narcissistic personality, 53-54, 55,
71; in paranoid schizophrenia,
239, 262; in schizotypal
personality, 107
Interest, diminished: in simple
schizophrenia, 245, 246, 263
Internalization, 259; positive, 131; in
psychopathic personality, 64, 66,
67, 68; in schizoid personality, 36
Interpersonal relations, 15-16; in